The Successors of the Mauryas

(*circa* 187 BC – 319 AD)

A Political History based on Coins and Inscriptions

The Successors of the Mauryas

(*circa* 187 BC – 319 AD)

A Political History based on Coins and Inscriptions

Prashant Srivastava

Agam Kala Prakashan

Delhi

First published 2017

ISBN : 978-81-7320-173-8

Published by :
Agam Kala Prakashan,
34, Central Market, Ashok Vihar,
Delhi-110 052.
Tel. : 91-11-27212195, 65688806-7
Fax : 91-11-27212195
E-mail : agambooks@gmail.com, agambook@yahoo.com
Website : www.agamkala.com

Composed by :
Elegant Printographics
Delhi-110085

Printed by :
Chawla Offset Printers
Ashok Vihar, Delhi-110 052

Printed in India.

Dedicated to
the memory of
my father,
Shri Priyonath Srivastava

Contents

Key to Illustrations

Coin no.	Ascription	Coin no.	Ascription
1-2	Audumbara : Dharaghosha	48	Strato I
3	Kuṇinda : Amoghabhūti	49	Telephos
4	Kuṇinda : *Chatreśvara*	50	Zoilos I
5	Ujjayinī	51	Zoilos II
6	Vemaki	52	Vonones with Spalahora
7-8	Yaudheya	53	Vonones with Spalagadama
9	Kauśāmbī	54-55	Spalirises
10	Mathurā	56-58	Maues
11	Pañchāla : Bhānumitra	59-60	Azes I
12	Pañchāla : Phalgunīmitra	61-64	Azilises
13	Agathokleia with Strato I	65-68	Azes II
14	Agathokles	69	Azes II with Aśpavarman
15	Amyntas	70	Gondopharnes with Aśpavarman
16-18	Antialkidas	71	Abdagases
19-20	Antimachos	72	Sasan
21-22	Apollodotos	73	Rañjuvula
23-24	Archebios	74	Soḍāsha
25	Demetrios	75	Hagāmasha
26	Diodotos	76	Sanabares
27	Diomedes	77	Kshaharāta : Nahapāna
28	Epander	78	Kārddamaka : Jīvadāman
29-30	Eukratides I	79	Heraos
31-32	Euthydemos I	80-81	Kujula Kadphises
33-34	Heliokles I	82-83	V'ima Takshuma
35	Heliokles II	84-85	V'ima Kadphises
36-37	Hermaios	86-89	Kanishka I
38	Hermaios with Kalliope	90-97	Huvishka
39-40	Hippostratos	98	Vāsudeva I
41	Lysias	99-100	Kanishka III
42-44	Menander I	101	Vāsudeva II
45	Nikias	102	Shāka : Saya
46	Pantaleon	103	Chandragupta I-Kumāradevī
47	Philoxenos	XX	XXX

Preface

The period *c* 187 BC to 319 AD, that is the period beginning with the decline and downfall of the Mauryas and ending with the rise of the Imperial Guptas, sandwiched as it is between these two great dynasties of ancient India, was, till very recent times, called the first dark age of ancient Indian history. However, it is one of the most interesting periods of ancient Indian history, and has received the attention of historians, most of them numismatists and epigraphists, as coins and inscriptions are the two major sources for the study of the political history of the period.

This work is meant as a textbook on the political history of the successors of the Mauryas, for the use of undergraduate and postgraduate students of ancient Indian history, particularly those students, who have opted for courses in ancient Indian numismatics and epigraphy. I hope that it shall equip them to appreciate the historical importance of coins and inscriptions, and locate them in their true historical perspective.

As always, the drafts of the work were read by Prof K K Thaplyal, and by my father, Shri Priyonath Srivastava; sadly, I lost the latter, while the work was in progress. My sincere thanks to both of them, for their appreciation, criticism, and valuable suggestions. My mother, Mrs Pushplata Srivastava, has been a constant source of inspiration. Thanks are also due to my wife, and my daughters, Pratichi and Purvi, and my nephews, Ayush and Raxit, for their untiring support during the progress of this book.

The Tagore Library, University of Lucknow, Lucknow; the State Museum, Lucknow; the Archaeological Survey of India, Lucknow Circle, Lucknow; the Central Library, Archaeological Survey of India, New Delhi; and the National Museum, New Delhi, provided facilities of study, for which I owe thanks to their respective librarians and staff.

The photographs of coins published have been provided by the State Museum, Lucknow, and the IIRNS, Nashik, for which I thank both the institutions.

Dr. Agam Prasad, of Agam Kala Prakashan, Delhi, promptly took up the book for publication; my thanks to him and his staff, especially Shri Ashok Kumar Pandey, for the care they have put in in the publication of the book.

18 November 2016 **Prashant Srivastava**

Chapter I

Introduction

I have been teaching numismatics and epigraphy to undergraduate and postgraduate students for the past about two decades. It is very difficult, both for the teacher and the student, to locate coins and inscriptions in their true historical perspective, without some knowledge of the political history of the period of their issue. The history of the period under study, that is from *c* 187 BC to 319 AD, has been reconstructed, in the main, on the basis of coins and inscriptions. I strongly feel that a student shall be better able to understand the historical significance of a numismatic or epigraphic source, if he is armed with knowledge of the political history, on which the source has a bearing. For instance, he shall be better able to follow the subtleties of Indo-Greek or Śaka-Pahlava numismatics, when he has some basic knowledge of their political history.

Unfortunately, in the present day scenario of history writing, political history has lost ground to socio-economic history. It is not unusual to come across established historians bemoaning the fact that, as students, they were made to plod through tomes on political history; they seem to regard it as a waste of their time and energy. Under the circumstances, there are few up-to-date works, dealing with the political history of the successors of the Mauryas, up to *c* 319 AD.

The present work, which treats of this subject, is divided into seven chapters, and has three appendices. Chapter I is introductory in nature, and deals with the nature and scope of the work, and the sources of study. Chapter II is concerned with the history of the Śuṅga and Kāṇva dynasties, and the monarchical and republican states of northern India. The Māhāmeghavāhanas of Kaliṅga and the Sātavāhanas form the subject of Chapter III.

Chapter IV makes a brief survey of the Indo-Greek rule in India. Extensive use of numismatic evidence has been made here in the reconstruction of their political history. Chapter V deals with the Śaka-Pahlavas and other rulers of Śaka extraction, mainly the Western Kshatrapas—the Kshaharātas and the Kārddamakas. The history of the Kushāṇa kings, and their successors, has been taken up for study in Chapter VI. In the last chapter, Chapter VII, the two predecessors of Chandragupta I, who would have belonged to the last quarter of the third century AD and the first quarter of the fourth century AD, have been taken up for discussion.

The Mauryas are not known to have ruled over any region in the Far South, and hence, the three major Tamiḷ powers—the Choḷas, Pāṇḍyas, and Cheras, as also the Toṇḍaiyar and Pallavas, cannot technically be called the successors of the Mauryas. However, a brief account of the Tamiḷ states, in the centuries preceding and succeeding the commencements of the Christian era, was felt desirable in order to project a complete picture of political conditions of ancient India in the period. This has been presented, not as a separate chapter, but as an appendix, Appendix 1.

Speaking roughly of the period under study, and particularly of the Indo-Greek period, A K Narain has rightly observed : 'For certain periods of Indian history the historian has to be a numismatist'. The general features of the coins of significant successors of the Mauryas have been dealt with in brief in Appendix 2. The other major source of information about the political history of the period under study are inscriptions. Appendix 3 gives a brief introduction of the significant epigraphs of the period, and their historical importance.

The work is meant primarily for undergraduate and postgraduate students, who have offered courses in ancient Indian numismatics and epigraphy. It was, therefore, deemed proper not to burden them with references and footnotes/endnotes. I hope that the Select Bibliography, which follows the three appendices, shall serve the purpose adequately, and also provide a list for further reading. In the selection of entries in the Bibliography, particular attention has been paid to works on numismatics and epigraphy, as they are the two main sources for the study of the political history of the successors of the Mauryas.

Sources of study

Literary sources

The literary texts, dealing with the political history of the period under study, fall into two broad classes—religious literature and secular literature.

Religious literature : It may further be divided into four categories—Brahmanical (that is the literature concerned with Brahmanical religion, which later on came to be known as Hindu religion), Buddhist, Jaina, and Christian.

Among the Brahmanical literary sources for the study of the political history of the period, the pride of place is occupied by the purāṇas. The historical value of the purāṇas, 18 in number with several upapurāṇas, was not appreciated by scholars, till F E Pargiter corrected the situation. The subject matter of the purāṇas is fivefold—*sarga* (creation), *pratisarga* (recreation), *vaṁśa* (genealogies of gods and sages), *manvantara*, and *vaṁśānucharita* (genealogies of kings). These are particularly important for the study of the cultural life in ancient India—social, economic, religious, as also for art and architecture. But the puranic lists of post-Maurya rulers are very helpful in the reconstruction of the political history of the period, as can be seen from *The Purāṇa Text of the Dynasties of the Kali Age*, by F E Pargiter (Oxford, 1913).

Of the Buddhist texts, which furnish information about the political history of the period, the *Divyāvadāna* is worth mention. Dated to the second century AD, it consists of *gāthās*, written both in prose and verse. The language is Sanskrit, with hints of Prakritisms. The text presents Pushyamitra Śuṅga as an oppressor of the Buddhists, who destroyed Buddhist monuments, and announced a reward of 100 *dīnāras* to one who brought him the head of a *śramaṇa*.

The *Milindapañho*, perhaps the most famous of the non-canonical Buddhist texts, deals with the questions of King Milinda concerning Buddhist philosophy, and the answers of the Buddhist philosopher, Nāgasena. Milinda of this text has been identified as the Indo-Greek king, Menander. The text provides information about that Indo-Greek king, and his interest in Buddhism, which is attested by the occurrence of the Buddhist *dharmachakra* on his coins.

The *Kālakāchāryakathānaka*, a 'well-known cycle of legends found in Jaina scriptures and texts', hints at the colonization of Śakakūla, the Patalene of Ptolemy, by the Śakas, before they settled in Saurāshṭra. It also refers to the Vikramāditya legend, and to the destruction of the Śakas at the hands of that hero.

Mention may also be made here of a Christian source, the Syriac version of *The Apocryphal Acts of Judas Thomas, the Apostle*, which refers to the Indian king, Gūdnaphar, who is said to have adopted Christianity, along with his mother, and brother Gad, due to the influence of St Thomas. This Gūdnaphar is identified as the Śaka-Pahlava ruler, Gondopharnes. It has been inferred on the basis of his Takht-i-Bahi inscription that Gondopharnes ascended the throne *c* 19/20 AD, and ruled for at least 26 years. This date for the reign of Gondopharnes is corroborated by this Christian source, which refers to him as a contemporary of St Thomas.

Secular literature : It might be divided into four broad classes—histories, biographies, foreign accounts, and romantic literature. India produced very few texts, which may technically be placed under histories. A famous text of this category is the *Rājataraṅgiṇī* of Kalhaṇa, which deals with the history of Kashmir. However, the account becomes reliable only from the seventh century AD onwards, and is of little help in the reconstruction of the political history of the period under study. For instance, it refers to three kings named Hushka, Jushka, and Kanishka, identified with the Kushāṇa rulers, Huvishka, Vāsishka, and Kanishka I, respectively, but makes them rule simultaneously.

Among the biographies, mention may be made of the *Harshacharita* of Bāṇa. It gives an account of the

Pushpabhūti dynasty, and, without dealing with the complete life of its hero, ends with the meeting of Harsha with his sister, Rājyaśrī, when the latter was about to perform *satī*. On the basis of such an 'abrupt' ending, it was earlier believed that the *Harshacharita* is a fragmentary work. But it appears that the author never intended to write a complete account of the life of Harsha, which task he regarded as beyond the comprehension of the omniscient, the capacity of the god of speech, and the strength of the goddess of eloquence. Incidentally, the text sheds some light on the history of the Śuṅgas, when, for instance, it refers to the assassination of Vasumitra by one Mūladeva/Mitradeva.

The accounts of foreign travellers and writers are also important. Indian literature is primarily normative. On the contrary, these foreign travellers described what they actually witnessed, although they sometimes seem to have experienced some difficulty in understanding Indian traditions and customs. Classical writers, like Plutarch, Justin, Apollodoros, Polybios, Trogus, and others, throw a flood of welcome light, mainly on the history of the Indo-Greeks, and, to some extent, on that of the Śaka-Pahlavas. The evidence provided by Strabo and Ptolemy, and the *Periplus Maris Erythraei*, is important for the reconstruction of the economic history and historical geography of the period, but has little value for political history. Marcus Agrippa (*c* 64/63 BC – *c* 12 BC) is believed to have prepared the 'design and memoranda' for the drawing of a map of the world. The map was set up in a portico built by Augustus Caesar at Rome, as reported by Pliny. Unfortunately, the 'design and memoranda' of Agrippa, as also the map of the world at Rome, no longer exist. However, later classical writers, like Pliny and Isidore of

Charax, refer to the notes of Agrippa. This so-called 'Agrippan Source' sheds light on the extent of authority, and history, of the Medes, Parthians, and Persians.

Among the Chinese sources for the political history of the period under study, the *Sse-ki* of Ssu-ma-chien, the *T'ien Han-shu* of Pan-ku, and the *Hou Han-shu* of Fan-ye, deserve mention. The *Sse-ki* speaks of the political upheaval, which forced the Yüeh-chihs to leave their original home in Central Asia. The *T'ien Han-shu*, the history of the first Han dynasty, and covering the period 206 BC – 24 AD, gives an account of the five Yüeh-chih principalities in Bactria. The *Hou Han-shu*, the history of the second Han dynasty, and covering the period 25 AD – 220 AD, provides information about the early rulers of the Kouei-chouang branch of the Yüeh-chihs, identified with the Kushāṇas.

The works of great Sanskrit *littérateurs*, like Kālidāsa, Bhāravi, Daṇḍin, and others, may be cited as examples of romantic literature. These help primarily in the reconstruction of the cultural life of the period of their composition. However, they sometimes shed light on political history as well. For instance, the *Mālavikāgnimitram* of Kālidāsa is an important source for the study of the history of the early Śuṅga rulers, Pushyamitra, Agnimitra, and Vasumitra.

The *Mahābhāshya* of the grammarian, Patañjali, a senior contemporary of Pushyamitra Śuṅga, throws light on the activities of the Indo-Greeks at Sāketa (Ayodhya) and Mādhyamikā (Nagari, near Chittor), during the reign of Pushyamitra Śuṅga. It also refers to the performance of a *yajña* by Pushyamitra, perhaps one of the two *aśvamedhas* he is said to have performed.

The *Gārgīsaṁhitā*, also known as *Vṛiddhagargasaṁhitā*, is a work on astrology, attributed to Vṛiddhagarga, who is mentioned by Varāhamihira. It has a section, the Yugapurāṇa, consisting of over 200 lines written in Sanskrit, with traces of Prakritism, which has been traced to a work, dated to the latter half of the first century BC by K P Jayaswal. It sheds some light on the Indo-Greeks, particularly on their invasion of India, in the course of which they are reported to have crossed Mathurā, Pañchāla, and Sāketa, and besieged Kusumadhvaja (Pāṭaliputra); they were, however, forced to return to their own land due to internal dissensions. It refers to the Indo-Greeks as barbarians, but alludes to them as well-versed in the science of astrology.

Tamiḷ literature : For the history of southern India, Śaṅgam literature is an important source, particularly for the closing centuries of the pre-Christian era and the first three or four centuries of the Christian era, and forms a class in itself. This literature is grouped into eight anthologies—*Naṟṟiṇai*, *Kuṟundogai*, *Aiṅguṟunūṟu*, *Padiṟṟuppattu*, *Paripāḍal*, *Kalittogai*, *Ahanānūṟu*, and *Puṟanānūṟu*. According to the traditional account of the Śaṅgams, as recounted in the commentary on the *Iṟaiyanār Agapporuḷ*, a work of the mid-eighth century AD, there were, in all, three Śaṅgams, which extended over a period of 9,990 years, with long intervals in between, attended by 8,598 poets, and patronized by 197 Pāṇḍya rulers. The extant Śaṅgam literature consists of 2,279 poems of varying lengths; 102 of these are anonymous works, while the rest have been attributed to 473 poets. The *Tolkāppiyam* is a work on Tamiḷ grammar by Tolkāppiyan, reputedly the most famous of the 12 disciples of Agastya.

The Tamiḷ epics, the *Śilappadikāram* and the *Maṇimekhalai*, also shed some interesting light on the history of the period. Of these, the latter is the earlier of the two, the work of a Buddhist poet, Sīttalai Sāttanār. Its heroine is Maṇimekhalai, the daughter of Kovalan and Mādhavī, who despairs of human love, and dedicates her life to the Buddha, *dhaṁma*, and *saṁgha*. The *Śilappadikāram*, though composed later than the *Maṇimekhalai*, is actually a prequel to the latter. Its author is Ilaṅgo-Adigal, the younger brother of the Chera ruler, Śeṅguṭṭuvan. The epic recounts the story of Kovalan, who lavishes all his wealth on Mādhavī, a courtesan of Puhār. But he is forgiven by his wife, Kaṇṇagī, and together they repair to Madurai, where Kovalan is executed on the orders of the Pāṇḍya king, Neḍuñjeḷiyan, who is to be distinguished from Neḍuñjeḷiyan, the victor of the battle of Talaiyālaṅgānam. Kaṇṇagī curses the royal couple, and the city of Madurai, and gives up her life to reunite with her husband in heaven. She is revered as the goddess of chastity among the Tamiḷs, and has a cult of her own.

Archaeological Sources

Archaeological sources for the study of the political history of the period may be divided into three broad classes—Coins, Inscriptions, and Sculpture.

Coins : They act as the primary source for certain periods of ancient Indian history—the periods of the Indo-Greeks, the Śaka-Pahlavas, and the Western Kshatrapas, may be cited as examples; other sources provide very little or no information about them. Coins help in the reconstruction of social, economic, religious, and cultural history of the period to which they belong. Coins being contemporary, their evidence is more valuable. As in the case of inscriptions, specific information supplied by coins is deemed reliable, although general information has to be treated with some caution. Space on coins is limited, leaving lesser scope for exaggeration. However, this lack of adequate space also results in the information furnished by coins being not as detailed as one might expect from a contemporary source. But for their coins, we would not have come across even the names of most of the three dozen odd Indo-Greek rulers so far known. Similarly, the chronology and genealogy of the Kārddamaka Kshatrapas would have remained a puzzle in the absence of their coins. General features of the coins of the significant powers of the period under study have briefly been dealt with in Appendix 2.

Inscriptions : They occupy a unique place among the sources of the political history of ancient India. On the one hand, they are written sources, and fall within the category of literary sources. On the other hand, they are the subject of study of an epigraphist, and fall within the category of archaeological sources. Inscriptions are mostly contemporary. Again, due to the limited space for writing available, there is relatively lesser scope for exaggeration. As such, specific information supplied by them is deemed reliable, although general information has to be treated with some caution. But due to the limited space, the information provided by inscriptions is often not as detailed as one might have expected from a contemporary source. The *Mahābhāshya* of Patañjali and the *Mālavikāgnimitram* of Kālidāsa do refer to the performance of the *aśvamedha* by Pushyamitra, but it is only in the Ayodhya stone inscription of Dhana[deva] that that Śuṅga ruler is given the credit for the performance of two horse sacrifices, when it refers to him as *dvirasvamedhayājin.* In the absence of his Hathigumpha inscription, Khāravela would have remained but a shadowy figure. The historical importance of some of the important inscriptions of the period under study has been dealt with briefly in Appendix 3.

Sculptures : Among sculptures, quite interesting are the inscribed stone figures of the Kārddamaka *kshatrapa*, Chashṭana, and the Kushāṇa rulers, V'ima Takshuma and Kanishka I, from Mat near Mathura. These are all dated to the last quarter of the first century AD, and executed in the famous Mathura style of sculptural art. Despite the rigid frontality and strict angularity of treatment, all the three figures are imbued with regal majesty. The kings are shown wearing the Central Asian type of dress. The representation of the Kārddamaka Chashṭana, in the Kushāṇa sanctuary, has led to the suggestion of some kind of relationship between the Kārddamakas and the Kushāṇas.

Another Kushāṇa *devakula* existed at Surkh Kotal, in southern Bactria, in the modern province of Baghlan, in Afghanistan. The sanctuary housed five major royal figures, and some fragments of divine figures. One royal figure, of which only the lower half is available, is shown wearing a heavy coat, trousers, and tunic. It resembles the statue of Kanishka I, from the Mat sanctuary. The second statue is much damaged. It wears a similar dress, and is of the same size as the first one. The third figure is that of an enthroned male, wearing a cone-shaped headdress. Flames are seen issuing from the shoulders, reminding one of similar royal figures on Kushāṇa coins. The fourth statue, only a torso, in fact, wears a topcoat and tunic, the dress reminding one of the figures of Kushāṇa kings, seen on coins. According to a report, the statue, believed to be that of Kanishka I, was destroyed during the height of Taliban iconoclasm, but has, since, been restored. It is interesting to note, that the Rabatak inscription of Kanishka I, found nearby, refers to the king ordering the construction of the images of himself, and his three predecessors—his father, V'ima Kadphises, his grandfather, V'ima Takshuma, and his great-grandfather, Kujula Kadphises.

There were, at Naneghat, images of some historical personages, each being accompanied by a label inscription, which makes possible, to an extent in some cases, the identification of the person represented. Due to damage, it is not possible to decipher two of the label inscriptions at all, and the reading of at least one more, mentioning *Kumāra* Vediśrī, the son of Sātakarṇi I and Nāganikā, is doubtful; the images, themselves, have not escaped the ravages of time. Of the personages represented, the most important appear to be Nāganikā and her husband, Sātakarṇi I, who appears to be the reigning at the time of the execution of these images and the incising of these inscriptions. Then, there are King Simuka, *Kumāra* Sātavāhana, *Kumāra* Vediśrī, and *Kumāra* Hakuśrī. Interestingly enough, Mahāraṭhī Traṇakayiro, the father of Nāganikā, too, is represented, perhaps because of the role he is believed to have played in the rise of the Sātavāhanas as a political power to be reckoned with in southern India. Some scholars suggest that one lost image, and the lost inscription accompanying it, might to be that of *Kumāra* Śaktiśrī, another son of Sātakarṇi I and Nāganikā. Scholars like D C Sircar and I K Sarma express the possibility that Kṛishṇa, too, might have been represented there, but the image is lost, as also the label inscription accompanying it; this view has not found universal acceptance among scholars. These images and label inscriptions shed welcome light on the political history of the Sātavāhanas.

Chapter II

The Śuṅgas, Kāṇvas, and their Successors

The decline and downfall of the Mauryas

The sources at our disposal give divergent information regarding the successors of Aśoka. The *Vāyupurāṇa* mentions Kuṇāla as the son and successor of Aśoka. There is a view that he might be the same as Suyaśas, mentioned in the *Vishṇupurāṇa* as the successor of Aśoka. If Buddhist tradition is correct in recording that he was deprived of his eyesight by Tishyarakshitā, a queen of Aśoka, there is not much likelihood of his ever ascending the throne, and Aśoka seems to have been succeeded by his grandson, Daśaratha, as per the testimony of the *Matsyapurāṇa*. According to puranic tradition, Daśaratha ruled for eight years. His cave inscriptions from the Nagarjuni hills show that he excavated three caves, and donated them to the Ājīvika monks, immediately after his coronation.

According to Jaina sources, Aśoka was succeeded by Samprati, who was inclined towards Jainism. The *Divyāvadāna*, too, informs us that Aśoka had declared

Samprati as his *yuvarāja*. However, in the purāṇas, he is described as the son and successor of Daśaratha, who ruled for a period of nine years. According to the *Pariśishṭaparvan*, the Mauryas lost Maharashtra and Andhra regions during the reign of Samprati. It is noteworthy that in the puranic lists of Maurya rulers, three rulers—Bandhupālita, the son of Kuṇāla; Indrapālita, perhaps the brother of Bandhupālita; and Daśona, the grandson of Bandhupālita, are mentioned between Kuṇāla and Daśaratha, the three having ruled for eight, ten, and seven years, respectively. D R Bhandarkar suggests that Bandhupālita should be identified with Daśaratha, and Indrapālita, with Samprati.

The *Rājataraṅgiṇī* of Kalhaṇa refers to Jalauka as the son and immediate successor of Aśoka in Kashmir. This devotee of Śiva repulsed some *mlechchha* (Indo-Greek ?) invasion, and extended his dominions up to Kanauj. Tāranātha would have us believe that Vigatāśoka, the grandson of Aśoka, ruled over Gandhāra, and was followed by his own son, Vīrasena. It appears that the death of Aśoka was followed by a division of his empire among his descendants, with Daśaratha establishing himself as an independent ruler in the eastern parts of the Maurya empire, Samprati, in the western parts, Jalauka, in Kashmir, and Vigatāśoka, in Gandhāra.

According to the purāṇas, Samprati was succeeded by Śāliśuka, who enjoyed a reign of 13 years. Like his predecessor, he was inclined towards Jainism, and has been described in the *Gārgīsaṁhitā*, as a wicked person, who prohibited the performance of sacrifices. Most of the scholars are of the view that the Indo-Greek expedition, described in the Yugapurāṇa section of the *Gārgīsaṁhitā*, in the course of which, the Yavanas crossed Sāketa, Pañchāla, and Mathurā, and besieged Pāṭaliputra, occurred during his reign. A K Narain, however, regards this Indo-Greek invasion as an event of the reign of Pushyamitra Śuṅga. If D R Bhandarkar is correct in identifying him with Subhāgasena (Sophagasenos of Polybios), the Seleukid ruler, Antiochos III Megas, would have led his eastern expedition during his reign. According to the *Divyāvadāna*, however, Samprati was followed by his son Bṛihaspati, grandson Vṛishasena, and great grandson Pushyadharman, in that order, the last ruler being Pushyamitra, the son of Pushyadharman. The inclusion of Pushyamitra in the list of Maurya king would seem to render the information of the Buddhist text, rather unreliable.

In the puranic lists of Maurya rulers, Śāliśuka is followed by Devadharman, and the latter's son, Śatadhanus, in that order, and they have been assigned a reign of seven years and eight years, respectively. The last Maurya ruler was Bṛihadratha, to whom, the purāṇas ascribe a reign of seven years. According of the *Harshacharita* of Bāṇabhaṭṭa, he was assassinated by Pushyamitra, the commander of his army (below). The rule of the Maurya dynasty, extending over a period of 137 years according to the purāṇas, thus, ended *c* 187 BC.

The foreign, internal, and religious policies of Aśoka are sometimes held responsible for the downfall of the Maurya empire. After the war of Kaliṅga, he gave up military conquests, and even advised his decendants to eschew all wars. It is felt by some scholars that this would have had an adverse effect on the efficiency and war-preparedness of the Maurya army. His messages of piety seem to have had no impact on the Indo-Greeks in northwestern India, who poured into India, almost immediately after the close of the reign of Aśoka, reaching even as far as Pāṭaliputra, and the Maurya army, which, under Chandragupta, had successfully repulsed the invasion of Seleukos, was unable to drive away the Indo-Greeks, who had besieged the capital; it was only due to internal bickering among them, that they raised the siege of Pāṭaliputra, and repaired to Bactria.

In order to make his administration more efficient, Aśoka introduced several reforms. However, his policy of entrusting high officials with the task of imparting instructions of piety to the subjects, turned civil administrators into 'religious propagandists', and this would, understandably, have had an adverse effect on the efficiency of the administrative machinery.

After adopting Buddhism, Aśoka extended patronage to that religion, and there are indications that the brāhmaṇas were deprived of certain previleges, which they had been enjoying till then. Of the two predeccesors of Aśoka, Chandragupta seems to have been inclined towards Jainism, and Bindusāra, towards Ājīvikism. It has been suggested that this would have alienated the brāhmaṇas, and the assassination of Bṛihadratha, at the hands of his brāhmaṇa *senānī*, was the revolt of the brāhmaṇas against the Mauryas, who are known to have patronized heterodox sects. However, it seems more likely that when Pushyamitra assassinated the last Maurya emperor, he was leading the revolt of the army, and not of the brāhmaṇas.

If the testimony of the *Divyāvadāna* is to be believed, Aśoka, in his religious zeal, became reckless while making donations to the Buddhist *saṁgha*, and his heir apparent, Samprati, and the minister, Rādhagupta, had to intervene to save the treasury from depletion. The philanthropic activities of Aśoka, not only within his empire, but also without, too, would have drained the royal exchequer.

It has been observed that, at a time, when India was being threatened with foreign invasions from the northwest, she 'needed men of the caliber of Puru and Chandragupta to ensure her protection against the Yavana menace. She got a dreamer.' However, in view of the significant role played by Aśoka in ensuring 'the moral ascendancy of Indian culture' over a considerable part of the then known world, history can afford to overlook the shortcomings of some of his policies, which might have been responsible for the downfall of the Maurya empire.

If the testimony of the *Divyāvadāna* is to be given any credence, even during the lifetime of Aśoka, political and family intrigues were quite common. The confusion regarding the order of succession after Aśoka would hint at the political uncertainty, which prevailed after the death of Aśoka. His descendants seem to have divided the empire among themselves, which would have added to the political instability. The empire started disintegrating. The inroads of the Indo-Greeks further compounded the situation. And the Maurya empire ceased to exist within less than half a century of the death of Aśoka.

The Śuṅga dynasty

According to the *Harshacharita* of Bāṇabhaṭṭa, Pushyamitra, the *senāpati* of the Maurya ruler, Bṛihadratha, assassinated his emperor, when the latter was reviewing his army (above). The *Divyāvadāna* informs us that Pushyamitra was related to the Mauryas, but this is not acceptable in view of the fact that he attained kingship by assassinating the last Maurya ruler. In the *Mālavikāgnimitram* of Kālidāsa, Agnimitra, the son of Pushyamitra, is called a scion of the

Baimbika family. The *Harshacharita* of Bāṇabhaṭṭa, which does not refer to Pushyamitra as a Śuṅga, uses the dynastic appellation for the last ruler of his line, namely Devabhūmi. However, in the purāṇas, Pushyamitra is called a Śuṅga. H C Raychaudhuri expresses the possibility that the purāṇas might have, inadvertently, placed the Baimbika and Śuṅga rulers under the common dynastic name of Śuṅga.

Pushyamitra, and most of his successors, have *mitra*-ending names. On this basis, H P Sastri suggested that the Śuṅgas might have been of Iranian origin, as the worship of the sun god, Mithra, was quite popular in Iran. But a number of Indian rulers, of indigenous origin, with *mitra*-ending names are known, and even H P Sastri later gave up this view. The Śuṅgas are generally regarded as brāhmaṇas of Indian origin. The *Vaṁśabrāhmaṇa* mentions a teacher named Śauṅgāyani, and the *Bṛihadāraṇyakopanishad* refers to another teacher named Śauṅgīputra. In the *Āśvalāyanaśrautasūtra*, too, Śuṅgas are referred to as *āchāryas.* Since, in the vedic period, teaching as a profession was generally associated with the brāhmaṇa *varṇa*, there is a great likelihood of the Śuṅgas being brāhmaṇas. This is supported by Pāṇini, who refers to the Śuṅgas as brāhmaṇas, of the bhāradvāja *gotra.* Curiously, according to the *Harivaṁśa*, the brāhmaṇa commander, who restored the *aśvamedha* in the *kaliyuga*, that is Pushyamitra according to K P Jayaswal, belonged to the kāśyapa *gotra.* The *Baudhāyanaśrautasūtra* refers the Baimbikas to the kāśyapa *gotra*, and Baimbika is the name of the family of Agnimitra in the *Mālavikāgnimitram* of Kālidāsa.

In the declining phase of the Maurya rule, disintegration had set in, and parts of northern India had already become independent. In the northwest, the Indo-Greeks had established their principalities. There is also no definite evidence for the Mauryas exercising any authority much to the south of the Vindhyas and the Narmada. The *coup* of Pushyamitra, thus, seems to have made him the master of only the central parts of the former Maurya empire.

From the *Mālavikāgnimitram* of Kālidāsa, it appears that during the reign of Bṛihadratha, there were two rival factions in the Maurya court, with his commander, Pushyamitra, leading one faction, and a minister leading the other. The minister seems to have used his influence to get Yajñasena, the husband of his sister, appointed as the governor of Vidarbha. When Pushyamitra occupied the throne, and imprisoned the minister, Yajñasena declared himself independent in Vidarbha. Agnimitra, the son of Pushyamitra and his viceroy at Vidiśā, was on friendly terms with Mādhavasena, a cousin of Yajñasena. Once, when Mādhavasena was going to meet his friend at Vidiśā, he was arrested by the governor of the frontier of the kingdom of Yajñasena. When the ruler of Vidarbha was asked by Agnimitra to set Mādhavasena free, Yajñasena demanded the release of his brother-in-law in return. Agnimitra retaliated by ordering Vīrasena, the brother of his wife and in charge of a fortress situated on the southern borders of Vidiśā, to invade Vidarbha. The recently established kingdom was, according to Kālidāsa, weak like a newly planted sapling, and Yajñasena was defeated. Vidarbha was divided between Yajñasena and Mādhavasena, with the river Varadā (modern Wardha) acting as the dividing line. Thus, the Vidarbha region came within the sphere of political influence of the Śuṅgas.

Pushyamitra also had conflicts with the Indo-Greeks. Patañjali, in his *Mahābhāshya*, states that the Yavanas had besieged Sāketa (Ayodhyā) and Mādhyamikā (modern Nagari, near Chittor in Rajasthan). That this commentator on the *Ashṭādhyāyī* of Pāṇini was a contemporary, and a senior one, of Pushyamitra is shown by the use of the present tense in his statement, 'Here we perform the sacrifices for Pushyamitra.' It seems that, moving from the northwest, the Indo-Greeks had crossed Rajasthan and the intervening territories, and reached as far east as Ayodhyā. But Pushyamitra seems to have succeeded in repulsing their invasion. The Indo-Greeks seem to have been led by Demetrios, who might have been accompanied by his general, Menander. The view, that Pushyamitra successfully faced this Indo-Greek invasion as the commander of the Maurya forces, is not based on any definite evidence.

Some conflict of Pushyamitra with the Indo-Greeks is also referred to in the *Mālavikāgnimitram* of Kālidāsa, which tells us that Pushyamitra performed the *aśvamedha*, during which Vasumitra, the son of Agnimitra, was made responsible for the safety of the sacrificial horse. This horse was caught by the Indo-Greeks, whom Vasumitra defeated on the banks of the river Sindhu (Indus ?). This conflict between the Śuṅgas and the Indo-Greeks seems to have taken place quite late in the reign of Pushyamitra, when his grandson was old enough to be entrusted with the task of safeguarding the sacrificial horse, and was different from the one referred to by Patañjali, the senior contemporary of Pushyamitra. This Indo-Greek invasion might have been led by Menander, who had, by that time, ascended the throne.

The statement of Patañjali, 'Here we perform the sacrifices for Pushyamitra', has been taken to refer to the performance of the *aśvamedha* by the Śuṅga ruler, although that sacrifice is not specifically mentioned in the commentary. But the *Mālavikāgnimitram* of Kālidāsa make a clear reference to the *aśvamedha* of Pushyamitra. However, the Ayodhyā stone inscription of Dhana[deva] describes Pushyamitra as *dviraśvamedhayājin*, 'performer of two horse sacrifices'. It seems that the first *aśvamedha* was performed by Pushyamitra in the initial years of his reign, and it is the one mentioned by his senior contemporary, Patañjali; the second horse sacrifice was performed by him towards the close of his reign, and it is the one mentioned by Kālidāsa. These performances of the sacrifices might have had something to do with his successes against the Indo-Greeks.

The performance of the *aśvamedha* by Pushyamitra marks the revival of Brahmanism during the rule of the Śuṅgas. Buddhist tradition regards Pushyamitra as intolerant of Buddhism. According to the *Divyāvadāna*, after three unsuccessful attempts to destroy the famous Kukkuṭārāma *vihāra* at Pāṭaliputra, he destroyed several sacred places of the Buddhists, and, at Śākala, he promised to pay a hundred *dīnāras* to the person who brought to him the head of a monk. This information about the anti-Buddhist activities of Pushyamitra seems to be corroborated by the testimony of Tāranātha, for whatever it is worth. But, in view of the Buddhist building activities in the Śuṅga period—the reconstruction of the great *stūpa* at Sanchi, the construction of the railing of the *stūpa* at Bharhut, it seems difficult to regard this information of the Buddhist sources as reliable.

Pushyamitra ruled for 36 years, and was succeeded by his son, Agnimitra, who had earlier served him as his viceroy at Vidiśā. According to the purāṇas, he ruled for eight years. The next Śuṅga ruler in the puranic lists is Vasujyeshṭha or Sujyeshṭha (called simply Jyeshṭha, in a manuscript of the *Matsyapurāṇa*), who is said to have ruled for seven years. Attempts have been made to identify the Śuṅga ruler, Agnimitra, with the homonym, known from some Pañchāla coins, and the Śuṅga ruler, Jyeshṭhamitra, with the homonym, known from the coins of Kauśāmbī, but without much success, as these Śuṅga rulers exercised sway over a considerable part of northern India, and one would expect the coins of the Śuṅga rulers to be found in areas other than Pañchāla and Kauśāmbī, too.

The fourth Śuṅga ruler was Vasumitra, the son of Agnimitra. In the *Mālavikāgnimitram* of Kālidāsa, he is depicted as a brave youth, who was entrusted with the security of the sacrificial horse at the time of the performance of the *aśvamedha* by his grandfather. But the *Harshacharita* of Bāṇabhaṭṭa portrays him as a prince, given to the pleasures of the senses, who was killed by one Mūladeva/Mitradeva, while he was enjoying some theatrical performance. This Mūladeva/Mitradeva might have been some ancestor of Dhana[deva] of the Ayodhyā stone inscription, and it is possible that, after killing Vasumitra, he founded the rule of a collateral branch of the Śuṅgas at Ayodhyā. Independent kingdoms seem to have been established at Pañchāla, Mathurā, and Kauśāmbī, too.

The next three rulers in the puranic lists are Āndhraka, Pulindaka, and Ghosha, who ruled for a total period of eight years. The first of these three rulers is also called Antaka in the *Matyapurāṇa*, Bhadraka in the *Bhāgavatapurāṇa*, and Ārdraka and Odruka in the *Vishṇupurāṇa*. K P Jayaswal would identify him with Udāka of the Pabhosa inscription mentioning Āshāḍhasena. A king named Bhāgabhadra is known from the Besnagar *garuḍa* pillar inscription of the Indo-Greek envoy, Heliodoros. Marshall identifies him with Bhadraka/Āndhraka. But the inscription refers to the fourteenth year of the reign of Bhāgabhadra, while the total reign of Āndhraka, Pulindaka, and Ghosha, extended over a period of a mere eight years. K P Jayaswal seems to be right in identifying this Bhāgabhadra with Bhāgavata, who, according to the purāṇas, ruled for 32 years. Nothing much is known about these three rulers, and there is even some doubt regarding their Śuṅga affiliations. According to the purāṇas, the Śuṅgas ruled for a total period of 112 years. If the eight years of the rule of Āndhraka, Pulindaka, and Ghosha are counted together with the reign periods of the other seven Śuṅga rulers, the total comes to 120 years. It seems more likely that Āndhraka, Pulindaka, and Ghosha were not Śuṅga rulers at all. Taking advantage of the troubled times, which followed the assassination of Vasumitra at the hands of Mūladeva/Mitradeva, they usurped the Śuṅga throne, and ruled for eight years.

The fortunes of the Śuṅga family seem to have been restored by Vajramitra, who is known to have reigned, for nine years, after Ghosha. The next in line was Bhāgavata, who seems to be identical with Bhāgabhadra of the Besnagar *garuḍa* pillar inscription. In that inscription, Heliodoros, the Yavana envoy of the Indo-Greek king, Antialkidas, refers to Bhāgabhadra as *trātā*, the Sanskrit equivalent of the Greek epithet, *soter*, 'saviour'. The use of the title of saviour for Bhāgabhadra by the envoy of Antialkidas is taken as indicative of some help, which the Indo-Greek king received from the Śuṅga. This might give us some idea of the political might and influence of the Śuṅgas during the reign of Bhāgavata. D R Bhandarkar is of the view that another *garuḍa* pillar inscription from Besnagar refers to the twelfth regnal year of Bhāgavata.

The last Śuṅga king was Devabhūti or Devabhūmi, who ruled for 10 years. According to the purāṇas, he was a worthless prince, and was dethroned by one of his ministers, Vasudeva. This seems to be supported by the *Harshacharita* of Bāṇabhaṭṭa, which informs us that the minister, Vasudeva, got 'over-libidinous Śuṅga' murdered, with the help of the daughter of his *dāsī,* disguised as the queen. Thus, the reign of the main branch of the Śuṅga dynasty came to an end around 75 BC. They seem to have maintained their hold, perhaps in the Vidiśā region, for almost half a century more, till their power was ultimately destroyed by Simuka.

The Kāṇva dynasty

Vasudeva, the minister of Devabhūti or Devabhūmi, who got his master assassinated by a slave girl, founded a new dynasty, called the Kāṇva or Kāṇvāyana dynasty. In the *Ṛigveda,* Kāṇvāyanas are described as the descendants of the sage, Kaṇva. This would show that the Kāṇvas were brāhmaṇas. Vasudeva ruled for nine years, as per the evidence of the purāṇas. His rule seems to have been confined to Magadha and its surrounding areas, as the Vidiśā region was under the later Śuṅgas, the Indo-Greeks were masters of northwestern India, and the western Ganga valley was being ruled by the so-called Mitra rulers. The purāṇas mention only three successors of Vasudeva, namely Bhūmimitra, Nārāyaṇa, and Suśarman, who ruled in that order. The same texts also inform us that Bhūmimitra ruled for a period of 14 years, Nārāraṇa for 12 years, and Suśarman, for 10 years. Attempts have been made to identify Bhūmimitra with the homonym of the coins of Pañchāla, though without much success. Some scholars propose to associate King Sarvatāta, known from the Ghosundi-Hathibada inscription as the performer of an *aśvamedha,* with the Kāṇvas. The Kāṇvas enjoyed sovereignty for a total period of 45 years, before their rule was brought to an end by Simuka, who established the rule of the Sātavāhana dynasty.

The purāṇas state that Simuka not only overthrew the Kāṇvas, but also destroyed the remnants of the power of the Śuṅgas. On this basis, R G Bhandarkar drew the conclusion that, towards the close of the Śuṅga rule, the Kāṇvas, also called Śuṅgabhṛitya, wrested the real power from their masters, and acted as *de facto* rulers, without uprooting the Śuṅga dynasty. Thus, the 45 years of the rule of the Kāṇvas should be included in the 112 years, assigned to the Śuṅgas in the purāṇas. But this view of R G Bhandarkar has been found untenable, on the grounds that the purāṇas clearly mention the overthrow of the last Śuṅga ruler, Devabhūti or Devabhūmi, by his minister, Vasudeva, the founder of the Kāṇva dynasty. The destruction of the remnants of the Śuṅga power by Simuka, mentioned in the purāṇas, seems to refer to his vanquishing the later Śuṅgas of Vidiśā (above).

Northern India after the Śuṅgas and Kāṇvas

The period, following the decline of the Śuṅgas and the Kāṇvas, saw the disintegration of northern India, with a number of powers emerging on the political horizon—some monarchical, and the others, republican. Some of these powers are known to have played a role in the history of India, often up to the rise of the Imperial Guptas, or even thereafter.

Ayodhyā. One such kingdom was that of Ayodhyā. The coins of the kings of Ayodhyā have been divided into two distinct series: (i) square cast coins, and (ii) round die-struck coins. The rulers known from the coins of Series I are (alphabetically), Dhanadeva, Jyeshṭhadatta, Mūladeva,

Naradatta, Poṭhadeva (Praushṭhadeva), Śivadatta, Vāyudeva, and Viśākhadeva, although some scholars would place Naradatta and Śivadatta of Ayodhyā coins among the rulers of Mathurā. Dhanadeva may be identical with the homonym of Ayodhyā stone inscription, who has been referred to therein as sixth in descent from Pushyamitra. Coins of Dhanadeva, Vāyudeva, and Viśākhadeva have similarity of device—Gajalakshmī, standing, while Śivadatta's coins show Gajalakshmī, sitting. Praushṭhadeva and Mūladeva, known from bull type of coins alone, are to be placed earlier than Dhanadeva. Bela Lahiri proposes the following chronological order—Praushṭhadeva, Mūladeva, Vāyudeva, Dhanadeva, Viśākhadeva, Śivadatta, Naradatta, and Jyeshṭhadatta. The rule of the kings, who issued square cast coins, could be dated from the middle of the first century BC to the second half of the first century AD. Their rule seems to have terminated with the conquest of this region by Kanishka I.

The series of round die-struck coins seems to have been issued when the Kushāṇa rule over the region slackened after Kanishka. The kings known are (alphabetically), Ajavarman, Āyumitra, Devamitra, Kumudasena, Mādhavavarman, Saṅghamitra, Satyamitra, and Vijayamitra. According to Bela Lahiri, of these rulers, Kumudasena, Ajavarman, and Mādhavavarman seem to be earlier as is indicated by the presence on their coins of a square incuse, which is characteristic of the earliest die-struck coins of India. Curiously, of the Ayodhyā kings, Kumudasena alone has the title of *rājan* on his coins. On the basis of the forms of the letter *ma* on the coins, Bela Lahiri suggests the following order of succession of the other rulers—Saṅghamitra, Vijayamitra, Devamitra, Satyamitra, and Āyumitra. The coins of this series may be placed between *c* 150 AD and the end of the third century AD, the latter date marking the beginning of the Imperial Gupta period. It seems that the rule of the local dynasty of Ayodhyā was brought to an end by one of early Imperial Gupta rulers, for the puranic evidence shows that Chandragupta I exercised authority over Sāketa.

From some seals discovered at Rajghat are known Dhavasena, his son Vishṇumitra, and the latter's son Saṅghamitra, and also one Vijayamitra and his son Śivamitra. Saṅghamitra and Vijayamitra of these seals may be identical with the homonyms of coins.

Kauśāmbī. This ancient capital of the Vatsa *janapada* has been identified with modern Kosam, near Allahabad. The early coins from this site are of four classes, namely uninscribed and inscribed cast coins, die-struck coins of early kings, Dhanadeva's coins and their degenerate copies, and Magha coins. The cast coins form the earliest coinage of Kauśāmbī. The second class of coins of Kauśāmbī belongs to the period from the second century BC till the region was conquered by Kanishka I, whose coins and a seal have been found at Kosam. Coins provide evidence for more than two dozen kings who ruled for about two centuries. Since it gives an average reign of less than eight years, some of these kings would have ruled contemporaneously over different parts of the *janapada*. The kings known from these coins are (alphabetically) Agrarāja, Agnimitra, Aśvaghosha, Bahasatimita (Bṛihaspatimitra II), Īśvaramitra, Jyeshṭhabhūti, Jyeshṭhamitra, Parvata, Prajāpatimitra, Praushṭhamitra, Priyamitra, Rāḍhamitra, Rājamitra, Rajanīmitra, Rāmamitra, Sarpamitra, Satyamitra, Suramitra, Varuṇamitra, and Vavaghosha. It has been suggested that the Kauśāmbī rulers, particularly kings with *mitra*-ending names, had blood relationship with the Śuṅgas. In view of the lack of any other evidence for the chronology of kings, one has to fall back on typology and palaeography of the coin legends. There seems to be a break in the issue of the local coins of Kauśāmbī during Kanishka's rule. Shortly thereafter, the coins of Dhanadeva, and their imitations, were struck. Then follow the coins of Nava, and those of the Magha kings.

Magha. The Maghas, known from coins, seals, and inscriptions ranging from years 51 to 139 (= 128 to 217 AD), are identified by some scholars with the Meghas known from the purāṇas as rulers in Kosala. There is a view that the dynasty should be taken as Māgha, named after its founder, and the name-endings of the kings of this dynasty should also be read as *māgha.* The Magha kings known from coins are King Magha, Vāsishṭhīputra Bhīmasena (also known from inscriptions of years 51 and 52), Poṭhasiri (also known from epigraphs of years 87 and 88), Bhadramagha (also known from inscriptions of years 83, 87, and 88), Śivamagha (also known from a seal and an epigraph), Vaiśravaṇa (also known from inscriptions, one being dated 107), and Bhīmavarman (also known from inscriptions dated years 130 and 139). Kings Satyamagha and Vijayamagha are known from coins alone. There are coins, on which the legends have been tentatively read as *Puramagha* (?), *Yajñamagha* (?), *Śaṅkhamagha* (?), and *Jayamagha* (?). The succession of kings from Bhīmasena to Bhīmavarman can be determined by the dated inscriptions; the other rulers seem to be later than Bhīmavarman. The Maghas appear to have ceased to exist as a political power before *c* 300 AD.

The epigraphs of the Maghas have been ascribed to the Gupta era by Cunningham, Fleet, and Sohoni, the Kalachuri era by K P Jayaswal, and the Śaka era by Marshall, Sten Konow, and Motichandra. Of these, the Gupta era is ruled out on the grounds that the Guptas could not have allowed members of a feudatory family to issue coins in their own name, and also that the Maghas should have mentioned the Guptas as their overlords in their epigraphs, which is not the case. These inscriptions appear to be dated in the Śaka era.

Mathurā. Situated on the right bank of the river Yamuna, Mathurā was the capital of the Śūrasenas. The early coins of Mathurā may be classified as those of the indigenous rulers and those of the Śaka satraps. In the first group, there are two different families, with *mitra-* and *datta-*ending names, respectively. Of the thirteen early rulers, six have *mitra-*ending names : Brahmamitra, Dṛiḍhamitra, Gomitra, Satyamitra, Sūryamitra, and Vishṇumitra. The kings with *datta-*ending names are Bhavadatta, Kāmadatta, Purushadatta, Rāmadatta, Śeshadatta, and Uttamadatta. Of these, Purushadatta, with the title of *rājan,* is placed as the earliest. After the Datta kings came Balabhūti, who has a different name-ending. The Datta kings ruled immediately after the Mitra kings, though some scholars hold that Śaka rule intervened and that the Datta kings were vassals of the Kushāṇas.

The rule of the Śaka *satrap,* Rañjuvula, who is placed in the beginning of the first century AD, seems to have followed that of the Mitra and Datta kings. He was followed by his son, Śoḍāsha, the other Śaka rulers of Mathurā being Taraṇaḍāsa, Ghaṭāka, Hagāna, Hagāmasha, Śivadatta, and Śivaghosha, who have all been discussed in

Chapter V. The Śakas in Mathurā were replaced by the Kushāṇas. The city was an important centre, perhaps the eastern capital of the Kushāṇas, and remained under their hold at least till the rule of Vāsudeva I. After *c* 200 AD, it came under the rule of the Nāgas. In the post-Kushāṇa phase, coins of Śiśuchaṁdāta (or Śaśachaṇḍāta, as Goyal suggests) and Vīrasena are found. The latter is taken as a Nāga ruler, and is identified with the homonym known from an inscription from Jankhat (district Farrukhabad).

Nāgas. The Nāgas are an ancient people, whose origin is shrouded in mystery. Most of the scholars are of the view that they were originally serpent worshippers, and came to be named after their totem, the *nāga.* Literary, epigraphic, and numismatic evidence, as also the presence of several localities bearing their name, testify to the wide distribution of their habitation. The existence of several Nāga ruling families is vouched for by the finds of their coins and inscriptions. Puranic evidence shows that the three main centres of their power were Padmāvatī, Kāntipurī, and Mathurā. Of these, Padmāvatī has been identified with Padmapura in Vidarbha, or Narwar near Shivpuri, but its identification with Pawaya, 25 miles to the northeast of Narwar in Madhya Pradesh, suggested by M V Lele, seems to be supported by the discovery of the remains of an ancient city and of a large number of Nāga coins at the site. K P Jayaswal identified Kāntipurī with Kantit between Mirzapur and Vindhyachal, but Wilford and Cunningham seem to be right in identifying it with Kutwal or Kutwar near Moraina, about 20 miles north of Gwalior in Madhya Pradesh. Nāga coins have also been found at Mathurā. K P Jayaswal had suggested that three different lines of Nāga kings ruled from these three centres, and of these, the

Bhāraśiva Nāgas of Kāntipurī represented the imperial line, while the ruling families at Padmāvatī and Mathurā were collaterals. But the coins from all these three centres often represent the same kings, and are similar to each other in types. Thus, it is concluded that all the three centres were ruled by the same family of Bhāraśiva Nāgas; Padmāvatī, which has yielded the greatest number of Nāga coins, was, perhaps, the main centre of their power, while Kāntipurī and Mathurā were 'two other important cities of the Nāga kingdom'. From the *provenance* of the Nāga coins, it is concluded that this kingdom comprised the areas of Bharatpur, Dholpur, Gwalior, Bundelkhand, as also some parts of Malwa, and was bounded by Yamuna in the north, Narmada in the south, Chambal in the west, and Ken in the east. Jayaswal had also suggested that the Nāga rulers formed a confederacy against the Kushāṇas, in which the tribal republics, like the Kuṇindas, the Mālavas, and the Yaudheyas, were their subordinate allies. Although there is no evidence to support this, there is no gainsaying that the Nāgas, like all these and other powers, played their part in liberating northern India from the yoke of Kushāṇa supremacy. The rulers represented by the Nāga coins are (alphabetically) Bhavanāga, Bhīmanāga, Bṛihaspatināga, Devanāga, Gaṇapatināga, Prabhākara, Ravināga, Skandanāga, Vasunāga, Vibhunāga, Vṛishabha, Vṛishanāga, and Vyāghranāga.

Pañchāla. The *Mahābhārata* associates Pañchāla with the Kurus. The country came to be known as Pañchāla as here, five vedic tribes merged into the predominant Kṛivis. Pañchāla was one of the 16 *janapadas* of northern India in the sixth century BC. The region constituted the area under Bareilly, Badaun, Farrukhabad, and the adjoining districts. It was divided into two parts, with Ahichchhatrā (modern Ramnagar near Aonla) forming the capital of northern Pañchāla, and Kāmpilya (modern Kampil, between Badaun and Farrukhabad), that of southern Pañchāla. The kings known from the Pañchāla series of coins are (alphabetically), Achyu[ta], Agnimitra, Anamitra, Bahasatimitra (= Bṛihaspatimitra or Bṛihatsvātimitra), Bhadraghosha, Bhānumitra, Bhūmimitra, Damagupta, Dhruvamitra, Indramitra, Jayagupta, Jayamitra, Phalgunīmitra, Prajāpatimitra, Rudraghosha, Rudragupta, Śivanandiśrī, Śrīnandi, Sūryamitra, Vaṅgapāla, Varuṇamitra, Vasusena, Vishṇumitra, Viśvapāla (?), Yajñapāla, and Yugasena. Thus, most of the kings have *mitra*-ending names. The other rulers variously have the following name-endings—*ghosha*, *gupta*, *nandi*, *pāla*, and *sena*. The latter are, however, interconnected by types and symbols with kings having *mitra*-ending names. There is hardly any justification for considering the Pañchāla kings, many of whom bore *mitra*-ending names, as belonging to the Śuṅga dynasty. Achyuta and Nandi of coins are identified with the homonyms mentioned in the Allahabad pillar inscription, and hence, should be dated to the fourth century AD. The rest of the Pañchāla coins have been dated variously between 200 BC and the end of the first century BC by Allan, between 100 BC and 100 AD by Smith (mainly on palaeographical ground), and between *c* 50 BC and 250 AD by Sircar.

Some republican tribes

Agra. The earliest mention of this tribe is to be found in the *Ashṭādhyāyī* of Pāṇini. Other references are met with in Baudhāyana and Patañjali, the *Mahābhārata, Mahāmāyūrī, Chāndravyākaraṇa, Kāśikā*, and *Sarasvatīkaṇṭhābharaṇa*. Yāska, in his Nirukta, refers to a teacher named Āgrāyaṇa.

The classical writers refer to the Agalassoi in the neighbourhood of the Siboi, in the context of the invasion of India by Alexander, and this tribe has been identified by some scholars with the Agras of Indian literature and coins; the Greek form of the name has been regarded as the rendering of Sanskrit, *Agrāsaḥ*. The chief city of the Agras seems to be Agrodaka, which is mentioned in the *Mahāmāyūrī*, and has been identified with Aggalapura of the *Vinayapiṭaka* and with modern Agroha, about 14 miles from Hissar in Haryana, from where a hoard of 51 Agra coins has been found in the course of excavations in 1938-1939. According to a local tradition, the city of Agroha was founded by one *Rājā* Agra (later named Agrasena), from whom the Agravālas claim their descent. The Agras issued die-struck coins in copper, barring one in silver. On the basis of palaeography, and the similarity of these coins with those of the Rājanyas, the Agra coins are placed in the second-first centuries BC, or even a little earlier. On most of the coins, the legend is *Agodaka* (or *Agodake*) *Agāchajanapadasa*, '[coin] of the *Agrātyajanapada* [issued from, or current at] Agrodaka'. Agra or Agrātya seems to be name of the tribe as well as the *janapada*. But on some coins, there is a different legend, which has been read by Barnett as *Agāchamitra-padābhishṭhāyinām̐* or *Agāchamitrapadābhishṭhāyinaḥ*, and interpreted as '[coin] of the rulers (or ruler) of the Allied State of the Agāchas'. On this basis, it has been suggested that the Agras had formed some confederacy with other tribes, like the Rājanya, Vṛishṇi, and Mālava, to tackle the problem posed by foreign rule in northwestern India. Sircar, however, taking Agrātyamitra (literally, 'friend of the Agrātyas) as a tutelary deity, translates the legend as '[This is the coin] of those who dwell at the feet of Agrātyamitra'. But Agrātyamitra as name of a deity is not known.

Ārjunāyana. This tribe finds mention in the *Gaṇapāṭha* of Pāṇini, the Allahabad pillar inscription of Samudragupta, the *Bṛihatsaṁhitā, Chāndravyākaraṇa, Kāśikā, Sarasvatīkaṇṭhābharaṇa*, and the *Abhidhānachintāmaṇi*. On the basis of the information supplied by the *Mahāmāyūrī*, this tribe is placed between eastern Punjab and western Uttar Pradesh. Cunningham places their territory in northern Rajasthan to the north of Malwa and south of Madradeśa, Smith in Bharatpur and Alwar region, and Allan in Delhi-Jaipur-Agra triangle. Handa procured two coins of the tribe from the ancient mounds of Nohar and Dhanasia in the Ganganagar district of Rajasthan, and, on this basis, regards the Ārjunāyanas as the western neighbours of the Agras. The tribal name connects them with Arjuna, the Pāṇḍava hero. There is a view that Ārjunāyana coins were issued after Huvishka, when the Kushāṇa power was on the decline. The Ārjunāyans continued to be a political power till they came to owe allegiance to Samudragupta (*c* 350 AD), as per the testimony of the Allahabad pillar inscription of that ruler.

Aśvaka. The *Mahābhārata* mentions Aśvaka and Aśmaka as variants of the name of the same tribe living in the northwest. The Aśvakas of coins are, in all probability, identical with the Assakenoi, who, according to the classical writers, offered a tough resistance to Alexander. The Assakenoi territory has been located in the Swat valley and its city, Massaga, is identical with Maśkāvatī of Pāṇini's *Ashṭādhyāyī*. It is difficult to say if the Aśvakas had any connection with the Aśmakas of the Godavari region (referred to as *dākshiṇātyas* in Pāṇini).

A few coins found near Taxila bear the device of a pile of balls, crescent-on-hill, a human figure, and a taurine, and the Brāhmī legend, *Vaṭasvaka.* Cunningham is inclined to include these coins under Taxila coins. *Vaṭāśvaka* as the name of a tribe is not known. Bühler rendered *Vaṭasvaka* into Sanskrit as *Vaṭāśvakaḥ*, 'the Aśvaka tribe of the *vaṭa* or fig tree clan'. Allan takes the legend in the singular and as a place name. *Vaṭa* also means a *cowrie*-shell, which, like coin, was a medium of exchange, and hence, *Vaṭasvaka* may be equal to Sanskrit *Aśvakānāṁ vaṭaḥ*, 'the coin of the Aśvakas'. These coins are datable to *c* third or second century BC, on palaeographical grounds. The find of Aśvaka coins at Taxila may indicate that they, at least some of them, had migrated to that region, or the presence of these coins in the area may be due to trade contacts.

Audumbara. Audumbara, a *tadddhita* form of *udumbara*, means people connected with the fig tree (*udumbara*) or a country where fig trees grow in abundance. The Audumbaras are referred to in the *Gaṇapāṭha* of Pāṇini, which locates them near Jalandhar. Besides, they are also mentioned in the *Mahābhārata, Bṛihatsaṁhitā, Vishṇupurāṇa*, and the Sanchi inscriptions. In the *Chāndravyākaraṇa*, the *Kāśikā* and the *Vaijayantī*, the Audumbaras are referred to as one of the sections of the Śālvas. Patañjali refers to them as kshatriyas, Jayaswal takes them as of Aryan origin, while Przyluski regards them as speakers of Austro-Asiatic languages. The Adamviras or Admeras, a section of the Johiya Rajputs, as also Gujarat brāhmaṇas of Audumbara caste and Viśvāmitra *gotra*, are taken as reminiscent of the Audumbaras. Audumbara coins have been found from the Pathankot-Gurdaspur region, and a few other sites of Punjab, and at Irippal, district Kangra, and a few other sites of Himachal Pradesh. The tribe seems to have occupied Kangra, Gurdaspur, Hoshiarpur areas. Pliny's reference to Odombeores in Kuchchh region suggests that some of them might have migrated there from Punjab and Himachal Pradesh.

The coins of this tribe are divided into two classes. The four chiefs represented by these coins are Śivadāsa, Rudradāsa, Dharaghosha, and Mahādeva. On palaeographical grounds, the coins of Class I are placed in the second or first century BC, while those of Class II at the end of the first century BC or the beginning of the first century AD, on the basis of the Indo-Greek influence on them. The names of chiefs, like Śivadāsa and Rudradāsa, and the devices of a Śaiva temple, trident, trident-battleaxe, and bull, attest to the Śaiva affiliations of the tribe.

Kshudraka. The Kshudrakas are mentioned in the *Gaṇapāṭha* of Pāṇini, and are identified with the Oxydrakai or Hydrakes of the classical writers. According to Megasthenes and Arrian, the Persians hired the Hydrakes as mercenaries. The historians of Alexander inform us that the Oxydrakai were quite powerful, and allied with the Malloi (= Mālavas) against the Macedonian invader. The confederation of the two tribes is, perhaps, hinted at in the formation *Kshudraka-mālavī-senā* by Pāṇini, and the *Kshatriya-dvandva* in the *Kāśikā* on Pāṇini. The mention of this confederation in Pāṇini seems to suggest that it was a 'permanent arrangement' between the two tribes. The confederate army against Alexander comprised 90,000 infantry, 10,000 cavalry, and 500 chariots. The find of their coins would render untenable the view that they had completely merged with the Mālavas. Smith is of the view that, as the eastern neighbours of the Malloi, the Oxydrakai occupied the Kangra, Gurdaspur, Hoshiarpur, and Amritsar regions. The coins of this tribe have been assigned to the second century BC on palaeographical grounds.

Kulūta. Of the 12 coins of the Kulūta tribe known so far, 11 were found at Taxila in the course of the archaeological excavations conducted by Marshall; the *provenance* of the twelfth coin is not known, but as Cunningham included this among the Audumbara coins, it probably came from Punjab or Himachal Pradesh. Earlier, the name of the tribe was wrongly read as *Koputa* by Cunningham, and *Kolūta* by Bergny; it was later corrected as *Kulūta.* The *Ashṭādhyāyī* of Pāṇini has Kulūtara, perhaps a variant of Kulūta. The *Rāmāyaṇa* mentions the Kolūkas or Kaulūtas together with the western tribes. The *Mahābhārata* refers to them as Ulūta and Kaulūta, and mentions them along with such north Indian powers as Kaśmīras, Gandhāras, Bāhlīkas, and Yavanas. At another place, it refers to a country called Kulūta. The tribe is also mentioned in the *Bṛihatsaṁhitā*, Bāṇa's *Kādambarī*, the *Bālabhārata*, and the account of Hiuen-tsang. Kulūna of the *Kāśikā* may also be a variant of Kulūta.

Most of the texts place them in northern India, though they might have had offshoots in eastern and southern India also. P L Gupta has suggested that the Kulūtas seem to have formed two distinct groups, one residing in the neighbourhood of the Trigartas, and the other, in that of the Madras. But this should not be taken to imply that they were two different peoples. The Kullu valley is taken, with a great deal of justification, as their original home. The *Mahābhārata* and the *Mudrārākshasa* label the Kulūtas as *mlechchhas*, which term is generally used for the people of foreign origin. Perhaps, they were of foreign (Mongoloid) origin and got Hinduized (the names of their chiefs are purely Indian) and mixed up with the local population.

The Kulūta coins mention the names of four rulers, namely, Ārya[mitra ?], Satyamitra, Vijayamitra, and Vīrayaśas, who, according to Bela Lahiri, might have ruled in that chronological order. The *provenance* of the coins, the use of both Brāhmī and Kharoshṭhī scripts, and the devices, link these coins with the Audumbaras and the Kuṇindas (second-first centuries BC), but the use of Sanskrit suggests for them a later date of first-second centuries AD, which is supported not only by the palaeography of the coin legends but also by the stratigraphical evidence of Marshall's excavations at Taxila showing that the Kulūta coins were buried in early Kushāṇa period.

Kuṇinda. While the coin legend gives the form Kuṇinda, literature has the forms Kulinda, Kauṇinda, Kaulinda, Kulindrene, etc. The evidence of the *Mahābhārata*, which mentions them as a mountainous people having hundreds of groups (*śata-saṁkulam*), associates them with the Pāṇḍavas and suggests that the tribe was widely diffused. The *Rāmāyaṇa* also mentions the tribe, as also the *Bṛihatsaṁhitā* which places it in the northwestern division, with the Kaśmīras, Kulūtas, etc. Ptolemy refers to them as Kulindrene, and places them in the mountainous region. According to the *Mahāmāyūrī*, the worship of Yaksha Ushṭrapāda was popular among the Kuṇindas. Kuṇinda coins have been found at Behat near Saharanpur, Srinagar in Garhwal, and the areas around Jwalamukhi, Karnal, Sunet,

Tappa Mewa, and Ropar. According to Cunningham, they inhabited the hill districts on both sides of the Sutlej, with their capital at Srughna (or Sugh), on the west bank of the Yamuna. Allan considers the strip of land at the foot of the Siwalik hills between the Yamuna and the Sutlej and the territory between the upper courses of the Beas and the Sutlej as their home. To this should be added the Garhwal-Kumaon region, where also their coins have been found.

The Kuṇindas, who were *rājaśabdopajīvī* (that is members of the central assembly bore the title of *rājan*), seem to have risen as a political power after the fall of the Mauryas. Tarn suggests that the Kuṇindas, along with some other tribes, were subjugated by Menander. It appears that during the Kushāṇa period also, they lost their independence; but later, along with the Yaudheyas and the Ārjunāyanas (with whom they might have formed a confederacy), they were responsible for the decline of the Kushāṇa power. They do not find mention in the Allahabad pillar inscription of Samudragupta (*c* 350 AD), which suggests that, by that time, their power had declined. Some scholars suggest that they were incorporated with the Yaudheyas, whose coins, datable to the second-third centuries AD, show influence of the Kuṇinda coins. The coins of the tribe have been divided into two series—the Amoghabhūti series, and the *Chatreśvara* series. Amoghabhūti seems to be the name of the tribal chief, or the title of the Kuṇinda chiefs. *Chatreśvara* in the legend of the second series is taken to stand for Śiva, who also appears in his anthropomorphic form on these coins, and there is a suggestion that the Kuṇindas might have dedicated their state to their patron deity, and, in this theocracy, coins were issued in the name of Śiva.

Mālava. According to the *Mahābhārata*, the Mālavas were the descendants of the 100 sons, whom King Aśvapati begat on his queen, Mālavī, as a consequence of the boon Sāvitrī obtained from Yama. This tribe (Malloi) is mentioned by the classical writers as unsuccessfully resisting Alexander by forming an alliance with the Oxydrakai (= Kshudrakas), in the fourth century BC. The epics, the purāṇas, the *Mahābhāshya*, the *Chāndravyākaraṇa*, and the *Kāśikā* also refer to the Mālavas, often along with the Kshudrakas, and the last two texts mention them as a *saṁgha*, whose members lived by the profession of arms. Hiuen-tsang refers to them as Mo-la-po. References to the Mālavas are also found in the Nasik inscription of Ushavadāta, the Nandsa *yūpa* inscription of (Vikrama) year 283 (= 225 AD), and the Allahabad pillar inscription of Samudragupta. The classical writers place them in Punjab near the river Ravi. The *Mahābhārata* also mentions them in association with the tribes inhabiting the Punjab region, like the Trigartas, Madras, and Śibis, thus showing that the Mālavas inhabited the Punjab region. The *Vishṇupurāṇa* and the evidence of the inscriptions and their earlier coins, however, suggest that they inhabited eastern Rajasthan. *Mālavagaṇa-vishaya,* mentioned in the Nandsa inscription, is believed by Altekar to comprise the former states of Udaipur, Jaipur, and Tonk, and the district of Ajmer. They appear to have migrated to Rajasthan from Punjab under the pressure of the Greek invasion; then they moved further south and occupied the region in western Madhya Pradesh, now called Malwa after them. In *c* 350 AD, they submitted to Samudragupta. Perhaps, the Mālavīya brāhmaṇas of Gujarat, Madhya Pradesh, and Uttar Pradesh are the descendants of the Mālavas.

Mālava coins are all in copper, and mostly round in shape, although square and rectangular coins are also known. Cunningham places these coins between 250 BC and 250 AD, but most of the scholars prefer the date from the second or first century BC to the fourth century AD, when the Mālavas submitted to Samudragupta; Rapson, however, believes that the upper limit for these coins may be as late as the fifth century AD. Some Mālava coins bear some enigmatic legends like *Magaja, Mapojaya, Bhapaṁyana, Yama, Pachha, Jāmaka, Paya, Māśapa, Magachha*, etc. In these curious legends, some scholars recognize the names of Mālava chiefs, though this is by no means certain.

Paurava. According to the *Mahābhārata*, the Paurava tribe was founded by Pūru, the son of Yayāti and Śarmishṭhā. In the *Ṛigveda*, the powerful Pūru ruler, Sudāsa, won a spectacular victory in the Dāśarājña battle fought on the banks of the river Parushṇī (modern Ravi). In the *Rāmāyaṇa*, it is told that Purūravas, the great-grandfather of Pūru, was the son of a ruler who had migrated from Bāhli in Central Asia. The *Ṛigveda* locates the Pūrus somewhere in the vicinity of the river Sarasvatī. The *Mahābhārata* refers to a city protected by the Pauravas, which was located somewhere near Kashmir. At the time of the invasion of India by Alexander, the land between the rivers Jhelum and Chenab was ruled by Poros, which seems to be the Greek form of Pūru or Paurava. The *Bṛihatsaṁhitā* also refers to the Pauravas with such northern tribes as the Madrakas, the Mālavas, and the Trigartas. There are some seven copper or billon coins in the collection of the British Museum, London, which seem to have been issued by the Pauravas. Names of three Paurava chiefs—Mahādeva,

Datamita/Iṁdrotamita, and Vijayanaya/Vijayayayī, along with the title *rājña* and the tribal name, have been read in the coin legend on some of these coins. The Paurava coins have been placed in the first century BC or first century AD, on palaeographical grounds.

Rājanya. First discovered by James Prinsep, the coins issued by the Rājanya tribe were earlier ascribed to the Mahārāja *janapada* due to the faulty reading of the legend on these coins, and Jayaswal postulated the existence of a state of that name and tried to trace its antiquity to Pāṇini. Later, the legend was correctly read by V A Smith as *Rajaña janapadasa.* Rājanya in the Purushasūkta of the *Ṛigveda* and the epics stands for the kshatriyas. It has been variously suggested that the Rājanyas might be the Kshatriyas mentioned in the *Arthaśāstra* along with the Kambojas and the Surāshṭras as subsisting by arms, and the Kshatriyas (Khatiyas) whose pride Gautamīputra Sātakarṇi subdued, and the Kathaoi and Xathroi of the classical writers. But Rājanya as a people are known in the *Gaṇapāṭha* of Pāṇini, the *Mahābhārata, Mahābhāshya, Chāndravyākaraṇa, Kāśikā, Sarasvatīkaṇṭhābharaṇa,* etc. The *Mārkaṇḍeyapurāṇa* locates them in the northeast. But the *Mahābhārata* groups them with such north Indian tribes as the Śibis, Yaudheyas, Madras, etc, and this is supported by the *Bṛihatsaṁhitā,* which refers to the Rājanyas as a people of the north. The Rājanyas of coins should be identified with them.

Of about 26 known coins of the tribe, some were found from regions around Mathurā, but most of them come from the Hoshiarpur district of Punjab. The *provenance* and the use of the Kharoshṭhī script suggest that the Rājanyas inhabited eastern Punjab, and later migrated to Mathurā and eastern Rajasthan. Their coins are datable, on palaeographical grounds, to second-first centuries BC.

Sāvitriputra. Among the Rājanya coins, Allan published a die-struck square copper coin, resembling the coin of the Trigarta *janapada.* The reading of the obverse Kharoshṭhī legend was doubtful, but Devendra Handa, after examining the coin in the collection of the British Museum, London, restores it as *Sāvitriputra janapadasa.* A tribe named Sāvitriputraka is mentioned by Pāṇini among the Dāmnyādi group of *āyudhajīvi saṁghas.* It is also mentioned in the *Mahābhārata,* amongst the people who fought by the side of the Kurus. The tribe seems to have traced its origin from the 100 sons the Śālva prince, Satyavān, and his wife, the Madra princess Sāvirtī, obtained as a boon from Yama. On the basis of the use of only the Kharoshṭhī script on these coins, Handa locates the Sāvitriputras in the region to the north of the river Sarasvatī.

Śibi. The *Ṛigveda* mentions Śivas as one of the tribes defeated by Sudāsa in the Battle of Ten Kings. The *Aitareyabrāhmaṇa* has a tribal name Śivi (= Śibi). The *Mahābhārata,* at one place, groups the Śibis with the Rājanyas, Yaudheyas, Trigartas, Madras, and Kekayas, and places them in the Punjab, while at another place, it refers to the Śibis along with the Trigartas and the Mālavas in the context of Nakula's western expedition. In this epic, Sunandā, the mother of Śāntanu, is described as a Śibi princess, while Yudhishṭhira marries a daughter of the Śibi king, Govāsana. Classical writers, like Diodoros, Strabo, and Curtius, refer to a Punjab tribe as Siboi or Sibae (= Śibi), who wore skin and had the club as weapon, and lived in the area between the rivers Beas and Chandrabhāgā. The Śibis are also mentioned in the Jātaka tales, which refer to Ariṭṭhapura and Jetuttara as two of their cities. The *Mahābhāshya* shows the existence of a tribe called Śibi and refers to their town, Śivapura, as *udīchyagrāma*, 'northern village'. Śivapura also finds mention in the *Mahāmāyūrī*, which text also refers to Śiva as the tutelary deity of that town. A fifth century inscription from Shorkot in the Jhang district, between the Ravi and Chenab, mentions Śibipura, and Vögel considers the mound of Shorkot as representing the city of the Śibis. Though Śibi coins have been reported from Punjab, their association with that region may be accepted.

The Sibia Jats of Haryana and Rajasthan might be the descendants of the Śibis. King Śibi Uśīnara, who is referred to in the *Mahābhārata*, the Jātaka tales, and the purāṇas, seems to have been the ancestor of the Śibis. The find of Śibi coins in and around Nagari in Rajasthan shows their migration to that area from Punjab region before the second century BC, to which period the coins are datable; Devendra Handa, however, feels that these coins should be dated from the latter half of the second century BC to mid-first century BC. The absence of any reference to them in the Allahabad pillar inscription of Samudragupta shows that they had ceased to exist as a political power by that time. The first part of the legend, *Majhamikāya Śibijanapadasa*, occurring on Śibi coins, may stand for *Mādhyamikāyāḥ* (for, or on Mādhyamikā), or *Mādhyamikāyāṁ* (in Mādhyamikā). Mādhyamikā is known as a city from literary and epigraphic evidence. The *Mahābhāshya* refers to the Yavana siege of Mādhyamikā. The *Mahābhārata* mentions Mādhyamikās along with Daśārṇa, and the *Bṛihatsaṁhitā* places them with the Yaudheyas and Ārjunāyanas, and in the central division of India. The Barli and Chittorgarh inscriptions also refer to Mādhyamikā. It was, in all probability, the capital of the Śibi *janapada* and is identical with Nagari near Chittor. There is a suggestion that the Mādhyamikās were neighbouring allies of the Śibis, who, like them, originally inhabited the Punjab region. Both tribes migrated to Rajasthan due to political and/or economic pressures; the Mādhyamikās probably came early and founded the city of Mādhyamikā, and the Śibis came after the siege of this city was a thing of the past.

Trigarta. The Trigartas are referred to as an *āyudhajīvī saṁgha* in the *Ashṭādhyāyī* of Pāṇini, which text also associates the bhārgāyaṇa *gotra* with this tribe. In the *Gaṇapāṭha*, they are referred to, along with the Yaudheyas and other tribes, and in the *Mahābhārata*, with the Yaudheyas, Śibis, Rājanyas, etc. *Trigarta-shashṭha* in Pāṇini is explained by *Kāśikā* as a confederacy of six members—(i) Kauṇoparatha, (ii) Dāṇḍaki, (iii) Kraushṭaki, (iv) Jālamāni, (v) Brāhmagupta, and (vi) Jānaki. V S Agrawala identifies Brāhmagupta with Bharmor (Chamba), and points out that, in the *Mahābhārata*, members of Jānaki confederacy are mentioned as helpmates of Trigarta king, Suśarman. The *Bṛihatsaṁhitā* locates the Trigartas, along with the Kulūtas and the Chīnas, in the northern region, and a puranic text, in the Himalayan region. The tribe also finds mention in various purāṇas, like the *Vishṇupurāṇa*, *Matsyapurāṇa*, *Vāyupurāṇa*, *Vāmanapurāṇa*, etc, as also in such texts as the *Chāndravyākaraṇa*, the *Daśakumāracharita* of Daṇḍin, the *Rājataraṅgiṇī* of Kalhaṇa, the *Sarasvatīkaṇṭhābharaṇa*, and the *Gaṇaratnamahodadhi*. A Trigarta king is mentioned in the Chamba copperplate inscription of 1050 AD. The word *trigarta* means 'three pits', and it has been suggested that the tribe occupied three valleys—those of the rivers Ravi, Beas, and Sutlej. Hiuen-tsang, and the *Vaijayantī* and the *Abhidhānachintāmaṇi*, take Trigarta as corresponding to Jālandhara, and Cunningham places the Trigarta region between Kangra and Jalandhar, to the south of Chamba.

A square copper coin, weighing 43 grains, shows a four-tiered structure and traces of a Kharoshṭhī legend on the obverse, and the branch of a tree, a *nandipada*, and another symbol on the reverse with the Brāhmī legend, *Trakata-janapadasa* (= Sanskrit, *Trigarta-janapadasya*, ie 'of the territory of the Trigartas') in second or first century BC characters.

Uddehika. The *Bṛihatsaṁhitā* locates the Uddehikas in northern India, and mentions them along with such other tribes as the Gaurgrīvas, Aśvatthas, Pāṇḍus, Guḍas, and the Pañchālas. Of these, the Pāṇḍus, who were, perhaps, identical with the Pandae of Ptolemy, may be located in Thaneshwar, while the Pañchālas occupied the Rohilkhand region. The Uddehikas, hence, might have lived in some region, 'not far from these tribes'. They are mentioned, together with the Pāṇḍus, Guḍas and the Madhyamikās, in the *Samāsasaṁhitā*. Alberuni places them near Bazana, which is identified variously with Narayanpur (former Alwar state), Naraina, and Bayana (Bharatpur district). Bela Lahiri regards the *madhyadeśa* as their area. Some others consider Bari Udai in the Gangasagar *tehsil* (old Jaipur state) as the old capital of the Uddehikas. Their territory would have comprised Rairh (Jaipur district, where their coins have been found), together with Bari Udai and the adjoining regions. Palaeographically, these coins can be ascribed to the second or first century BC, though Rapson placed them in the third century BC. The names of the chiefs—Sūryamitra and Dhruvamitra—are mentioned on coins, without any titles.

Vemaki. *Vemaka* in Sanskrit means 'weaver'. In the *Harivaṁśa* and the *Brahmapurāṇa*, as pointed out by D C Sircar, it is the name of a sage, perhaps the patron saint of the tribe. The Vaiyāmakas of the *Mahābhārata* are referred to along with the Audumbaras, and their inhabiting territories, close to each other, is corroborated by the find of Vemaki and Audumbara coins together. Some editions of the *Mahābhārata*, as also the *Mahāmāyūrī*, have the form Vairāmaka, which tribe has to be identified with the Vemakis. Bhaṭṭa Utpala, the commentator on the *Bṛihatsaṁhitā*, mentions a tribe named Vaimaka in the northern region. Coins reveal the existence of three Vemaki chiefs—Rudravarman, Bhavavarman, and Śivaghosha. The Vemaki coins may be assigned to the second-first centuries BC.

Vṛishṇi. The *Ashṭādhyāyī* of Pāṇini speaks of the Andhaka-Vṛishṇi *saṁgha*; the *Mahābhārata* includes some other tribes also in this confederation, and refers to Vāsudeva as its leader. The purāṇas and the *Arthaśāstra* also mention the tribe. In the epic-puranic tradition, they are associated with the Mathurā region, but the evidence of the *Śatapathabrāhmaṇa* seems to suggest that in the later vedic period, they inhabited some area in Haryana or Punjab. The *Harivaṁśa* informs that, when attacked, they left Mathurā under the leadership of Kṛishṇa, and settled in Dvārakā. The obverse legend on the only coin of this tribe has been read as *Vṛishṇi rājajñāgaṇasya tratarasya*, and interpreted variously as 'of the protector of the tribe Vṛishṇirājanya', ie 'of the protector of the Rājanya (or warrior) tribe of the Vṛishṇis'; or 'of a family whose name (?) is Vṛishṇirāja' or 'whose royal name (?) is Vṛishṇi'; or '[the coin] of him whose family are Vṛishṇi kshatriyas'; or '[coin] of the saviour of the host of Vṛishṇi kings', etc. P L Gupta regards this coin as a joint issue of a confederation of the Vṛishṇis and the Rājanyas. Some even take Jñāgaṇa as a personal name, and translate the legend as '[This is the coin] of Jñāgaṇa, King of the Vṛishṇis, the Saviour'. On the basis of the mention of *Vṛishṇi-rājanya-gaṇa* at the beginning of the legend on two sealings from Sunet, Devendra Handa proposes to the read the legend on the coin as *Vṛishṇi-rājanya-gaṇasya trātārasya*, and suggests that the coin was issued in the name of Vāsudeva-Kṛishṇa, who is mentioned in the *Mahābhārata* as the saviour (*trātā*) of the Vṛishṇis, and whose emblem, the wheel, occurs on the reverse of this coin. He further suggests that, the Vṛishṇis might have dedicated their state to Vāsudeva-Kṛishṇa, and issued the coin in his name.

Devendra Handa has published certain copper coins, mostly from Sunet, which bear, on the obverse, a Brāhmī legend, variously mentioning such names as Yajñasoma, Vyāghrasoma, Vyāghrasattra, Jayasa/Jiyasa, Vasusena, Jayasoma/Āryyasoma, Yajñadeva, Sattragupta, Balavighna/Balavāhana, Vesha (?), etc. Associating these coins with the Vṛishṇis, Handa proposes to identify the persons mentioned on these copper coins as Vṛishṇi generals (like the *mahāsenāptis* mentioned on the sealings from Sunet), who seem to have been elected by the *gaṇa* as their rulers, and were vested with the right to issue coins in their own names. Though the literary evidence places the Vṛishṇis in Mathurā, the likely *provenance* of the coin (Punjab), the *chakra* which also occurs on Kulūta coins, the epithet *tratara* which is a translation of the Greek *soter*, and the use of the Kharoshṭhī script, point out that at the time of the issue of the coin, Punjab was the homeland of the Vṛishṇis. Either these Vṛishṇis were different from those of Mathurā, or else originally the Vṛishṇis belonged to Mathurā, from where they migrated to Dvārakā, and, after the destruction of that city, some of them migrated thence to Punjab. The *Vishṇupurāṇa* states that after the destruction of Dvārakā, Arjuna settled the Vṛishṇis in the Pañchanada country (Punjab), and 20 seals of the Vṛishṇis have been reported from Sunet. Interestingly, the Vārshaṇeyas of today, who are considered as the descendants of the Vṛishṇis, claim Agroha in Hissar district as their original home. This would suggest that the Vṛishṇis, at some point of time, inhabited the area between the upper courses of the Ravi and Beas.

Yaudheya. The *Ashṭādhyāyī* of Pāṇini mentions the Yaudheyas as an *āyudhajīvī saṁgha*, but, recently, attempts have been made to trace the antiquity of this tribe up to the later vedic period on the basis of the occurrence of *Yaudheya* in the pre-Pāṇini *Śākaṭāyanavyākaraṇa* and the *Jaiminīyabrāhmaṇa.* The tribe also finds mentions in the *Mahābhāshya*, the purāṇas, *Bṛihatsaṁhitā*, *Chāndravyākaraṇa*, and *Kāśikā.* The *Mahābhārata* refers to Yaudheya as a son of Yudhishṭhira and his wife, Devikā or Devakī, but, according to the *Vishṇupurāṇa*, Yudhishṭhira won the hand of the Princess Yaudheyī in a *svayaṁvara.* The name of the princess (Yaudheyī) seems to show that she belonged to the Yaudheya tribe; if this be correct, the Yaudheyas must have existed before Yudhishṭhira, and the tribe could not have descended from Yudhishṭhira's son. The *Yaśastilaka* of Somadevasūri (tenth century AD) refers to the Rājapura city (identified with Rajapur in former Patiala state) of the Yaudheyas. Still later, the tribe is mentioned in the *Sarasvatīkaṇṭhābharaṇa* and the *Vaijayantī*. The *Harivaṁśa* and some purāṇas consider the Yaudheyas as descendants of Nṛiga, the son of Uśīnara. The Junagarh inscription of Rudradāman I, the Bijayagadh inscription, and the Allahabad pillar inscription of Samudragupta, also refer to this tribe. The first of these inscriptions refers to the defeat of the Yaudheyas at the hands Rudradāman I. The Bijayagadh inscription, of the third century AD, mentions their elected leader, a *mahārāja* and *mahāsenāpati*. A sealing from Agroha refers to *mahārāja*, *mahākshatrapa*, and *mahāsenāpati* as titles of Indramitra or Rājyamitra, who, as per the testimony of the sealing, had been selected as such by the Yaudheya *gaṇa*. Curiously, the classical writers make no mention of this tribe, although Arrian's description of a people beyond the Hyphasis as good agriculturists and gallant fighters and having a constitutional government, is taken by some scholars, like K P Jayaswal, to the refer to the Yaudheyas. Cunningham considers the Johiya Rajputs as the descendants of the Yaudheyas.

Yaudheya coins have been found in various parts of Punjab, Haryana, Himachal Pradesh, Delhi, Rajasthan, and Uttar Pradesh; or, in other words, from western Uttar Pradesh in the east to eastern Rajasthan in the west, and from Kangra in the north to Sambhar in the south. It has been suggested that the territory of the Yaudheyas extended 'from Ludhiana to Saharanpur and beyond in Garhwal in one direction and from there to Bahawalpur in another', with Rohtak and its environs as its core. Richard Mann, however, is of the view that at the time of the issue of their early coinage, the tribe inhabited the Rohtak-Naurangabad region. But it was forced to move towards the foothills of the Himalayas as a result of the invasion of V'ima Takshuma. According to him, there are no Yaudheya coins for the period when Kanisha I and Huvishka were ruling, and the Yaudheyas seem to have started issuing their coinage again only towards the end of the reign of Vāsudeva I. In this period, the tribe seems to have, once again, occupied the Rohtak-Naurangabad region, expanded its territories, at least up to Hissar in the west, and the river Yamuna in the east, and established Sunet as one of its centres. On the basis of the occurrence of the figure of Kārttikeya on some Yaudheya coins, as also of the coin legends of this class mentioning the god, it has been suggested that the Yaudheyas might have dedicated their state to their patron deity, and administered their territories in his name.

Chapter III

The Māhāmeghavāhanas, Sātavāhanas, and the Successors of the Sātavāhanas in the *Dakshiṇāpatha*

The Māhāmeghavāhana dynasty of Kaliṅga

After its conquest by Aśoka, not much is known about the history of Kaliṅga, till the Hathigumpha inscription of Khāravela sheds some welcome light on three generations of Chedi rulers of the Māhāmeghavāhana family. The name, Māhāmeghavāhana, might have been derived from Mahāmeghavāhana, who seems to be the eponymous founder of the ruling family and the grandfather of Khāravela. The immediate predecessor of Khāravela might have been Vakradeva, of the Māhāmeghavāhana family, who got the lower storey of the Manchapuri cave excavated on the Udayagiri hill. In the Hathigumpha inscription, Khāravela claims descent from the famous ancient Chedi ruler, Vasu [Uparichara]. This inscription is unique in ancient Indian history, in that it gives the account of the early life, and the first 13 years of the reign, of Khāravela, in a chronological order.

The inscription records that Khāravela spent the first six years of his life in the company of the women of the palace, as befitted a prince. For the next nine years, he received education in various branches of knowledge, like drawing of charters (*lekha*), currency (*rūpa*), accountancy (*gaṇanā*), protocol (*vavahāra*), and law (*vidhi*). At the age of 15, he was appointed the heir-apparent, and, in that capacity, received practical training of administration. When he completed 24 years of age, he was anointed king. The language of the inscription hints that the predecessor of Khāravela abdicated the throne in his favour. In the first year of his reign, Khāravela carried out extensive repairs of the fortifications of his capital, Kaliṅganagara, which had been struck by a cyclone, and beautified it with several ponds, thus consolidating his position against foreign aggressions. Thereafter, he lavished 35 lakh current coins on entertaining his subjects, thus endearing himself to his subjects.

In the second year of his reign, Khāravela despatched a huge army towards the west, 'unmindful' of Sātakarṇi, who is believed to be some Sātavāhana ruler, though his identity is not certain, and this information cannot be used to determine the date of Khāravela. The armies of Kaliṅga advanced up to the river, named Kaṇhabeṁṇā in the inscription, and struck terror in the heart of the inhabitants of a city, the name of which has been read as Asikanagara by most of the scholars, but as Musikanagara by K P Jayaswal. The river has been identified as Wainganga, together with its tributary, the Kanhan, by Rapson and B M Barua, but as Krishna by K P Jayaswal. Rapson and Barua identify the city of Asikanagara with the capital of the Assikas in the Godavari valley, but Jayaswal, who reads the name of the city as

Musikanagara, locates it near the junction of the rivers Musi and Krishna, at the borders of the district of Nalgonda. As the identification of the river and the city are not certain, it is not possible to determine the limits of the advance of the army of Kaliṅga in the west. The use of the words, *achitayitā Sātakaṁṇi*, 'unmindful of Sātakarṇi', in this context seems to indicate that this western expedition was not undertaken to occupy any new territories, but, rather, to challenge the Sātavāhana ruler. Although it did not lead to any acquisition of territories, the western expedition was represented in Kaliṅga as a successful one, and the third year of the reign of Khāravela saw the organization of festivals to celebrate the victorious campaign.

In the fourth year of his reign, Khāravela launched a campaign against the Raṭhikas of Khandesh and Ahmadnagar, and the Bhojakas of Berar, who were defeated and forced to worship the feet of the ruler of Kaliṅga. In this context, the inscription mentions an 'abode of the Vidyādharas', which had been established by some rulers of Kaliṅga, who preceded Khāravela. According to an inscription of Kumāragupta I, from Mathurā, Vidyādhara was a branch of the Jainas. The Hathigumpha inscription begins with an incantation to the Jaina *arhats* and *siddhas*, revealing the inclination of Khāravela towards Jainism. There is a suggestion that the Raṭhikas and the Bhojakas might have violated some place of Jaina worship, for which, they were punished by Khāravela.

In his fifth regnal year, Khāravela extended, up to his capital, the system of canal, which had been dug by some Nanda ruler, *ti-vasa-sata* earlier. This Nanda king has been identified with Mahāpadmananda, who, according to the purāṇas, conquered Kaliṅga. The date of the original excavation of the system of canals by this Nanda ruler is not known for certain. However, according to the Ceylonese sources, the Nandas ruled for 22 years, and their rule was brought to an end by Chandragupta Maurya, around 324 BC. To reduce the margin of error, the date of the excavation of the system of canals may be placed in the middle of their 22 year rule, that is *c* 335 BC. The phrase, *ti-vasa-sata*, could mean both one hundred and three years, and three hundred years. If it means one hundred and three years, the fifth year of the reign of Khāravela would come to (335-103 =) 232 BC. But this cannot be accepted, as, at that time, Kaliṅga was under the Mauryas. Taking *ti-vasa-sata* to mean three hundred years, the fifth year of the reign of Khāravela would come to (335-330 =) 35 BC, and his accession may be placed *c* 40/39 BC. The latter half of the first century BC, as the date of Khāravela, is also supported by the palaeography and style of the Hathigumpha inscription, and the use of the title of *mahārāja* for him.

In the sixth year of his reign, Khāravela demonstrated kingly pomp, which cost the royal treasury several lakhs of coins, by providing amenities for the inhabitants of his capital city, and remitting taxes. The word for kingly pomp in the inscription is *rājaseyaṁ.* K P Jayaswal proposed to amend the reading of the word as *rājasūyaṁ*, and suggested that Khāravela performed the *rājasūya* sacrifice in the sixth year of his reign. But Khāravela, a Jaina, could not be expected to perform a vedic sacrifice. Besides, to accept the suggestion of Jayaswal, one would have to amend the reading of the word, unnecessarily. The portion of the inscription, dealing with the seventh year of the reign of Khāravela, is damaged, and, consequently, the account of this year is not very clear. However, it appears that the wife of Khāravela, who belonged to the vajiradhara *gotra* and was the daughter of the great-grandson of King Hastisiṁha of the Lalāka dynasty, gave birth to a child, perhaps the heir to the throne.

In his eighth regnal year, Khāravela mounted his first attack on northern India. His armies advanced towards Gorathagiri (Barabar hills), destroyed its fortifications, and besieged Rājagṛiha. This great feat of Khāravela struck terror in the heart of the Indo-Greek ruler, who immediately retreated to Mathurā. The name of this Indo-Greek ruler has been read, variously, as Dimita, Dimiṭa, Ḍimiṭa, or Ḍimita. There is no unanimity among scholars regarding his identification, too, and Demetrios I, Demetrios II, and even Diomedes, have been regarded as the leader of the Yavana hosts. Under the circumstances, it would not be appropriate to determine the date of Khāravela on the basis of his contemporeinity with this Indo-Greek ruler. In the ninth year of his reign, Khāravela commemorated his successful northern campaign by building a magnificent palace, named Mahāvijaya-*prāsāda*, on both the banks of the river Prāchī.

The account of the tenth year of the reign of Khāravela is quite vague. The inscription merely informs us that, in that year, he mounted an attack of Bhāratavarsha. This is the name used for India, in general, but, in certain instances, this is the technical name for the Ganga valley. This enterprise does not appear to have borne any result.

In the eleventh year of his reign, Khāravela turned his attention towards the south. His armies captured Pithuṁḍa, which is identified with Pitundra of Ptolemy, and Pithuṇḍa of the Jaina text, *Uttarādhyayanasūtra*, and got it ploughed with ploughs yoked to asses. The same year, he is said to have defeated a confederacy of Tamiḷ states, which had been in existence for *terasa-vasa-sata* (one hundred and thirteen years, or thirteen hundred years).

Khāravela had mounted two attacks on northern India, one in the eighth year, and the other, in the tenth year of his reign. But, in the twelfth year of his reign, he led a third expedition against northern India, causing consternation to the kings there. The horses and elephants of his army watered in the river Ganga. Bahasatimita, the king of Magadha, was defeated, and forced to pay homage to Khāravela. K P Jayaswal rendered Bahasatimita into Sanskrit as Bṛihaspatimitra, and, on the basis of astrology, suggested his identification with Pushyamitra Śuṅga. As this Śuṅga king began ruling *c* 187 BC, Jayaswal placed Khāravela in the first half of the second century BC. This, however, has not found much favour with historians. The Prakrit rendering of Bṛihaspatimitra would be Bahapatimita, while the Hathigumpha inscription has Bahasatimita, which is the Prakrit rendering of Bṛihatsvātimitra. Scholars like D C Sircar identify this ruler with Bṛihatsvātimitra of the Mora and the Pabhosa inscriptions, who ruled after Indrāgnimitra and Brahmamitra, some time in the second half of the first century BC. The victorious arms of Khāravela also seem to have reached Aṅga, and he returned to Kaliṅga with enormous booty from those two countries. He is also said to have brought back from Magadha, the statue of a Jina, which had been taken from Kaliṅga to Magadha by the Nanda ruler. But Barua proposes to read *Kaliṅga jana*, the people of Kaliṅga, in place of *Kaliṅga jina*, and suggests that these people were the descendants of those inhabitants of Kaliṅga, whom the Nanda conqueror had taken away to Magadha as captives of war.

The same year, Khāravela is also said to have captured some horses, elephants, and pearls from the Pāṇḍya king. Some scholars, however, find it difficult to believe that Khāravela could have led two expeditions—one in northern India, and the other, in southern India, in one and the same year. It is also possible that, taking advantage of the absence of Khāravela from Kaliṅga, the Pāṇḍya king might have attacked that kingdom, but Khāravela succeeded in repulsing that attack, and, at the same time, in inflicting heavy losses on the invader.

In the thirteenth year of his reign, Khāravela was engaged in religious activities. In that year, he commissioned the construction of residential chambers for Jaina monks on the Udayagiri hill, and spent 75 lakh of the current coins on the beautification of a magnificent congregation hall for those Jaina monks. The very purpose of the Hathigumpha inscription is to record these pious acts of the king. Although Khāravela was a devout Jaina, he honoured all the religious sects, and repaired the temples of all the deities. The inscription, which illuminates the historical horizon of Kaliṅga like a meteor, ends with this account of the thirteenth year of the reign of Khāravela, and nothing further is known of the history of that part of India for quite some time.

The Sātavāhana dynasty

The history of the *dakshiṇāpatha*, after its conquest by Aśoka, remains shrouded in mystery for a long time. Of course, there are references to kings, like Kuberaka, who seem to have exercised independent authority, but a major part of the northern *dakshiṇāpatha* continued to remain under the political influence of the successors of Aśoka, and the Śuṅgas after them, till the rise of the Sātavāhanas, called Andhras or Andhrabṛityas in literature. There is a suggestion that Andhra might have been the lineage of these rulers, and that the ruling family was named Sātavāhana, after the eponymous founder, King Sātavāhana, known from some copper and lead coins. Some scholars have tried to identify this King Sātavāhana with Simuka, who is called Simuka Sātavāhana in an inscription from Naneghat.

The rule of the Sātavāhana dynasty came to an end *c* 225 AD. According to the *Matsyapurāṇa*, the Sātavāhanas ruled for 460 years. If this information be accepted, the Sātavāhanas would have started ruling around 235 BC. But that was the time of Aśoka and his successors. According to the puranic tradition, the Mauryas ruled for 137 years, the Śuṅgas, for 112 years, and the Kāṇvas, for 45 years, and Simuka established the rule of the Sātavāhanas by ousting Suśarman, the last Kāṇva ruler. This would imply that Simuka brought the rule of the Kāṇvas to an end, (137+112+45 =) 294 years after 324 BC (the initial year of Maurya rule), that is *c* 30 BC. The Sātavāhanas would, thus, have started ruling some time around the middle of the first century BC. The *Aitareyabrāhmaṇa* refers to the Andhras as dasyus, and Indian tradition refers to Simuka as *vṛishala*. However, in the Nasik cave inscription of year 19 of Vāsishṭhīputra Puḷumāvi, Gautamīputra Sātakarṇi is referred to as *eka bramhaṇa*, that is the 'unique brāhmaṇa'. According to the *Dvātriṁśataputtalikā*, the Sālivāhana (= Sātavāhana) were of mixed brāhmaṇa and Nāga lineage. This would, perhaps, explain the claim of brāhmaṇahood for Gautamīputra Sātakarṇi in the Nasik cave inscription, and the reluctance of the orthodox brāhmaṇas to grant brāhmaṇa status to the Sātavāhanas.

According to Indian tradition, and the information provided by Ptolemy, the Sātavāhanas are known to have ruled from Pratishṭhāna (modern Paithan, on the Godavari, near Aurangabad in Maharashtra). The epigraphic records and coins of the early Sātavāhana rulers, too, were, for a long time, known only from northern Maharashtra, and from Vidisha in Malwa. On this basis, it was suggested that their original home was situated somewhere in northern Maharashtra or central *dakshiṇāpatha*. However, the use of the terms, Andhra or Andhrabṛitya, for the Sātavāhanas in literature, led to the suggestion that they originally hailed from Andhradeśa; the recent discovery of the coins of some early rulers of the dynasty, like Simuka, from places like Karimnagar in Andhra Pradesh, has been cited as evidence in support of this view.

As seen above, the rule of the Sātavāhana dynasty appears to have been established by Simuka, who, according to the purāṇas, 'violently extirpated' the Kāṇva ruler, Suśarman, and destroyed the remaining power of the Śuṅgas. He seems to have conquered the territories around Vidiśā from the later Śuṅgas. But there is no evidence to show that he wrested Magadha, or any other part of northern India, from the Śuṅgas or the Kāṇvas. In all likelihood, Simuka exercised authority over parts of the *dakshiṇāpatha* and central India. He might also have captured some parts of western India, from the Indo-Greeks, or from the Śuṅgas or Kāṇvas.

According to the purāṇas, the next ruler of the dynasty was Kṛishṇa, the brother of Simuka (often called Śiśuka), who ruled for 18 years. He is also known from an inscription from Nasik, which records the excavation of a cave, for the use of Buddhist monks, by one of his high officials. The findspot of his inscription would show that, during his rule, the Sātavāhana dominions extended as far west as Nasik. The purāṇas refer to Sātakarṇi I, the successor of Kṛishṇa, as a son of the latter, although, on the basis of the probable absence of the figure of Kṛishṇa, between those of Simuka and Sātakarṇi I, at Naneghat, some scholars have concluded that Sātakarṇi I might have been a son of Simuka himself. Epigraphic and numismatic evidence seems to suggest that Sātakarṇi I ruled over a considerable part of northern *dakshiṇāpatha*, and parts of central and western India; northern Konkan and Saurashtra, too, were, perhaps, within the sphere of his political influence. He married Nāganikā, who belonged to the powerful Mahāraṭhī family, and was, perhaps, a daughter of Mahāraṭhī Tranakayiro Kalalāya of the Aṁgiya or Ambhiya family, and this matrimonial alliance might have helped him in his subsequent career. This Nāganikā is known from her Naneghat inscription, and from some silver coins bearing her name along with that of her husband. Sātakarṇi I appears to have performed a number of vedic sacrifices, including two *aśvamedhas*. It seems that, at the time of his death, his sons, Vediśrī and Śaktiśrī, were minors, and that his widow, Nāganikā, administered the Sātavāhana kingdom as a regent for some time. This is, however, not acceptable to V V Mirashi.

In the period of about a century, intervening between the close of the reign of Sātakarṇi I and the accession of Gautamīputra Sātakarṇi, the power of the Sātavāhanas was eclipsed, perhaps due to the rise of the Western Kshatrapas. In this period, the different lists of Sātavāhana rulers, found in the various purāṇas, mention 10, 12, 13, 14, and even 19 rulers. This confusion was, perhaps, the result of some purāṇas including in their lists, not only the rulers of the main branch of the Sātavāhanas, but also those of the collateral branches. Among these rulers, mention may be made of Sātakarṇi II, Āpīlaka, Kuntala Sātakarṇi, and Hāla.

However, the Sātavāhanas made a complete recovery under Gautamīputra Sātakarṇi, aptly called 'the greatest of the Sātavāhanas'. He was the grandson of

Chakora, and the son of Śivasvāti and Gotamī Balaśrī. The main source of information about him is the Nasik cave inscription of the nineteenth regnal year of his son and successor, Vāsishṭhīputra Puḷumāvi. Gautamīputra Sātakarṇi had begun the construction of a cave, which was to be donated to the Buddhist monks of the Bhadrayānīya sect. But death intervened, and the work of construction was completed by Gotamī Balaśrī. The main purpose of the Nasik cave inscription is to record this donation.

From some other sources, it is known that Gautamīputra Sātakarṇi was engaged in military activities in Māmālahāra (region around Poona) in the seventeenth year of his reign, and in southern Maharashtra in the eighteenth year. These regions had earlier been wrested by the Kshaharāta Kshatrapas from the Sātavāhanas. It appears that, after consolidating his power in the initial years of his reign, Gautamīputra Sātakarṇi made a concerted effort to destroy the power of the Kshaharāta Kshatrapas. The Nasik cave inscription informs us that he uprooted the Śaka rulers. This information is corroborated by literary and numismatic evidence. The commentary on a *gāthā* in the Jaina *Āvaśyakasūtra* relates that the Sātavāhana king, through one of his ministers, induced the Śaka ruler to spend all his wealth on charity, and that when the royal treasury was empty, he attacked the Śaka ruler, and defeated and killed him. That the defeated Kshaharāta ruler was Nahapāna, is shown by the Jogalthembi hoard, which has some 9,000 silver coins of Nahapāna, struck by Gautamīputra Sātakarṇi.

The Nasik cave inscription also states that Gautamīputra Sātakarṇi put to the sword, or drove out, the Śakas, Yavanas, and Pahlavas. The Śakas might have belonged to the Kshaharāta family, but as the utter destruction of the Kshaharāta power, at the hands of

Gautamīputra Sātakarṇi, is mentioned in the inscription elsewhere, it seems more likely that these Śakas, mentioned together with the Yavanas and the Pahlavas, belonged to the Vidarbha or Kārddamaka branch of the Western Kshatrapas. The Yavanas appear to be a people of Greek origin, who had settled in Maharashtra, and whose donations are recorded in some inscriptions from places like Kanheri. Nothing definite is known about the identity of the Pahlavas mentioned in this inscription. The Nasik cave inscription also refers to the victory of Gautamīputra Sātakarṇi over some confederacies of his enemies. It has been suggested that the Śakas, Yavanas, and Pahlavas, all of foreign stock, had made common cause with the Kshaharāta Kshatrapas, and Gautamīputra Sātakarṇi defeated them in the course of his struggle against the Kshaharāta Kshatrapas.

In the Nasik cave inscription, Gotamī Balaśrī gives a list of the provinces, over which her son had exercised authority. These include Ākara (eastern Malwa), Avanti (western Malwa), Anūpa (Narmada valley), Vidarbha (Berar), Asika-Asaka-Mulaka (all in northern Maharashtra), Aparānta (northern Konkan), Kukura (western Rajasthan), and Suraṭha (Saurashtra). Thus, it appears that, as a result of his successes against the Kshaharāta Kshatrapas, Gautamīputra Sātakarṇi not only reestablished Sātavāhana authority over the territories of Ākara, Avanti, Anūpa, Vidarbha, Asika-Asaka-Mulaka, and Aparānta, which had been wrested from the Sātavāhanas by the Western Kshatrapas, but also added to the Sātavāhana kingdom, the Kshaharāta provinces of Kukura and Suraṭha. There is a view that, although not mentioned in the Nasik cave inscription as parts of the dominions of Gautamīputra Sātakarṇi, Ānartta, Śvabhra, and Maru, which lay between

Kukura, Suraṭha, and Avanti, would also have been annexed by the Sātavāhana ruler.

The Nasik cave inscription, called 'the funeral oration of a disconsolate mother', also lists the hills and mountains situated within the dominions of Gautamīputra Sātakarṇi. These include Vijha (eastern parts of the Vindhyas), Achchhavata (Ṛikshavat), Pārīchāta (the Aravali and the western parts of the Vindhyas), Sahya (the northern parts of the Western Ghats), Macha-Siriṭana-Malaya (the southern parts of the Western Ghats), Mahīda (Mahendra in the Eastern Ghats), and Chakora (the southern parts of the Eastern Ghats). Interestingly, by mentioning Gautamīputra Sātakarṇi as lord of Mahīda, Gotamī Balaśrī seems to be claiming her son's authority over Kaliṅga, and by mentioning her son as lord of Chakora, she appears to be claiming Gautamīputra Sātakarṇi's authority over the Andhradeśa. The inscription also claims that 'his chargers had drunk the waters of the three oceans', which reminds one of the title of *trisamudrādhipati*, used by Bāṇabhaṭṭa for a later Sātavāhana ruler.

The Nasik cave inscription praises Gautamīputra Sātakarṇi in conventional style, comparing him to Rāma, Keśava, Arjuna, and Bhīmasena in prowess, to Nābhāga, Nahusha, Janamejaya, Sagara, Yayāti, and Ambarīsha in lustre, and to Vāyu, *garuḍa*, the *siddhas*, the yakshas, the rākshasas, the *chāraṇas*, the moon, the sun, the asterisms, and the planets in his battle skills. He administered his kingdom along the guidelines laid down by the śāstras, maintained *varṇāśramadharma*, and worked tirelessly for the welfare of his subjects. On the basis of the phrase, *varavaraṇavikama chāruvikama*, occurring in the Nasik cave inscription with reference to Gautamīputra Sātakarṇi, and the fact that he defeated the Śakas, attempts have been made to identify him with the legendary king, Vikramāditya, though this has not found universal acceptance. The inscription refers to Gotamī Balaśrī as *mahārājamātā mahārājapitāmahī.* This has led R G Bhandarkar and D R Bhandarkar to suggest that, for some time at least, Gautamīputra Sātakarṇi ruled conjointly with his son, Vāsishṭhīputra Puḷumāvi, but there is no corroborative evidence to support this contention.

According to the purāṇas, Gautamīputra Sātakarṇi was succeeded by his son, Vāsishṭhīputra Puḷumāvi, who ruled for 28 or 29 years. The findspots of his inscriptions—Nasik, Karle, and Amaravati, give us an idea of the extent of his dominions. Although the Sātavāhanas had lost some of the northern provinces of their empire to the Kārddamaka Kshatrapas during the reign of Vāsishṭhīputra Puḷumāvi, or even towards the close of the reign of Gautamīputra Sātakarṇi, the discovery of the inscription of Vāsishṭhīputra Puḷumāvi at Amaravati, and that of a large number of his coins at the same site and in its surroundings, testifies to the extension of Sātavāhana authority towards the south, as far as the river Krishna, during his reign. He also seems to have annexed the Bellary region of Andhra Pradesh. It was, perhaps, these two newly conquered provinces, which came to be called Andhrāpatha and Sātavāhanihāra.

The next Sātavāhana ruler in the puranic lists is Śivaśrī Sātakarṇi, who might be identical with Vāsishṭhīputra Śivaśrī Sātakarṇi of coins, discovered in the districts of Krishna and Godavari. An inscription from Kanheri refers to him as the son-in-law of *Mahākshatrapa* Ru[drāman I]. There is a suggestion that, before his accession, he might have served his father-in-law as his viceroy in the Aparānta region, which region he might have occupied later on, perhaps after the death of Rudradāman I.

He was succeeded by Śivaskanda Sātakarṇi, known from the purāṇas and some silver coins. Attempts have been made to identify him with Śivamaka Sāta[karṇi ?], known from an inscription found at Amaravati, and with Skanda Sātakarṇi of coins.

The last great Sātavāhana ruler was Yajña Sātakarṇi. The discovery of his inscriptions from Nasik, Kanheri, and Chinna Ganjam in the Krishna district, and of his coins from the districts of Krishna and Godavari in Tamil Nadu, Chandrapur (earlier, Chanda) in Madhya Pradesh, Vidarbha, northern Konkan, Baroda, and Saurashtra, shows that he ruled over most of the territories he had inherited from his predecessors. The resemblance borne by his silver coins from Sopara, to the silver coins of Rudradāman I, has led to the suggestion that, he might have taken advantage of the struggle for succession between Rudrasiṁha I and Jīvadāman, and of the rise of the Ābhīra chief, Īśvaradatta, and put to an end, the rule of the Kārddamaka Kshatrapas in Aparānta, and, possibly, also in parts of western India and the Narmada valley. Some of his coins bear the device of a ship with two masts, indicating, perhaps, his authority over the Coromondal coast. According to the purāṇas, he ruled for 19 years. He might have been succeeded by Māṭharīputra Śakasena of the two inscriptions from Kanheri, whose rule seems to have been confined to the Andhra and Vidarbha regions.

The Sātavāhana empire seems to have disintegrated after the reign of Yajña Sātakarṇi. Purāṇas, epigraphs, and coins reveal the existence of some Sātavāhana rulers, like Vijaya Sātakarṇi, Chandraśri, Rudra Sātakarṇi, and Puḷomā, who seem to have ruled in the period, when the power of their family was on the decline. Ultimately, the Ikshvākus and the Pallavas supplanted the Sātavāhanas in the Krishna,

Guntur, and Bellary regions. Some collateral branches of the family carved out independent kingdoms for themselves. One such collateral branch seems to be ruling in the Kuntala region, and another, in Dakshiṇa Kosala. The Sātavāhanas of the Kuntala branch seem to have continued to rule, till they were displaced by the Kadambas, some time before the fourth century AD. Some erstwhile feudatories of the Sātavāhana, too, seem to have asserted independence.

The successors of the Sātavāhanas in the *dakshiṇāpatha*

Among the successors of the Sātavāhanas in the *dakshiṇāpatha*, mention may be made of the Ikshvākus, the Ābhīras, the Bodhis, the Bṛihatphalāyanas, the so-called Chuṭu kings of Karwar—Muḍānanda, Chuṭukaḍānanda, Chuṭukulānanda, and others, and the so-called Kura rulers of Kolhapur—Vāsishṭhīputra Vilivāyakura, Māṭharīputra Sivalakura, and Gautamīputra Vilivāyakura.

In the territories near the mouth of the rivers Krishna and Godavari, the Sātavāhanas seem to have been supplanted by the **Ikshvākus**, in the first half of the third century AD. Their relationship, if any, with the Ikshvākus of Ayodhyā, is not known. The rule of this Ikshvāku ruling family, which had its headquarters, perhaps at Vijayapurī in the Nagarjunikonda valley, was founded by Śāntamūla I, who is known to have performed several vedic sacrifices, including the *aśvamedha*. He established matrimonial relations with a number of prominent ruling families of his time, like the Pukīyas, the Dhanakas, and the Hiraṇyakas. He was succeeded by his son, Māṭharīputra Vīrapurushadatta, who ruled for about 20 years. He seems to have married a princess of the Kārddamaka family, and to have given his daughter in marriage to some Chuṭu-Sātakarṇi ruler of Vanavāsī. These matrimonial alliances must have strengthened the political power and prestige of the Ikshvākus.

The son and successor of Māṭharīputra Vīrapurushadatta was Ehuvula Śāntamūla II, who is known to have ruled for at least 11 years. Another ruler, Ruḷupurushadatta, too, seems to be associated with Māṭharīputra Vīrapurushadatta. Although the Pallavas of Kāñchī occupied the Andhra region around the end of the third century AD, the Ikshvākus continued to maintain their existence as a local power for many years afterwards.

The **Ābhīras** appear to be of some foreign stock. Their arrival into India almost coincides with the advent of the Śaka-Pahlavas. Ābhīra settlements are known from various parts of western, central, and southern India, but the purāṇas specifically refer to the Ābhīras of Aparānta as the successors of the Sātavāhanas in the *dakshiṇāpatha.* The author of the *Periplus of the Erythraean Sea,* and Ptolemy, would locate the Aberia or Abiria, that is the country occupied by the Ābhīras, somewhere between the lower Indus valley and Saurashtra. Epigraphs reveal the existence of some Ābhīra generals, serving under the Kārddamaka Kshatrapas, like Bāpaka and his son, Rudrabhūti.

The coins of one *Mahākshatrapa* Īśvaradatta have been found in several hoards of Kārddamaka coins, and these bear a close affinity to the coins of the Kārddamaka Kshatrapas. However, he cannot be regarded as a Kārddamaka ruler, mainly on the bases of the facts that his name does not appear to fit in with those of the Kārddamaka rulers, and that he dates his coins in his regnal years while the Kārddamaka Kshatrapas date their issues in the Śaka era. It has been proposed that he was an interloper, who either usurped the Kārddamaka throne, or ruled simultaneously with some Kārddamaka ruler after wresting some of his territories from him. Although his coins make no mention of his antecedents, Bhagwanlal Indraji regarded him as associated with the Ābhīras mentioned in a Nasik inscription. Various dates have been proposed for his reign. Bhagwanlal Indraji places him between the years 171 and 176; Rapson, on the basis of the greater similarity of his coins with those of Vīradāman, Yaśodāman I, and Vijayasena, dates his coins between the years 158 and 161; Bhandarkar identifies him as the intruder who forced Rudrasiṁha I to revert to the position of a *kshatrapa* between the years 110 and 112; P L Gupta earlier dated his reign between the years 273 and 284, but later placed it between the years 254 and 270. On the basis of a coin, on which Shobhana Gokhale has read the date of year 154 in numerals on the obverse, and identifying Īśvaradatta with Īśvarasena of a Nasik record which is dated in the ninth regnal year of that ruler (below), she places the rule of Īśvaradatta between the years 151 and 162. Mirashi is of the view that Īśvaradatta ruled over northern Maharashtra, and wrested some parts of Malwa and Saurashtra from the Kārddamaka Kshatrapas. B N Mukherjee suggested that he might have occupied some Kārddamaka territories, and ruled for some time, simultaneously with, and independently of, some Kārddamaka ruler. Similar is the view of P L Gupta, who regards central Gujarat and western Malwa as having comprised the dominions of Īśvaradatta. But Amiteshwar Jha and Dilip Rajgor read the date on the coin published by Shobhana Gokhale as year 164, and suggest that Īśvaradatta ruled simultaneously with Vijayasena.

Most of the scholars regard Rājā Māṭharīputra Īśvarasena, son of Śivadatta, as an Ābhīra ruler of northwestern *dakshiṇāpatha*, who ruled in the first half of the third century AD, some time after the death of Yajña Sātakarṇi. Nothing is known about any other Ābhīra chief, although the purāṇas refer to as many as 10 of them. Around the middle of the fourth century AD, the Ābhīras came into conflict with the Kadamba ruler, Mayūraśarman. Some Ābhīras are also referred to in the Allahabad pillar inscription of Samudragupta, as a people, who came within the sphere of political influence of that Imperial Gupta ruler. The Traikūṭakas supplanted the Ābhīras in northwestern *dakshiṇāpatha*, perhaps some time in the latter half of the fourth century AD.

In the third century AD, some parts of northwestern *dakshiṇāpatha* appear to have passed from the Kārddamaka Kshatrapas to the Bodhi dynasty, perhaps founded by a ruler named Bodhi or Śrībodhi. Coins reveal the existence of three more rulers of this dynasty—Śivabodhi, Chandrabodhi or Śrīchandrabodhi, and Vīrabodhi or Vīrabodhidatta. Nothing definite is known about the achievements of any of these rulers.

Ptolemy refers to a people called Maisoloi, who had their capital at Pitundra. The town, also mentioned in the Hathigumpha inscription of Khāravela, and in the Jaina *Uttarādhyayanasūtra*, as Pithuṁḍa, has been located near Masulipatam. In the closing years of the third century AD, one Jayavarman of the Bṛihatphalāyana dynasty, known from the Kondamudi inscription, threw off the yoke of the Ikhsvākus in that area, and ruled for at least nine years, the date of his inscription. No other ruler of this dynasty is known so far. Shortly afterwards, the Pallavas of Kāñchī established their authority over that region.

Chapter IV

The Indo-Greeks

In the historical period, the Indians first seem to have come into contact with the Greeks of Ionia during the reign of Darius I, when the former were the easternmost, and the latter, the westernmost subjects of that Achaemenian emperor. During the post-Maurya period, northwestern India was subjugated by a number of foreign powers, the Indo-Greeks being the first among them. Around the middle of the third century BC, Bactria asserted its independence of the Seleukid emperor, Antiochos II, under its satrap, Diodotos I. The rebellion of Diodotos I is mentioned by Justin, Trogus, and Strabo. On the basis of the monograms occurring on the coins bearing the name of Diodotos, Macdonald and Tarn suggested that the revolt of Diodotos was not sudden; rather, Diodotos rose gradually to power. But Narain has rejected the idea, and believes that the 'breakaway was abrupt'. Not much is known about the subsequent career of Diodotos I, except that, besides Bactria, he also ruled over Margiana and Sogdiana. The Parthians seem to have held him in awe, and Arsakes was forced to keep a large army battle-ready for fear of an attack by Diodotos I. On the commemorative coins issued by Demetrios I and Agathokles in honour of Diodotos I, he is given the title of *soter*, but it is not known if this title was used by Diodotos I himself in his lifetime.

According to Justin, Diodotos I was succeeded by his son, Diodotos II. The Parthians maintained friendly relations with him, for mutual security, as also to foil any attempts on the part of the Seleukids to re-establish their authority over the two breakaway satrapies of Bactria and Parthia. He was able to the retain hold over Bactria and Sogdiana. On the basis of the portraits of Diodotos II appearing on his coins, it has been suggested that his rule ended *c* 235 BC. Polybios seems to suggest that Diodotos II lost his life at the hands of Euthydemos I.

According to Polybios, Euthydemos I belonged to the city of Magnesia, but it is not certain whether he meant the Ionian city of that name, or the Lydian. He might have been a high-ranking military official or a satrap (of Sogdiana or of Aria and Margiana) under Diodotos II. Polybios' account suggests that Euthydemos attained kingship of Bactria by 'destroying' the descendants of the original rebels. From this, it has been surmised that he killed Diodotos II and occupied his throne, *c* 235 BC, about the same time as the death of Aśoka. It has been suggested that Diodotos II might have formed an alliance with the Parthians against the Seleukids, and this might have provided Euthydemos with an excuse to 'destroy' the family of Diodotos. He appears from his coin portraits to have been young at the time of his accession to the throne, and to have had a long reign of around 30 years. Very little is known of the career of Euthydemos, till the eastern expedition of Antiochos III, around 208 BC, to reassert Seleukid authority over Parthia and Bactria. Euthydemos met the Syrian invader on the river Arius (modern Hari-rud), was worsted, and had to withdraw to his capital, Bactra, which Antiochos besieged for two years. Euthydemos made overtures for peace, emphasizing its need in view of the danger from the nomads from the north. Incidentally, this has been taken to indicate that the Śaka-Pahlavas, from the north of the river Jaxartes and from Sogdia, had begun their migration towards the south by this time. A treaty was agreed upon, after which Antiochos retired to Syria. It is not known whether Euthydemos acknowledged the suzerainty of Antiochos III; even if he did, 'it soon became a dead letter'. Euthydemos exercised control over Bactria, Sogdiana, Kabul, Kandahar, Seistan, southern Afghanistan, and adjoining parts of Iran. He, however, took care to extend his sway in such directions as would not invite a fresh Seleukid attack. The end of his reign is generally placed about 190 BC, though scholars like Narain and R C Senior would date it about ten years earlier.

Demetrios I, the son of Euthydemos I, had shown such promise even as a young prince, that the Seleukid, Antiochos III, decided to give him one of his own daughters in marriage. He succeeded his father, and scholars have attributed him wide-ranging conquests. According to Tarn, he annexed Aria, Arachosia, and Seistan to his kingdom. But Aria was already a part of the Indo-Greek kingdom during the reign of Euthydemos I, who met Antiochos III on the river Arius. The suggestion of the conquest of Seistan by Demetrios is based on the evidence of the find of a few of his coins in that region, and Justin's reference to the conflict of the 'Drangians' with the Bactrians. The conquest of Arachosia by Demetrios is proved by the reference to a city named Demetrias in Arachosia, by Isidore of Charax. He could also have occupied the eastern parts of Gedrosia.

The conquests of Sogdiana, and perhaps Ferghana, also seem to have been achieved by Euthydemos II, during his reign.

It was earlier almost universally believed that Demetrios crossed the Hindukush, and occupied the Kabul and the Indus valleys, on the basis of two bilingual types, one each in silver and copper, bearing the name of Demetrios, believed to be the son of Euthydemos I by scholars like Cunningham and Whitehead. It was argued that after his conquest of the Indian territories, Demetrios was obliged to introduce the Kharoshṭhī legend for the benefit of his Indian subjects. But the bust of the king on the obverse of the silver type is shown in a flat *kausia*, while that on the copper one is clumsily depicted wearing an elephant's scalp, and these are unlike the depiction of the king on the other coins of Demetrios I. Besides, on the bilingual coins, there occurs the additional epithet, *aniketos* (Kharoshṭhī, *aparajita*), which is not found on the other coins of Demetrios. On these grounds, scholars like Macdonald and Narain ascribe these bilingual coins to Demetrios II, although A N Lahiri includes these two types among the issues of Demetrios I. The other reasons for suggesting the conquest of some Indian territories by Demetrios I are that Justin calls him 'king of the Indians'; that Apollodoros' statement referred to by Strabo is interpreted to mean that Menander and Demetrios, between them, conquered Patalene, Saraostus, Segerdis, and regions as far as Seres and Phryni; that there is a mention of Demetrios as a *yavanādhipa*, and of a town Dattāmitrī in the *Mahābhārata*; that there is mention of Demetrios as Ḍimita in the Hathigumpha inscription of Khāravela; etc. But Narain has shown that Demetrios is called 'king of the Indians' in a very vague sense; Apollodoros, whom Strabo finds not always reliable, seems to have confused Demetrios the son of Euthydemos I, with Demetrios who subdued the Indians; Dattāmitra of the *Mahābhārata* was the epithet of Sumitra, a king of Sauvīra, and the name of the *yavanādhipa* was Vittala, and hence, the association of Dattāmitrī with Demetrios has no solid basis; even the reading of the name Ḍimita in the Hathigumpha inscription is not certain, much less the identification with Demetrios. Tarn says that 'it is just possible that Paropamisadae were his already; anyhow he took Gandhāra, crossed the Indus, and occupied Taxila'. But, according to Narain, no coins of Demetrios, the son of Euthydemos I, have been found in the Kabul valley, or at Taxila, and there is no impact of the local coinage of Taxila on the coins of Demetrios; lion, the only 'Taxila animal' to occur on Indo-Greek coins, is seen on the coins, not of Demetrios but of Agathokles. Thus, there is no evidence to support the theory of the extensive conquests of Demetrios in India, and there is nothing to prove Tarn's contention that Demetrios eyed the throne of Aśoka because he regarded himself as an heir to the Mauryas through alleged matrimonial relations of both his family and that of the Mauryas with the Seleukids, and that he succeeded in this endeavour through the help of his able generals and sons.

Demetrios had to face danger of the nomads from the north, and the Imperial Parthians from the west, besides restive elements in Sogdiana, Aria, Drangiana, and India. He, therefore, very wisely desisted from disturbing the powers on the other side of the Hindukush, and, rather, utilized his energies in consolidating the territories he had already conquered. But the subsequent discoveries of his coins from several places in the North West Frontier Province, and the use of the elephant's scalp as his headdress on coins, have led Osmund Bopearachchi to suggest that Demetrios I might have attempted conquests to the south of the Hindukush.

There are some silver coins bearing the name of Euthydemos, with a 'youthful bust with draped shoulders' on the obverse, and Herakles standing with a wreath in his extended right hand on the reverse. These coins were earlier attributed to Euthydemos I, but scholars, like von Sallet, Gardner, and Macdonald, regard these coins as the issues of a second ruler of that name, on the grounds that the youthful portrait of the king on these coins varies from those on the coins of Euthydemos I, and Herakles on these coins is standing 'in a singular way which is not typically Greek', while this deity is shown as seated on the coins of Euthydemos I. Some scholars regard Euthydemos II as a son of Demetrios, but he is generally believed to be a younger brother of the latter. There is a suggestion that he was dispatched by Euthydemos I to conquer territories in the north, and he finally succeeded in occupying the regions as far as Sogdiana, and even Ferghana in its north and north-east, possibly after the death of his father, when Demetrios had ascended the throne. It was this conquest which enabled him to strike in nickel, Euthydemos II being the first Indo-Greek ruler to issue nickel coins. He seems to have ruled as a joint-king or sub-king of Demetrios, and predeceased him, *c* 190 BC.

Pantaleon is believed to be a son of Demetrios I. It is suggested that after his conquest of Arachosia and Drangiana, Demetrios I left behind his two sons, Pantaleon and Agathokles, as joint subkings of those provinces, and the two ruled jointly after the death of Demetrios I in Bactria. Tarn proposed that after some time, Antimachos I occupied these regions. But Narain regards the find of only a few coins of Antimachos I in Arachosia and Seistan as not sufficient grounds to prove the hold of that king over those regions. Narain is of the view that, taking advantage of the conflict between Eukratides and Demetrios II, the two brothers occupied the Kabul valley and struck the coins bearing the figure of Dionysos, the mythical conqueror of the Kabul valley before Alexander. They then proceeded to conquer western Gandhāra in the east, but Pantaloen died before Takshaśilā could be occupied. Pantaloen would have ruled roughly from 185 BC to 175 BC. He predeceased Agathokles, and the latter alone established his authority over Takshaśilā, where he issued the *hirañasame* and the '*stūpa* and tree-in-railing' types of coins. Narain is of the view that the two brothers might have ruled from *c* 185 BC to 165 BC.

Some coins bearing the name of Zoilos use the title *dikaios*, while others use the title *soter*. On the basis of the *provenance* of these coins, the coins of Zoilos *Dikaios* have been placed to the west of the river Indus, and those of Zoilos *Soter*, to the east of that river. Scholars like Cunningham did not distinguish between Zoilos *Dikaios* and Zoilos *Soter*, but the remarkable difference in style of the two series has been taken as evidence of the existence of two Indo-Greek kings bearing the name of Zoilos, the one using the title of *dikaios* being Zoilos I, and the other with the title of *soter* being Zoilos II. Zoilos I is believed to have belonged to the family of Euthydemos I on the basis of the use of the Herakles type by him; there is a suggestion that he might have been a son of Demetrios I. He seems to have served under Menander as a subking, and was appointed in the Swat valley by Agathoklcia whcn shc transfcrrcd Antimachos II from there to northern Arachosia. The presence of his coins in the Mir Zakah hoard has been taken to suggest that the transfer might have been mutual. Osmund Bopearachchi regards Zoilos I, perhaps as a rival of Menander I, who might have been responsible for the death of the latter. Coins of Zoilos I have been assigned to the Paropamisadae and western Gandhāra. The rarity of his coins shows his brief reign in the eighth decade of the second century BC.

Lysias is believed to have been a grandson of Demetrios I and a son of Zoilos I. He seems to have ruled the region to the north of the Hindukush, the Kabul valley, and Ghazni. His coins in the Gandhāra region are relatively few. On the basis of the facts that Heliokles II restruck the coins of Philoxenos, and Antialkidas, those of Lysias, Narain suggests that Philoxenos and Lysias 'were in league against the family of Eukratides'. On the basis of the occurrence of the name of Lysias on the obverse and that of Antialkidas on the reverse of one bronze coin, and that of Antialkidas on the obverse, and that of Lysias on the reverse, of another bronze piece in the American Numismatic Society, it was suggested that the two kings issued joint coins, and Tarn regards it as an evidence of a *rapprochement* between the rival Indo-Greek families of Euthydemos and Eukratides, in view of the Śaka-Pahlava menace. But Narain regards the first piece as a 'mule'. Lysias seems to have ruled from *c* 120 BC to 110 BC, although R C Senior would place his reign from *c* 130 BC to 125 BC.

The last ruler in this line was, perhaps, Theophilos. He is believed to belong to the family of Euthydemos I on the basis of his Herakles type of coins, and he was, perhaps, a son of Lysias. Although some of his coins are reported from Rawalpindi and Sialkot, the *provenance* of most of his coins is difficult to establish. Narain suggests that he did not immediately succeed his father, but rebelled and set up an independent kingdom in some regions north of the Hindukush, some time in the second decade of the first century BC; R C Senior, however, places his reign between *c* 115 BC and 110 BC. His use of the title of *autokrator* is unique in Indo-Greek numismatics, and has been taken as suggestive of his rebellion. Shortly afterwards, he seems to have been overthrown by Amyntas.

Another notable family of Indo-Greek rulers was founded by Eukratides I. According to Justin, he started his career simultaneously with the Arsakid, Mithridates I of Parthia. As the Arsakid ruler is believed to have ascended the throne *c* 171 BC, Eukratides I would have started ruling around that date. On some of his coins, he commemorated his parents, Heliokles and Laodike. The obverse of these silver coins, struck on the Attic standard, bears the helmeted bust of the king, the legend mentioning the name and titles of Eukratides I. The reverse has the conjugate busts of Heliokles and Laodike, with the legend mentioning their names. As on these coins, Laodike is shown with a diadem, the mark of royalty, while Heliokles is bareheaded, scholars like Tarn believe that Laodike was a Seleukid princess, a daughter of Seleukos II, and Heliokles was, perhaps, a governor under Antiochos III. Tarn further suggested that Eukratides was sent by his cousin, Antiochos IV, to stir up a revolt against Demetrios in Bactria, in which endavour he was successful. But Narain feels that Antiochos IV had 'neither the statesmanship to envisage nor the resources to carry out' such a plan. He regards Eukratides as an upstart, who was born of a princess, perhaps a daughter of Diodotos II or Euthydemos I. Recently, R C Senior has suggested that Laodike was a daughter of the Seleukid ruler, Antiochos III. Justin informs us that when Demetrios [II] was busy in his southern campaigns, Eukratides I occupied Bactria. Demetrios II rushed to Bactria, and besieged Eukratides I with a large army. But Justin states that, in spite of having only 300 soldiers with him, Eukratides was able to defeat Demetrios II, who might even have been killed in this encounter. Justin also refers to his wars in Sogdiana, Aria, Arachosia, Drangiana, and India. From Justin's account, it appears that after consolidating his position in Bactria, Eukratides I embarked upon an ambitious campaign. Aria and Margiana would have been inherited by Demetrios II from Antimachos I, and the victory of Eukratides over Demetrios II must have resulted in these territories also passing into the hands of the victor. He would also have occupied the Kabul valley before he proceeded towards Arachosia and Drangiana, and assumed the title of *megas*, 'the great', perhaps to commemorate this achievement. The discovery of his coins in Arachosia and Seistan, and in the Mir Zakah hoard near Ghazni, has led to the inference that, from the Paropamisadae, he advanced to Arachosia and Seistan *via* Ghazni, and occupied a considerable part of these provinces. He also advanced towards Gandhāra, but the rarity of his coins in that region shows that he was not very successful in this direction, and could not cross the river Indus.

Justin informs us that when he was returning in triumph to Bactria, his son, whom he had left behind in Bactria as his joint king, killed him, 'drove his chariot through his blood', and cast away his corpse. Justin does not name this parricide. One of the sons of Eukratides was Heliokles I, but as he assumed the title of *dikaios*, some scholars hesitate in identifying him as the parricide. Narain proposes that this parricide son of Eukratides I be identified with Plato, on the grounds that the head of Plato on his coins closely resembles that of Eukratides I, and that Plato is the only Indo-Greek king to issue coins with the device of Helios on quadriga, which device, according to Narain, might have something to do with the parricide son of Eukratides I driving his chariot through the blood of his father. He feels that no other Indo-Greek king used this device because it had come to be associated with the parricidal act of Plato. Justin says that the Arsakids were interested in Tapuria and Traxiana, the two satrapies of the kingdom of Eukrarides, and Mithridates I seems to have occupied them soon after. On this basis, Narain suggests that Plato might have been instigated to kill his father by the Arsakids. But he himself was done away by Heliokles I, who perhaps called himself 'just' after punishing the killer of his father. He seems to have ruled for a short time from *c* 155 BC, his brief reign being suggested by the rarity of his coins. The possibility of the parricide being Eukratides II, has also been expressed.

R C Senior, on the basis of a statement of Justin, that the Bactrians lost their territories, and even their liberty, as a result of their defeats at the hands of Mithridates, suggests that Eukratides I was responsible for the 'final decline' of the Greek power in Bactria, and that due to this, he was killed by one of his sons. But it must be remembered that, according to Justin, Eukratides I was returning to Bactria from a *victorious* campaign, when he was killed. Tarn, however, believes that Eukratides I was killed, not by his own son, but by the son of Demetrios, and that this information of Justin is erroneous. Eukratides I ruled from *c* 171 to 155 BC, although Senior would take his reign up to 145 BC.

Another son of Eukratides I was Heliokles I, who ascended the throne of Bactria, perhaps after removing his brother, the parricide (?) Plato. Besides Bactria, his authority extended over the territories of Badakshan and Sogdiana. During his reign, the Arsakids wrested the outlying Indo-Greek provinces, and Mithridates I seems to have conquered territories as far east as Aria. The coins of Heliokles come mostly from the regions to the north of the Hindukush; the regions to the south were under Menander. Heliokles was believed to be the last Indo-Greek king to the rule over Bactria, but, according to some scholars, with the discovery of the Attic *tetradrachms* of later Indo-Greek kings, like Eukratides II, Archebios, and others, in the Qunduz hoard, this view can no longer be entertained. He seems to have ruled from *c* 155 BC to 140 BC, although Osmund Bopearachchi would place the end of his reign *c* 130-129 BC. Some scholars, like Cunningham and Marshall, believed in the existence of only one Indo-Greek king named Heliokles. However, Gardner expressed the possibility of the existence of two Indo-Greek kings bearing that name, on the basis of the marked contrast between the portraits of Heliokles appearing on the monolingual coins bearing the name of Heliokles on the one hand, and that on the bilingual coins on the other. This suggestion of Gardner has been supported by Tarn, Whitehead, Narain, and others, with the monolingual coins being attributed to Heliokles I, and the bilingual ones, to Heliokles II.

Scholars expressed the possibility of the existence of two Indo-Greek kings named Eukratides as early as 1738, but other scholars, like Cunningham and Trever, opposed this view, while some others, like Whitehead, refused to commit themselves. However, with the discovery of more coins bearing the name of Eukratides and the title *soter*, the possibility of a second Eukratides has increased, with most of the modern writers on the subject accepting the existense of Eukratides II. Tarn regarded him as a son or brother of Heliokles I, appointed as the governor of the territories to the north of the Hindukush. But as his coins are nearer to those of Heliokles I than to those of Eukratides I, Narain prefers to take him as a son of Heliokles I. He seems to have ruled over Bactria and Badakshan. The possibility of his rule over regions to the south of the Hindukush is precluded by the presence of Menander in those regions. There is a suggestion that during his reign, the Śaka-Pahlavas of the Jaxartes-Oxus area crossed the river Oxus, and occupied Bactria, which would make Eukratides II the last Indo-Greek king to the rule over Bactria proper. Henceforth, the authority of the Indo-Greeks to the north of the Hindukush remained confined mainly to Badakshan. Eukratides II seems to have ruled from *c* 140 BC to 130 BC, and was succeeded by Archebios, perhaps his son.

Rapson, Tarn, and Marshall regard the type, *pilei* of the Dioskuri, as associated with Takshaśilā, and as Archebios issued this type of coins, it was suggested that he ruled over that region, which, after him, passed into the hands of the Śaka-Pahlavas; Osmund Bopearachchi is also in favour of associating Archebios with Takshaśilā. But Narain feels that the association of this type with the Takshaśilā region is by no means certain, and that there is no definite evidence to suggest Archebios' hold over Takshaśilā. He, however, occupied the territories of Kabul and Ghazni to the south of the Hindukush by taking advantage of the death of Menander, and also parts of western Gandhāra. He ruled for about seven or eight years from *c* 140 BC, and was succeeded by his uncle, Heliokles II; R C Senior, however, places him between *c* 95 BC and 80 BC.

On the basis of the marked contrast between the portrait of Heliokles on the monolingual coins, and that on the bilingual coins, Gardner has expressed the possibility of the existence of two Indo-Greek kings named Heliokles, and this is supported by a number of scholars, with the monolingual coins being attributed to Heliokles I and the bilingual ones to Heliokles II. Narain regards Heliokles II as a son of Heliokles I, and a brother of Eukratides II. He seems to have come to power after his nephew, Archebios. He ruled over the Kabul and Ghazni regions, and parts of western Gandhāra where his coins are quite numerous. He is identified with that Heliokles who restruck the joint coins of Agathokleia and Strato I, as the restruck pieces are also bilingual. It is generally believed that he expanded his dominions at the expense of Strato I, then a minor. Almost all his coins show him as 'a man well advanced in middle age', and he seems to have had a brief reign from *c* 120 BC to 115 BC, although R C Senior places his reign between *c* 85 BC and 75 BC, and Osmund Bopearachchi, between *c* 110 BC and 100 BC.

Heliokles II was succeeded by his son, Antialkidas. He retrieved the fallen fortunes of his family some time around 115 BC, and the *provenance* of his coins shows that he established his sway over the Kabul valley, western Gandhāra, and Takshaśilā. As mentioned earlier, there are certain coins bearing the name of Lysias on one side, and that of Antialkidas on the other, which are regarded by some scholars as joint issues of the two kings, while others regard such pieces as 'mules'. Antialkidas also restruck a coin of Lysias. He is mentioned in the Besnagar *garuḍa* pillar inscription of the time of King Bhāgabhadra, and the language of the inscription gives the indication that the seat of his power was Takshaśilā. He sent an envoy, Heliodoros, to the court of that Indian ruler, and in the inscription the envoy uses the title of *trātāra* (Prakrit equivalent of the Greek title, *soter*) for Bhāgabhadra, leading to the inference that the Indian king might have saved Antialkidas from some enemy. Narain, however, believes that towards the close of his reign, the authority of Antialkidas was confined to the Takshaśilā region alone, with Apollodotos occupying almost all his territories to the west of the river Indus, and Strato I ruling over the Jammu-Sialkot region to the east of the river Jhelum. Beleaguered by these problems, Antialkidas might have sought the help of Bhāgabhadra, but to no avail. He ruled up to *c* 100 BC, when he was, perhaps, overthrown by Apollodotos. Senior, however, places his reign from *c* 127 BC to 120 BC.

On the basis of the use of the mounted Dioskuri type, which is generally associated with the family of Eukratrides, it was suggested by Cunningham that Diomedes might have been a son of Eukratides. But his use of monograms associated with later kings shows that he was, perhaps, a son of Antialkidas, who managed to establish himself in parts of western Gandhāra, apparently after the death of Apollodotos, *c* 95 BC, and ruled for about 10 years, when he was supplanted by Amyntas in that region. R C Senior, however, places him between *c* 100 BC and 90 BC, and regards him as a contemporary, and, perhaps, also an assistant, of Philoxenos.

Telephos is believed to be a son of Antialkidas on the basis of the enthroned Zeus type of his coins, and to have ruled over Takshaśilā in the period between the end of the reign of Apollodotos *c* 95 BC, and its occupation by Maues *c* 85 BC. But Tarn regards him as a usurper and even doubts if he was at all a Greek. His rare coins are reported mostly from Gandhāra and Takshaśilā, and one coin even comes from the Hazara region; he might have conquered the Takshaśilā region from Nikias. There is no evidence to support Tarn's claim that he ruled over Kapiśā or the Kabul valley. He ruled from *c* 95 BC to 80 BC; R C Senior, however, places him *c* 60 BC.

A third son of Antialkidas was Amyntas, who did not immediately succeed his father. After the death of Antialkidas, the territories to the north of the Hindukush were occupied by Theophilos, the Pushkalāvatī region and the Kabul valley by Peukolaos, and western Gandhāra by Diomedes, while Apollodotos ruled over the remainder of the kingdom of Antialkidas. But some time after the death of Apollodotos, Amyntas regained the territories his father had lost to Apollodotos, and also overthrew Theophilos and Peukolaos in the region to the north of the Hindukush and in the Pushkalāvatī region and the Kabul valley, respectively. Coins of Amyntas from western Gandhāra show that he superseded Diomedes in that region. Narain suggests that he might have issued the two types of his double-*decadrachms* and assumed the title of *nikator* to commemorate the re-establishment of his authority. On the basis of the appearance of Athena-Pallas, a type usually associated with Menander and his successors, on some coins of Amyntas, it has been suggested that the descendants of Eukratides I and those of Menander, might have formed an alliance in view of the Śaka-Pahlava and Yüeh-chih menace. The marriage of his son, Hermaios, with Kalliope of the family of Menander, might have been the result of this alliance. Coin portraits reveal that Amyntas was able to establish himself as a king in his middle age around 85 BC, although R C Senior would date his accession about a decade later, and Osmund Boearachchi places it between 95 BC and 90 BC; he seems to have ruled for about 10 years.

The last ruler of the line of Eukratides I was Hermaios, the son of Amyntas. There are some coins on which the name and/or portrait of Hermaios is associated with the Kushāṇa ruler, Kujula Kadphises. The suggestion of scholars like Percy Gardner, V A Smith, R B Whitehead, and Alberto M Simonetta, that Kujula Kadphises began his career as a subordinate ally of the Indo-Greek ruler and later displaced him, as also that of other scholars like, Cunningham, Whitehead, Smith, and initially also Rapson, that in view of the Śaka-Pahlava menace, Hermaios formed an alliance with the Kushāṇa ruler and they issued these coins conjointly, and then Kujula Kadphises immediately succeeded Hermaios, on the basis of these coins, can no longer be entertained in view of the strong evidence indicating an interval of at least 70 years between the end of the reign of Hermaios and the accession of Kujula Kadphises. This long gap was suggested by F W Thomas, and supported by the result of the excavations at Taxila. The *Hou Han-shu* also informs us that the Yüeh-chihs conquered the Kabul valley from the Śaka-Pahlavas [not from the Indo-Greeks]. Tarn suggested that these coins were issued by Kujula Kadphises, who desired to legitimize his hold over the Kabul valley by proclaiming his relationship with Hermaios, a princess of whose family was married to Heraos, a predecessor of Kujula Kadphises. But Bachhofer proposed that when Kujula Kadphises occupied the Kabul valley, he imitated the type of Hermaios which was popular in that region. The *provenance* of the coins of Hermaios shows his hold over an extensive dominion, comprising the Paropamisadae, some regions to the north of the Hindukush, upper Arachosia, and perhaps even eastern Gandhāra and Takshaśilā. There seems to have been an alliance between the descendants of Eukratides and those of Menander against the Śaka-Pahlavas and the Yüeh-chihs, during the reign of Amyntas, and perhaps as a result of this alliance, Kalliope, a princess of the family of Menander and, perhaps, a daughter of Hippostratos, was married to Hermaios. The joint coins of Hermaios and Kalliope seem to show that Kalliope was a 'queen regnant', and there is a possibility that, following the death of Hippostratos, Hermaios and Kalliope might have jointly exercised authority over some territories previously ruled by Hippostratos. But towards the end of his reign, Hermaios lost most of his provinces to Azes I. Narain suggests that the Śaka-Pahlava ruler first occupied upper Arachosia, and then Gandhāra and the Paropamisadae. Hermaios also lost the regions to the north of the Hindukush to the Yüeh-chihs. The reign of Hermaios seems to have come to an end *c* 55 BC, although some scholars, like Osmund Bopearachchi and R C Senior, would place the end of his reign around 70 BC.

A third family of Indo-Greek rulers was founded by Antimachos I, a 'myterious king', who was earlier regarded as one of the three original founders of the Indo-Greek kingdom. But there can be no doubt that he was one of the early Indo-Greek kings of Bactria. He has been variously described as a son or close relative of Diodotos II, a son of Euthydemos I, a Sogdian with a Greek name, etc. He is believed to have ruled after Euthydemos I, and there is a suggestion that he might have risen to power around 190 BC by 'eliminating' Euthydemos II. From eastern Bactria, he moved on to the Kabul valley and the Upper Indus valley, and occupied parts of Paropamisadae. Whitehead and Allan even postulate his temporary occupation of Takshaśilā on the basis of his unique square coin of Taxila type. He is not known to have struck bilingual coins; had his occupation of the Takshaśilā region been permanent, he would have started the practice of issuing bilingual coins. After the death of Demetrios I, he seems to have annexed the whole of Bactria, and even conquered Margiana. The appearance of the Greek sea-god, Poseidon, on his coins has led to the suggestion that he might have gained some naval victory on the river Oxus, but some scholars associate the depiction of this god on his coins with his hold over some territories where the 'heavenly horses' of the Chinese sources were bred. However, the suggestion of a naval victory seems to gain ground in view of the fact that he issued a round copper type, the reverse of which is occupied by the figure of Nike standing on the prow of a ship. Antimachos I assumed the title of *theos* on coins, perhaps under the influence of some local tradition. He seems to have started ruling late in his life, his career coming to an end around 180 BC. He was succeeded by a son named Demetrios.

Coins reveal the existence of two Indo-Greek kings bearing the name of Demetrios—Demetrios the son of Euthydemos I (that is Demetrios I), and Demetrios *Aniketos* (that is Demetrios II). On the basis of the rules of nomenclature, Demetrios II might be regarded as a younger son or a grandson of Demetrios I, but Narain has shown very convincingly that Demetrios II was related to Antimachos I, and was perhaps the son and successor of the latter. He is believed by some scholars to be the first Indo-Greek king to issue bilingual coins, the Kharoshṭhī legend on the reverse being meant for his Indian subjects. This has led to the inference that Demetrios II was perhaps the first Indo-Greek king to cross the Hindukush, and occupy the Kabul valley. He seems to have assumed the title of *aniketos* after this achievement. He might also have conquered Gandhāra and some of its western territories. One of his coins has been found during the excavations at Taxila, but it would not be fair to assume his occupation of that city on the basis of the discovery of a solitary piece alone. But when he was busy in these southern ventures, Eukratides I occupied Bactria. Demetrios II rushed to Bactria, and besieged Eukratides I with a large army. But Justin informs us that, in spite of having only 300 soldiers with him, Eukratides was able to defeat Demetrios II, who might even have been killed in this encounter. If Demetrios II succeeded Antimachos I around 180 BC, he might have ruled up to *c* 165 BC. Two of his sons, Menander and Antimachos II, are known to have ruled after him.

Menander I is generally believed to be identical with King Milinda of the Buddhist text, *Milindapañho.* Therein, it is related that he was born in a village called Kālasī near Alasanda (Alexandria of the Caucasus), and he belonged to a royal family. He seems to be a scion of the family of Demetrios II, mostly probably his son, as Pallas is the commonest device on the coins of both these rulers. His wife was Agathokleia, who might have been a daughter of Demetrios I. Tarn suggested that he was initially a general of Demetrios I, and assumed kingship on the death of his master, the marriage with Agathokleia being the basis of his claim to royalty. If this be accepted, it stands to the reason that Menander would have been a mature person when he ascended the throne, but it has been pointed out that he appears as a very young man on his earliest coins. Narain suggests that he started his career immediately after the end of the reign of Eukratides I, *c* 155 BC; R C Senior, however, places the end of the reign of Eukratides I *c* 145 BC, and says that the reign of Menander overlaps that of Eukratides I. Osmund Bopearachchi expresses the possibility that Menander might have started ruling as early as 165 BC, and regards him as a close contemporary of Eukratides I. Although Tarn felt that there is not enough evidence of his rule over the Paropamisadae, the find of his coins from Begram and Kabul, and in the Mir Zakah hoard, leaves little doubt that he ruled over the Kabul valley. From there, he may have endeavoured to occupy Gandhāra, Arachosia, and Seistan. The discovery of his coins in the excavations at Taxila, in the Sheikhano Dheri hoard near Charsadda, at Charsadda itself, and at places like Rajjar, Mardan, Peshawar, and Rawalpindi, shows that he ruled over Gandhāra, with its two centres of Takshaśilā and Pushkalāvatī. However, no coin of this ruler is reported from Arachosia and Seistan, and hence, there is no evidence of his hold over these two regions; they seem to have been occupied by the Arsakids after Eukratides I. Narain, however, feels that some parts of northern and eastern Arachosia might have been included in his dominions. Menander also conquered Hazara and the Swat valley, as is evident from the discovery of his coins in the two Bajaur hoards, and also from his mention in the Shinkot-Bajaur relic-casket inscriptions of the time of Viyakamitra, who seems to have served under him as his governor in the Swat valley. Udyāna, the country between the rivers Suvāstu and Gaurī, and the Sind-Sagar *doab*, too, seem to have been under his control. There is nothing definite to testify to his conquest of the Jhelum-Chenab *doab*, or the Kashmir valley. The classical accounts give Menander the credit for conquests in India, and Strabo, quoting Apollodoros, says that he crossed the Beas, and also, perhaps, the Yamuna. Kālidāsa refers to an Indo-Greek invasion of India towards the end of the reign of Pushyamitra Śuṅga. The Yugapurāṇa section of the *Gārgīsaṁhitā* states that the Indo-Greeks crossed Sāketa, Pañchāla, and Mathura, and besieged Pāṭaliputra, but retired due to internal dissensions. Most of the scholars generally suggest that this Indo-Greek expedition was led by Demetrios (above, Chapter II), but Narain believes that the two sources speak of the same Indo-Greek invasion, and as it occurred towards the end of the reign of Pushyamitra Śuṅga around 150 BC, it must have been led by Menander.

Menander's coins are generally not found to the east of the river Ravi; such coins as have been reported from places like Saharanpur, Sonipat, Bundelkhand, Kangra, and Hoshiarpur, seem to be the result of the popularity of his coins in those regions, and not of the extension of his rule over those territories. Tarn's view that his kingdom included the territories of the Audumbaras, Kuṇindas, Yaudheyas, and the Ārjunāyanas, as also the Broach region in Gujarat, does not seem to rest on solid grounds. The suggestion that Menander ruled over Mathurā, also seems to be unwarranted; had Indo-Greek rule intervened between the rule of the local kings of Mathurā and that of the Śaka Kshatrapas, the latter would have copied Indo-Greek coin types, and not the local types of Mathurā as done by Rañjuvula and Śoḍāsha. Scholars generally believe that beyond the Ravi and the Beas, the incursions of Menander in the Yamuna valley were more in the nature of raids, rather than regular conquests. Plutarch and Strabo refer to Menander as a Bactrian king, on which basis scholars like Cunningham and Narain suggest that, encouraged by his military successes in India and regions to the south of the Hindukush, Menander might have made a bid for Bactria, but died in the course of this expedition; Plutarch refers to his death in camp, although the Buddhist tradition says that he retired from the world after handing over his realm to his son. His reign seems to have ended around 130 BC.

The coins bearing the name of Menander use the titles of *soter* and *dikaios* for him. Narain ascribes the coins with both these titles to one king only, and feels that as the coins with the title of *dikaios* are rarer than those with the title of *soter*, and as the king on the former coins is depicted as older than that on the latter coins, Menander would have issued the coins with the title of *dikaios* towards the end of his reign. But a number of scholars, on the basis of the use of two different epithets, as also on some other grounds, postulate the existence of two Indo-Greek kings named Menander (below).

Menander seems to have appointed several subkings, like Antimachos II, Polyxenos, and Epander, to help him in the administration of his vast kingdom. Polyxenos is believed to have governed some territory to the west of the river Indus. His coins, which are very rare, are reported from the Mir Zakah hoard, and from Peshawar and Utmanzai, but none from Taxila. Although he assumed the high-sounding titles of *epiphanes* and *soter*, he seems to have had a very short reign, sometime around 130 BC, although R C Senior places his reign between *c* 110 BC and 105 BC. The rare coinage of Epander does not help us in identifying the province governed by him, but Cunningham places him in the upper Kabul valley. He seems to have ruled very briefly sometime in the seventh decade of the second century BC, although R C Senior places him *c* 80 BC. Their relationship with other Indo-Greek kings in not known.

There are some silver and copper coins, all struck on the Indian standard, which bear the name of Menander *Dikaios*. These coins have 'nothing in common' with the coins bearing the name of Menander *Soter* [Menander I], and even the canting type (thundering Athena) of Menander *Soter* is not known for Menander *Dikaios*. The monograms on the two series are also not common. The *omicron* on the coins of the Menander *Soter* series is normal, while that on the coins of the Menander *Dikaios* series takes the form of a dot, suggesting a late date for the latter series. On these grounds, some scholars regard Menander *Soter* as Menander I, and Menander *Dikaios* as Menander II, who is believed to have had a 'short and comparatively insignificant reign'. In view of the use of the reverse device of king on prancing horse by both Menander II and Artemidoros, the two might be regarded as near contemporaries, ruling over Taxila, and Menander II might be assigned to the first-second decades of the first century BC, although R C Senior would place him *c* 65 BC.

Menander I had married Agathokleia, who is believed to belong to the family of Euthydemos on the basis of the presence of seated Herakles on her coins, and most of the scholars regard her as the daughter of Demetrios I, and sister of Agathokles. She struck joint coins with Strato I. Earlier scholars, like Cunningham and Gardner, described her as the wife of Strato I, but Prinsep, and following him, Rapson, Smith, Brown, Tarn, Narain, A N Lahiri, B N Mukherjee, and others, regard her as the mother of Strato I. For, on the coins showing their conjugate busts, Agathokleia is a mature woman, while Strato I looks to be in his teens. Also, if they were man and wife, it would become very difficult to explain as to how the queen had come to occupy the more important position on the obverse, while the king had been relegated to the reverse of some of their joint coins. On the basis of the close resemblance between the bust of Athena on the coins of Menander and that of Agathokleia on her own coins, Rapson suggests the possibility of Agathokleia's being the wife of Menander. According to Plutarch, Menander died in camp. Perhaps his son, Strato I, was a minor at that time, and Agathokleia assumed the regency of the kingdom during the minority of her son. Her tenure as regent has been placed between *c* 130 BC and 123 BC, after which, Strato I assumed independent charge of his kingdom. He is depicted on his various coins in different stages of life, from a young boy in his teens to an old man 'with toothless jaws and sunken cheeks', and on this basis it was suggested by scholars like Rapson that he had a long reign of around 70 years. But there is no portrait, which might link his middle-aged portrait on the coins bearing the title of *epiphanes*, with those, which show him as an old man of around 70 years of age. On this ground, Narain suggests that after he had ruled for about 35 years, Strato I was superseded by other kings for about 15 years, till he could regain authority. He dates the first phase of his reign between *c* 130 BC and 95 BC, and the second phase between *c* 80 and 75 BC. Osmund Bopearachchi, however, ascribes to him a single reign of only about 15 years, from *c* 125 BC to 110 BC.

Towards the beginning of his reign, he might have lost some provinces to Heliokles II, who restruck some joint coins of Agathokleia and Strato I. But he seems to have regained most of the lost provinces with the help of his younger brother, Apollodotos, whom he appointed his subking or joint king. His coins, though relatively few in number keeping in view his long regin, are very widely distributed, being found in western Gandhāra and Takshaśilā, Ghazni, and the Jammu-Sialkot region, thereby showing that, at least in the first phase of his reign, he retained authority over the larger part of the territories he inherited from Menander. But encouraged by his successes, Apollodotos seems to have replaced Strato I, and declared himself an independent king. After a gap of some 15 years, Strato I regained his throne, perhaps with the help of his grandson, Strato II, and also the Śaka-Pahlava ruler, Maues. During the second phase of his reign, he seems to have appointed Strato II as his co-ruler, and issued joint coins with him. But on a coin issued by Strato I alone, housed in the British Museum, London, Rapson sees an even older Strato I, leading to the suggestion that Strato II might have predeceased his grandfather, leaving him alone to the rule for some time more. A N Lahiri and some other scholars have expressed the possibility of the existence of three kings named Strato, and they regard Strato *Soter* of these joint coins as Strato II, and Strato *Philopator* as Strato III. But others do not agree with this, on valid grounds.

Another Indo-Greek ruler, Thrason, is known from a single coin in a hoard of the coins of Menander I. The portrait on this coin shows the king as 'a young boy'. The coin bears a strong resemblance to the issues of Menander. On this basis, R C Senior regards him as another son of Menander, besides Strato I and Apollodotos, and places him *c* 130 BC.

Apollodotos, too, is believed to be a son of Menander I. On the basis of the amendation in a statement of Justin suggested by Bayer, a number of scholars express the possibility of the existence of two Indo-Greek kings named Apollodotos, but Narain feels that the numismatic evidence does not support such a hypothesis. Subsequent writers on the subject, however, still believe in the existence of two Apollodoti. Apollodotos is believed to be a son of Menander I, and a younger brother of Strato I, who began his career as a subking or joint king of Strato I around 115

BC, initially ruling over the Swat valley. He seems to have proved to be a very effective joint ruler, and to have helped Strato I in recovering most of the western regions he had earlier lost to other kings. He reoccupied western Gandhāra, the Kabul valley, and the Ghazni area. Around 100 BC, he seems to have overthrown Antialkidas in Takshaśilā, and perhaps this encouraged him to declare his independence; he might even have replaced Strato I. The *provenance* of his coins shows that, for some time at least, he ruled over almost the whole of the kingdom of his father. However, taking advantage of his engagements in Gandhāra, Kabul, and Ghazni regions, Maues might have occupied some territories in the Swat valley and the Hazara region, and perhaps also Takshaśilā. The fact that Apollodotos restruck a copper coin of Maues seems to show that the former tried to the recover the territories he had lost to the Śaka-Pahlava ruler, although the recovery proved to be of a short duration. His reign ended *c* 95 BC. R C Senior, however, regards him as a contemporary and rival of Antimachos I, and the first Indo-Greek ruler to conquer territories to the south of the Hindukush and issue square silver coins based on the Indian weight standard. But Osmund Bopearachchi regards Apollodotos as the immediate successor of Pantaleon, Agathokles, and Antimachos I, and a predecessor of Menander I.

Artemidoros is believed to be a subking of Apollodotos, who might have later asserted his independence for a short while. Tarn associates him with the Pushkalāvatī region, but Narain feels that his authority was confined to the Peshawar area. Tarn's suggestion that, in the Peshawar region, Artemidoros was succeeded by Maues, according to Narain, is not based on sufficient grounds. R C Senior has read a Greek legend, meaning

'Artemidoros, son of the king of kings, Maues', on a coin, and, on this basis, as also on the basis of the similarity of devices, suggested that Artemidoros was a son of Maues. Osmund Bopearachchi associates him with the Takshaśilā region. His reign may be placed some time in the period *c* 95-85 BC, although Senior would place his reign between *c* 65 BC and 60 BC, and Osmund Bopearachchi, in the second decade of the first century BC. He is known to have restruck the joint coins of Hermaios with Kalliope.

Peukolaos, too, is believed to be a subking of Apollodotos, who later asserted independence for a short while. Tarn associates him with the Pushakalāvatī region, but according to Narain, he seems to be ruled over the Kabul region also. His coins are, however, not reported from Takshaśilā and Ghazni. His reign may be placed some time during the period *c* 95-85 BC. Recently, attempts have been made to associate him with Maues, through Machene. Their relationship with other rulers of the Indo-Greek stock is not clear.

Apollodotos was followed by three rulers, namely Zoilos II, Dionysios, and Apollophanes. The coins of Zoilos II seem to associate him with Apollodotos, and he appears to have ruled over the Jammu-Sialkot region in the interval between the two phases of the reign of Strato I, perhaps immediately after Apollodotos whose coins he restruck. His reign may be placed in the latter half of the first decade of the first century BC. Dionysios, too, appears to have ruled over the Jammu-Sialkot region in the interval between the two phases of the reign of Strato I, perhaps succeeding Zoilos II, and preceding Apollophanes. His reign may be placed in the second decade of the first century BC. Apollophanes appears to have ruled over the Jammu-Sialkot region towards the end of the interval between the two phases of the reign of Strato I, after Zoilos II and Dinysios; Osmund Bopearachchi associates him with western Punjab. Strato I seems to have regained his authority by overthrowing him around 80 BC, possibly with the help of Strato II and Maues, as seen earlier.

It appears that, after the end of the rule of Menander I, a minor branch of the family of Antimachos I established its independent rule, under Antimachos II. He is believed to be a subking and general of Menander, and to have belonged to the family of Antimachos I and Demetrios II, with whom he shares several coin types; Osmund Bopearachchi, however, suggests that Menander I succeeded Antimachos II. Narain regards him as a grandson of Antimachos I, and a brother of Menander. Tarn would make him a subking of Gandhāra. But no coin of Antimachos II has been found in the excavations at Taxila, while they are reported in the Bajaur hoards and the Mir Zakah hoard, from which Narain infers that he first governed the Swat valley and was later transferred to northern Arachosia by Agathokleia during her regency. The large number of his coins shows that he might not have submitted to the regency of Agathokleia, and set himself up as an independent king in northern Arachosia some time after the death of Menander, perhaps from *c* 130 BC to 125 BC. Several of his direct successors are known to have ruled, till the amalgamation of the kingdom, with that of Hermaios. There is, however, a view suggesting the overlapping of the reigns of Antimachos I and Antimachos II. The discovery of his coins from Charsadda shows the extension of his authority in western Gandhāra. R C Senior, however, suggests that he might have succeeded Apollodotos in the territories to the south of the Hindukush. Bopearachchi suggests his hold over Paropamisadae as well.

The son of Antimachos II was Philoxenos, with whom he shares the type of 'equestrian king', and also the use of some common monograms. From the evidence of the Mir Zakah hoard, Philoxenos seems to have succeeded Archebios in northern Arachosia. The *provenance* of his coins shows that he, at times, ruled over parts of the Kabul valley, western Gandhāra, and Takshaśilā. He started his career *c* 125 BC, and seems to have been replaced by Heliokles II, around 115 BC. R C Senior, however, dates Philoxenos between *c* 110 BC and 95 BC, and regards him as, perhaps, the last Indo-Greek ruler 'to control a unified kingdom south of the Hindu Kush'.

Nikias, believed to be a son of Philoxenos, was appointed as a subking by Apollodotos, perhaps in some parts of western Gandhāra, from where most of his silver coins are reported; his copper ones come from the Jhelum area. It is possible that he might have ruled over the Takshaśilā region for some time before being overthrown by Telephos; no coin of Nikias was, however, found during the excavations at Taxila. On the basis of the depiction of the figure of Poseidon on some of his coins, Tarn suggested that he might have achieved some naval victory on the river Jhelum, perhaps against the Śaka-Pahlavas, but Narain feels that the speed of the currents in this river preclude such a possibility, and agrees with Tarn's alternative suggestion that Nikias might only be imitating the Poseidon type of one of his ancestors, Antimachos I. The small number of his coins shows that he had a short reign, from *c* 95 BC to 85 BC, although R C Senior has placed him between *c* 120 BC and 115 BC.

The last ruler of the line Antimachos II was Hippostratos. Tarn regarded him as the father of Nikias, but Narain seems to be right in suggesting that he was actually the son of the latter; Nikias depicted Poseidon on his coins, while his son Hippostratos depicted Poseidon's son, Triton, on his coins. Hippostratos seems to have succeeded Nikias in western Gandhāra. Whitehead has placed him in the Peshawar and Hazara regions, but, according to Narain, this seems doubtful in view of the scarcity of his coins at Takshaśilā. He, however, might have controlled some territories to the east of the river Indus. Osmund Bopearachchi regards him as the last Indo-Greek king to the rule over western Punjab, including Takshaśilā and Pushkalāvatī. He started ruling *c* 85 BC, and was, perhaps, overthrown by Azes I, around 70 BC, and this marked the end of the rule of the Indo-Greeks in the regions to the east of the Kabul valley; R C Senior, however, places his reign between *c* 60 BC and 50 BC. Some parts of his territories were, however, inherited by Kalliope.

Known from the coins she issued conjointly with her husband, Hermaios, Kalliope seems to be a descendant of Antimachos because her joint coins bear on the reverse the device of equestrian king, popular in the family of Antimachos; it has been suggested that she might be a daughter of Hippostratos. As Hermaios belonged to the family of Eukratides, Cunningham believes that these joint coins 'refer to a royal alliance' between the families of Antimachos and Eukratides. It seems that the father of Kalliope had no male heirs, and on his death, the part of his kingdom, which was not occupied by Azes I, passed on to her. From the fact that the device of equestrian king was adopted by Hermaios for the joint coins, as also for the obverse of some of his other coins, it has been inferred that the family of Kalliope might have been more powerful than that of Hermaios. She ruled over this kingdom conjointly with Hermaios, and issued joint coins with him.

The Indo-Greek rule seems to have come to an end, with Hermaios, sometime around the middle of the first century BC. The fact that so many Indo-Greek rulers have to be placed within less than two centuries goes to show that there were several Indo-Greek principalities in northwestern India, and that they were often engaged in internecine struggles. However, in view of the emerging Śaka-Pahlava menance, the rival Indo-Greek ruling families seem to have made an attempt at *rapprochement*, the evidence for which we find, perhaps, in the joint coins of Lysias and Antialkidas, and in the marriage of Hermaios and Kalliope, but with no success, and soon, their territories were occupied by the Śaka-Pahlavas.

Chapter V

The Śaka-Pahlavas and the Western Kshatrapas

The Śaka-Pahlavas

The origin of the Śaka-Pahlavas is a much debated subject among scholars, and various theories have been proposed, of which the most reasonable one seems to be that of R C Senior, which is mainly based on the account of the Śakas as given by Laszlo Torday. The Śakas were confederations of a number of apparently racially and linguistically homogenous tribes or clans, originally from Central Asia, although sometimes they may have also assimilated other ethnic nomadic tribes. These people referred to themselves as Śaka. The Chinese called them Sai. The Greeks called these people Skythians, from their supposed founder, Skulatai, which name was corrupted by the Greeks into Skolotai, Skules, Skylas, or Skythes. According to Herodotos, he was a descendant, either of Targitaus, a son of Zeus, or of Herakles, another son of that deity. The name, Skythes, may mean 'shooter or archer', which suits the Śakas well. It may also be connected to Sogdia

(Transoxiana)—Skytha becoming Skuda<Suguda<Sogdia. The Skythians had been migrating from their original homeland towards the west since the beginning of the first millennium BC. Arsakes I, the founder of the Parthian dynasty, belonged to the Aparni tribe, which was a part of the Dahae confederation of Chorasmia, the Dahae themselves being a part of the Śaka confederation. This, incidentally, shows a close connection between the Skythians and the Parthians, and, hence, the use of the term Śaka-Pahlava throughout this work.

In the latter half of the third century BC, the Hiung-nu tribe inhabited some region to the north of the Mangolian plateau, while the Yüeh-chih tribe occupied Kansu to the west of the Ordoṣ plateau, which lay outside the Great Wall of China, but within a loop formed by the river Hwang-ho. The two tribes often fought with each other over the possession of Ordos. Sometimes before 221 BC, the Yüeh-chih defeated the Hiung-nu *Shan-yü* (king), T'ou-man, and took his son, Mao-tun, as hostage. In 221 BC, the Chinese emperor, Cheng, forced the Hiung-nu to retreat towards the north, but on his death in 210 BC, they returned and attacked the Yüeh-chih, and Mao-tun escaped. He became the king, occupied Ordos, and defeated a number of nomadic tribes, forcing them to join his confederation.

Around this time (208-206 BC), intense volcanic activity seems to have led to a decline in world temperatures, and a number of peoples migrated south from Siberia towards the river Oxus. In 200 BC, the first Han emperor, Kao-tsu, attacked the Hiung-nu, but was besieged and forced to sign a treaty in 198 BC. In 177 BC, during the reign of the next emperor, Wen-ti, the Hiung-nu crossed the Hwang-ho, and breached the Great Wall. According to the *Shih Chi*, Mao-tun sent a letter to Wen-ti, claiming that he had punished his commander, 'Right Wise King', for this breach of the treaty, and sent him west to give fight to the Yüeh-chih, whom he had succeeded in wiping out. He also claims that he had defeated the Wu-sun, Hu-chieh, and 26 states, and that 'all the people who live by drawing the bow are now united into one family'. The Yüeh-chih, however, did not join this confederation. Some scholars believe that the Yüeh-chih migration from their original homeland began after this battle in *c* 177-176 BC. But it was Left Wise King (called Old Shan-yü by the Chinese), the son and successor of Mao-tun, who finally defeated the Yüeh-chih sometime before 159 BC, killed their ruler, and forced them to migrate. Most of the Yüeh-chih, called Ta Yüeh-chih by the Chinese, migrated westwards from Kansu, and then north to Etsin Gol, in the Turfan basin, crossed the Tien Shan mountains, and settled in the Ili valley, the homeland of the Śakas; in 128 BC, Chang Ch'ien, the emissary of the Chinese emperor, Wu-ti, found the Ta Yüeh-chih in K'ang-chü, along the north bank of the river Jaxartes. Some Yüeh-chih remained in Kansu and Etsin Gol, at least up to 121 BC, and they are called Hsiao Yüeh-chih by the Chinese. Under the pressure of the Ta Yüeh-chih, the Śakas fled their homeland in the Ili valley, and moving towards the south, occupied Ki-pin (Kashmir). The tribe spilt repeatedly, and established several states, like the Hsui-hsn and Chan-tu to the northwest of Shu-lo (Kashgar).

According to the Chinese accounts, the Śakas invaded India only from the north, which is not entirely correct. However, some Śakas from the Ili valley did cross the Pamirs, and entered India, settling in the Hazara-Kashmir region. Maues belonged to this branch of the Śakas, who colonized the Hazara and Kashmir regions, and he later advanced west into the Indo-Greek territories. This is suggested by the high quality of his silver coins in the Hazara-Kahsmir region, as also by several of his coin types being imitated from Indo-Greek coinage.

A western branch of the Śakas was pushed by the Yüeh-chih across the Jaxartes and the Oxus. Another branch was already moving from Sogdia. They first occupied Merv and northern Bactria, and then crossed the Hindukush into India, occupying Kapiśā, the Kabul valley, and western Gandhāra, that is they advanced east into the Indo-Greek territories. Vonones and the related rulers, Spalahora, Spalagadama, Spalirises, Azes I, Azilises, and Azes II, belonged to this branch of the Śakas. This branch began the posthumous Hermaios coinage, which developed into the initial coinage of the family of Vonones in the Gandhāra region, there being strong monogram links between the posthumous Hermaios coinage and the initial coinage of the family of Vonones. The two branches of Maues and Vonones were mainly responsible for the end of Indo-Greek rule, and were finally united by Azes.

The Parthian emperor, Phraates II, hired Śaka mercenaries, perhaps from Margiane, Traxiane, and Aria, for his campaign against Antiochos VII. But after the campaign, he had a dispute with the Śakas, and he, as also his uncle and successor, Artabanos I, lost their lives at the hands of these Śaka mercenaries. The next ruler, Mithridates II, initially fought with these Śakas. But later, he reversed his policy *vis-à-vis* the Śakas, and settled them in Drangiana, which henceforth became known as Sakastene (Seistan). There is a view that Orthagnes, Gondopharnes, Guḍa, Abdagases, and perhaps, also Pakores, probably belonged to this branch of the Śakas from Seistan, although there is a strong possibility that they were related to the family of Vonones.

The earliest known Śaka-Pahlava ruler was, perhaps, Vonones. Cunningham regards him as originally a lieutenant of Maues, left behind in Seistan to govern the region when Maues himself pushed forward into India. Later, Vonones was either installed as the king of Seistan by Maues himself, or he rebelled against Maues and declared himself the supreme sovereign in Seistan. But Tarn regards Vonones as originally serving under the Arsakid emperor, Orodes II, as his vassal, and later asserting his independence. It is generally believed, by scholars like Alexander Cunningham, J H Marshall, and G K Jenkins, that the 'chief centre of rule' of the family of Vonones was Arachosia. As seen earlier, he belonged to that branch of the Śaka-Pahlavas, which had first occupied Merv and northern Bactria, and then crossed the Hindukush into India, occupying Kapiśā, the Kabul valley, and western Gandhāra. In the Kabul valley, they imitated the coins of Hermaios. Senior associates Vonones with this branch of the Śaka-Pahlavas, and regards the coins issued by him and his associates as 'successors of the imitation Hermaios coinage'. On the evidence of the *provenance* of coins, Senior places the circulation of the coins of the family of Vonones mainly in 'the great Gandhāra region, west of Taxila'.

Vonones appears to have employed some subordinate rulers. On some coins bearing the name of Vonones on the obverse, the reverse legend mentions Spalahora as 'brother of the king', without according him any royal title. While Tarn regards 'king's brother' as a title of honour, most of the scholars believe that Spalahora was, indeed, a brother of Vonones, the 'king' mentioned on the obverse of these coins. Most of the scholars believe that the coins of Vonones with Spalahora belong to Arachosia, showing that the former served under Vonones in that region. R C Senior, however, places the circulation of these coins in 'the greater Gandhāra region, west of Taxila'. Spalahora also issued copper coins with his son Spalagadama, which bear the name of Spalyris (= Spalahora; Osmund Bopearachchi would, however, identify him with Spalirises) on the obverse, and that of Spalagadama on the reverse. Neither he, nor his son, uses any royal title, showing that they issued these coins as subordinate rulers, serving under Vonones.

There are certain satrapal coins, which mention one Spalirises as 'brother of the king', and do not use any royal title for him, showing that he began his career as a subordinate ruler of the latter. Although the name of the 'king' is not mentioned on these coins, most of the scholars identify him with Vonones; the suggestion, that he might be Maues, is not acceptable. The publication of a silver coin bearing the name of Vonones on the obverse, and the legend, *Maharajabhrata dhramiäsa Spalirishasa*, on the reverse, would seem to set the controversy at rest. Spalirises also issued coins with his son, Azes I, on which, both Spalirises and Azes I are called 'great king'. Most of the scholars believe that these coins were issued during the reign of Vonones, with both Spalirises and Azes I serving as his subordinate rulers. But Marshall feels that by assuming the title of 'great king', they are announcing the end of Vonones' overlordship. Spalirises also issued copper coins on which he assumed the sovereign titles of *basileos basileon megalos*. He restruck the joint coins of Vonones with Spalahora (or Spalagadama), and of Spalahora with Spalagadama as well. This seems to show that Spalirises overthrew Vonones in Arachosia, and also removed Spalahora and his son from power. Most of the scholars believe that the coins of Spalirises come from Arachosia (although R C Senior would place their circulation in 'the greater Gandhāra region, west of Taxila'). But his son, Azes I, ruled only in northwestern India. This shows that Spalirises was himself overthrown by some one, perhaps some direct descendant of Vonones, and Azes I had to move to northwestern India.

Meanwhile, in northwestern India, one of the earliest Śaka-Pahlava rulers to issue coins bearing the king's name was Maues. He has been associated with that branch of the Śaka-Pahlavas, which crossed the Pamirs from the Ili valley, and settled in the Swat-Hazara-Kashmir (Chinese Ki-pin) region, some time after 160 BC. On some of his coins, Maues bears the subordinate titles of *basileos* and *maharaja*, while on others, he is given the sovereign titles of *basileos basileon megalos* and *rajatiraja mahata*. This has led to the suggestion that Maues, perhaps, started his career as a subordinate ruler of Vonones, and asserted independence in northwestern India, when Spalirises overthrew Vonones. But on the coin Maues issued in association with his mother, Machene, he has the titles of *rajatiraja mahata*, showing his sovereign status even during his minority. This indicates that, if his family ever served under the family of Vonones, it must have thrown off the yoke of vassalage some time before the accession of Maues. Attempts have been made to associate him with the Indo-Greek ruler, Peukolaos, through Machene, although there are certain difficulties in accepting this suggestion. He seems to have ruled in the first century BC; his dates are not certain, although R C Senior is in favour of placing him between *c* 95/85 BC and 60/57 BC. Maues imitated the coin types of the Euthydemid and Eukratid families of Indo-Greek rulers, like Demetrios I, Antimachos, Menander,

Antialkidas, Strato I, Peukolaos, Theophilos, Heliokles II, and Polyxenos, showing that he must have ruled over territories wrested from both of the families. He is believed to have advanced west into the Indo-Greek dominions from the Swat-Hazara-Kashmir region. However, the scarcity of his 'westernmost coinage' has been taken to suggest that this advance was not 'too successful or of long duration'. His rule over Gandhāra is vouched for by the Taxila copperplate inscription of [Vikrama *saṁvat*] 78, and there is a suggestion that the year might belong to some era founded by Maues, *c* 95 BC. He, however, seems to have lost Takshaśilā, perhaps to the Indo-Greeks, towards the end of his reign. His name might have been mentioned in the Mathura lion capital inscriptions of the time of Rañjuvula and Śoḍāsha, as also in some inscriptions from Chilas. Numismatic evidence suggests that Maues was succeeded by Azes I. Some scholars believe that Maues might have married his daughter to Azes I, and the succession from Maues to Azes I might have been peaceful. But it seems to be more likely that, when Spalirises, the father of Azes I, was overthrown in Arachosia, Azes I was forced to come to northwestern India, where he defeated Maues, occupied his throne, and forced him to the rule as a subordinate ruler. It was during this period that Maues issued coins with the subordinate titles.

A large number of coins bearing the name of Azes have come to the light. From the fact that on some coins, the name of Azes occurs in Greek, on the obverse, and of Azilises (Ayalisha), in Kharoshṭhī, on the reverse, while on some others, the order is reversed, it has been suggested that there were two Śaka-Pahlava kings, bearing the name Azes. Of these, the elder, that is Azes I, associated his son, Azilises, in government, perhaps in his old age, and the latter, in his turn, associated his own son, Azes II, in government towards the close of his reign. The issue of the existence of two kings named Azes is a contentious one, and needs to be addressed in some detail, as it has a bearing on the history of the Śaka-Pahlava rulers. Whitehead, on the contrary, is of the view that there might have been two kings named Azilises, and only one Azes. His argument is that as the 'best didrachms of Azes compare unfavourably with the fine silver coins of Azilises', hence, Azilises preceded Azes. However, in view of the fact that the coins of Azilises do not show any great difference in style and execution, while the same cannot be said of the coins bearing the name of Azes, there is a greater likelihood of there being two rulers named Azes. Scholars like Ernst Herzfeld and J E van Lohuizen-de Leeuw suggested that Azes, Azilises, Aya, and Ayilisha (the last two being the Prakrit forms of Azes and Azilises, respectively) are the different names of one and the same king. But this view has not been taken seriously by scholars. Sten Konow was earlier of the view that there was only one Azes. But, later on, he accepted the theory of the existence of two kings named Azes. Jenkins has shown that some coins bearing the name of Azes are of fine quality silver, bear the obverse device of horseman king with spear, and have the early form of the Kharoshṭhī letter *sa* in the reverse legend; other coins bearing the name of Azes are in debased silver, bear the obverse device of horseman king with whip, and have the late form of the Kharoshṭhī letter, *sa.* He ascribes the former coins to Azes I, and the latter to Azes II.

R C Senior has recently pleaded the case for a single king named Azes. He regards all the joint issues in the name of Azes/Azilises or Azilises/Azes as 'mules'. He says that 'mules', by their very nature, are extremely rare, while joint coins should be more prolific and produced from several dies. But he himself admits that thc Azilises/Azes copper coins are 'more problematic since more than one die is known and so far no coin exists with an Azes obverse (ie, no coin of this type known of Azes alone)'. He has tried to explain away this problem by suggesting a number of possibilities and 'unusual' situations. The evidence of coin hoards, too, has been cited, but it cannot be said to be conclusive. For instance, the Nul Guniar hoard, which has coins of both the 'King mounted with spear' and 'King mounted with whip' types of Azes, but no coins of Azilises, has been taken as confirmation of the suggestion that Azilises did not intervene between Azes I and Azes II series of coins. It is further argued that all the coins were patinated to the same extent, showing that they were deposited 'within a short period of issue'. But should such conclusions be drawn on the basis of a hoard of mere 11 coins ? Would the patination become markedly different within a period of, say, some 20 years ? The stratified evidence of the Azes coins from Taxila also supports the existence of two kings, bearing the name of Azes. The occurrence of the early form of the Kharoshṭhī letter, *sa*, on the coins of Azes found in the lower strata, when compared with the occurrence of the later form of the same letter on the Azes coins from the upper strata, also indicates the existence of two Azes. Moreover, the coins of Azilises themselves show no debasement, and, as such, the debased coins of Azes [II] cannot be placed before him. The view of R C Senior, that Azilises started ruling at the same time as Azes, and predeceased the latter, is difficult to accept.

But the most clinching evidence in favour of the existence of two kings named Azes is as follows : The dates of Vijayamitra are available from several inscriptions. The

Shinkot-Bajaur relic-casket inscriptions refer to his regnal year 5. Then, there is the Indravarman reliquary inscription of Azes year 63, which mentions year 25 of Vijayamitra. A third inscription, the Prahodia inscription, is reported to refer to year 32 of Vijayamitra, and this may be the reason for identifying *apracharaja*, whose regnal year 25 is mentioned in the Indravarman reliquary inscription, with Vijayamitra. Finally, there is the so-called 'Bhagamoya' inscription of year 77 of Azes, which also mentions Vijayamitra. If Azes year 63 of the Indravarman relic-casket inscription, is regnal year 25 of Vijayamitra, then Azes year 77 of the 'Bhagamoya' inscription will make regnal year 39 of Vijayamitra. This shows that Vijayamitra must have ruled for 39+ years. The era of Azes is generally identified with Vikrama *saṁvat*, commencing 58/57 BC. On this basis, year 63 of Azes, mentioned in the Indravarman relic casket inscription, comes to 5 AD. This is believed to be the 25th regnal year of Vijayamitra. Hence, Vijayamitra would have started ruling *c* 20 BC. The 'Bhagamoya' inscription shows that he was ruling in Azes year 77, ie, 19 AD. We have joint coins to show that Azes had Indravasu, the son of Vijayamitra, as his subordinate ruler, and Aśpavarman, the son of Vijayamitra's nephew, Indravarman, as his *strategos*. If there were only one Azes, this would mean that he survived, not only Vijayamitra, but also received the services of Vijayamitra's son, Indravasu, and of Aśpavarman, the son of Vijayamitra's nephew, Indravarman. According to the 'Bhagamoya' inscription, Vijayamitra was ruling in Azes year 77. To have Aśpavarman serve under him, Azes would require an exceptionally long reign of 77+ years. But if we accept the existence of two kings named Azes, this problem would be solved. We would have an Azes whose year is mentioned in these records, and a second king of that name as overlord of Indravasu and Aśpavarman. Azes I would have been dead at the time of the issue of the Indravarman reliquary inscription of Azes year 63 (= 5 AD), for this epigraph refers to the era as *maharajasa Ayasa atidasa*, 'of the *Maharaja* Aya deceased'. It is quite possible that Azes I was not alive even in the early years of the reign of Vijayamitra. R C Senior seems to be right, when he suggests, on numismatic grounds, that Vijayamitra asserted himself immediately after the death of Azes, *c* 20 BC.

Numismatic evidence shows that, later on, Azes I succeeded, not his father Spalirises in Arachosia, but Maues in India. Sircar suggests the possibility that Azes I might have been the son-in-law of Maues, and succeeded to the territories of Maues peacefully. But it is more likely that Spalirises was overthrown in Arachosia, and Azes I had perforce to go to northwestern India, where he defeated Maues, occupied his territories, and even forced Maues to serve under him. Azes I extended Śaka-Pahlava sway towards eastern Punjab, where he seems to have defeated Indo-Greek kings of the family of Antimochos I. He not only imitated the Athena Promachos type of Menander and his successors, but also restruck the coins of Apollodotos and Hippostratos. Some of the monograms of these two princes appear on the coins of Azes I also. He is regarded as one of the great rulers of ancient India, who unified a great part of northwestern India. His 'huge output of coinage' testifies to the prosperity of his kingdom. He seems to have founded an era, perhaps at the time of his accession, which came to be known as Vikrama *saṁvat*. Towards the end of his rule, he associated his son, Azilises, in government, as shown by their joint coins.

Azilises, on succeeding his father, ruled over the extensive territories, which had earlier been under the authority of Maues and Azes I, his coins showing his hold over the Hazara-Kashmir region, and parts of western Gandhāra. His silver coins, bearing the device of Gajalakshmī on the reverse, remind one of the coins of Mathurā depicting a similar device, and might be indicative of the extension of his sway up to Mathurā in the east. The Herakles seated type of his coins might be indicative of his hold over parts of southern Afghanistan. Towards the end of his reign, Azilises seems to have associated his son, Azes II, in government as a junior co-ruler, and issued joint coins with him. R C Senior, however, regards these joint issues as 'mules'. He tentatively proposes new interrelationships between the Śaka-Pahlava rulers. He is of the view that Azilises was the '*sole* successor' of Maues in Hazara, and might have been his son, although he also expresses the possibility of Azilises being a son of Spalirises. On the basis of the close proximity of some types of Azilises with those of 'Azes', he regards the two as 'closely related', perhaps as brothers or as father and son. According to him, hoard evidence seems to show that Azilises' coins from Hazara predate some coins of 'Azes', and that if the two were father and son, Azilises would have been the father of 'Azes'. All these difficulties in the chronology of the Śaka-Pahlava rulers seem to arise out of the fact that Senior believes in the existence of only one Śaka-Pahlava king named Azes.

Azes II started his career as a junior co-ruler of his father, Azilises, and issued joint coins with him. Ultimately, Azes II succeeded his father to the throne and issued his independent coinage. He also struck joint coins with Indravasu, and with Aśpavarman, both of whom belonged to the family of the Apracharajas. Aśpavarman is known to have served under both Azes II and Gondopharnes, in the capacity of *strategos.* There is a possibility that when Gondopharnes invaded the kingdom of Azes II, Aśpavarman switched over his loyalty to the invader and helped him in defeating Azes II. The victorious invader permitted Aśpavarman to continue as *strategos*, as a reward for the help received from him. Scholars like Rapson and Sten Konow, however, believe that Gondopharnes succeeded Azes II peacefully.

Orthagnes was a successor of Spalirises in Arachosia, or, more probably, the successor of the person who overthrew Spalirises in that region. There are some silver and copper coins bearing the name of Orthagnes with full sovereign titles on the obverse, and those of Gondopharnes and Guḍa, or that of Guḍa alone, on the reverse. Scholars, like Cunningham, Smith, Whitehead, and Allan, regard Orthagnes as a successor of Gondopharnes, while Sten Konow and J E van Lohuizen-de Leeuw are of the view that the names Orthagnes and Gondopharnes refer to one and the same person. But Rapson suggests that Orthagnes was the overlord of Gondopharnes and Guḍa, and this is supported by the occurrence of the name of Orthagnes on the obverse, and of Gondopharnes and/or Guḍa on the reverse of the coins. It appears that, initially, Orthagnes ruled over Arachosia with the help of his subordinates, Gondopharnes and Guḍa. This Guḍa seems to be identical with Gad, mentioned in the Syriac version of *The Apocryphal Acts of Judas Thomas, the Apostle*, as a brother of Gūdnaphar (= Gondopharnes). Gondopharnes conquered territories in northwestern India, dissociated himself from the administration of Arachosia, and consequently, Orthagnes nominated Guḍa to succeed Gondopharnes as the viceroy of Arachosia.

Gondopharnes, after his successes in northwestern India, seems to have declared himself independent. Later, however, Gondopharnes issued Arachosia type of coins, on the reverse of which occurs the name of Guḍa. This shows that, perhaps after the death of Orthagnes, Gondopharnes occupied Arachosia, and Guḍa continued to serve there as his viceroy. The hold of Gondopharnes over the Kabul valley is attested by Philostratos and Fan-ye. The Takht-i-Bahi inscription shows that the Gandhāra region formed a part of his empire. Interestingly, this inscription, dated in [Vikrama *saṁvat*] 103 (= 46 AD), refers to [regnal] year 26 of Gondopharnes, showing that he ruled from *c* 19 AD to 46+ AD. He is identified with Gūdnaphar or Goundaphoros, 'the king of India', who received Apostle Thomas, about the middle of the first century AD, and this Christian tradition also supports the date *c* 19 AD to 46+ AD for Gondopharnes. However, attempts have been made, by scholars like J E van Lohuizen-de Leeuw, and, recently, by R C Senior, to place Gondopharnes in the first century BC, by rejecting the legend of St Thomas' visit to India and regarding the year 103 of the Takht-i-Bahi inscription as referring to some earlier Śaka-Pahlava era commencing 129-128 BC. The copper coins of Gondopharnes from the Pathankot area were copied from the crude copper issues of Rañjuvula in that region, showing that Gondopharnes conquered that region from Rañjuvula.

According to the Rapson, the peculiar Gondopharnes symbol is found struck on some coins of Orodes II (57-37/36 BC). The same mark was found by Alexander Cunningham on some coins of Artabanos III, who ruled from 11/12 AD to *c* 38 or 40 AD. Rapson, however, doubted this, and suggested that Cunningham might have meant 'Orodes'. But there is a coin type of

Artabanos III, the reverse of which shows the king mounted on horse, left, and being offered a palm-branch by Tyche standing before him. This type was issued *c* 27/28 AD. This coin type of Artabanos III seems to have served as the prototype for the obverse device of a bronze type of Gondopharnes, which has king on horseback, left, and being received by a female figure, identified as Nike by Gardner, though some doubts have been expressed regarding this identification. If this suggestion regarding the inspiration for the coin device of Gondopharnes be correct, Gondopharnes might have ruled over some Arsakid provinces.

Gondopharnes was served, not only by Aśpavarman, but also by the latter's nephew, Sasan, with whom he issued joint coins, and his own nephew, Abdagases. He was the last great Śaka-Pahlava ruler, and after him, Abdagases, Pakores, and Sasan are known to have ruled as independent kings, though their order of succession is not certain. There is numismatic evidence to show that, among these successors of Gondopharnes, Abdagases, who had served his uncle, perhaps in western Gandhāra, exercised sway over Arachosia, Seistan, and Takshaśilā. Pakores ruled over Arachosia. The fact that some of his Arachosian types of coins are overstruck on pieces of *Soter Megas*, has been taken to indicate his success, howsoever temporary it might have been, against the Kushāṇas in that region. Sasan, the nephew of Aśpavarman, ruled over Takshaśilā, Seistan, Arachosia, and the lower Indus regions. His authority over Pushkalāvatī-Gandhāra region is not proved by the available sources; perhaps it was occupied by Phraotes and/or the Kushāṇas after Gondopharnes.

There are also some other Śaka-Pahlava rulers, known mainly from their coins. Sanabares, assigned to the middle of the first century AD, seems to have some relation with Gondopharnes, as the peculiar Gondopharnes symbol occurs on some of his coins. The occurrence of an Arsakid symbol, on a number of his coins, shows some connection with the Parthian empire also. Numismatic evidence suggests that he exercised authority over Arachosia and Seistan. Gardner feels that the conspicuous absence of any Indian script on his coins suggests that he ruled 'exclusively or principally to the north of the Indian Caucasus'. Mamvadi, known from a unique *tetradrachm*, seems to have ruled somewhere in the Gandhāra region after Azes. Nastene is known from a *tetradrachm*, bearing the device of the helmeted bust of the king on the obverse, and equestrian king on the reverse. The legend introduces him as son of Xatran. The coin has been placed in mid-first century AD. It has been suggested that Nastene might have been of Śaka-Pahlava, Kushāṇa, or 'mixed parentage', who rose to power, perhaps somewhere to the north of the Hindukush.

Gondopharnes was the last great Śaka-Pahlava ruler. His empire disintegrated soon after, paving the way for the establishment of Kushāṇa supremacy in northwestern India. There were also certain satrapal families, which ruled under the Śaka-Pahlavas, and/or the Kushāṇas; some of them ruled virtually as independent powers.

A Śaka satrapal family is known to have ruled over Mathurā, of which, Rañjuvula was the first known *kshatrapa*. As his son and successor, Śoḍāsha, was ruling in 15 AD, he may be placed in the beginning of the first century AD. R C Senior, however, places him between *c* 25 BC and 5 AD. His coins show that he first ruled as a *kshatrapa*, the coins referring to him as such being rather rare, and later attained the position of a *mahākshatrapa*. His coins testify to his hold over Takshaśilā, or territories to its northeast, Hazara to Akhnoor-Jammu, the Punjab and western Uttar Pradesh, particularly Mathurā. It has been pointed out that his earlier coins bear legends in both Brāhmī and Kharoshṭhī, while the later ones have legends in Brāhmī only. Also, his commonest type is copied from Indo-Greek coins (particularly those of Strato I), while his rarest coins are modelled after the local issues of Mathurā. These facts seem to suggest that he occupied Mathurā 'late in life', but made it the centre of power of his family, towards the end of his rule. The Mathura lion capital inscriptions of the time of Rañjuvula and Śoḍāsha refer to the consecration of Buddhist relics by Nada Diäka, the chief queen of Rañjuvula, who, according to different interpretations, was either the daughter or the mother of Kharaösta. Rañjuvula, in his records, does not refer to his overlord. The Greek legend of his coins refers to him as *basileos basileon soter*, probably meaning 'king of kings, the saviour', while the Kharoshṭhī legend gives him the title of *kshatrapa* or *mahākshatrapa*, often with the additional title, *apratihatachakra*. All this seems to suggest that, for all practical purposes, he was ruling as an independent king.

Śoḍāsha was the son and successor of Rañjuvula. His known date is 15 AD. The Mathura lion capital inscriptions of the time of Rañjuvula and Śoḍāsha refer to the former as *mahākshatrapa*, and to the latter as *kshatrapa*. On his earlier coins also, Śoḍāsha refers to himself as a *kshatrapa*, and as 'son of Rañjuvula' or 'son of *mahākshatrapa*'. But later, he issued coins as a *mahākshatrapa*, and, interestingly, dropped the patronymic in the coin legend. The paucity of his *mahākshatrapa* coins indicates his short reign. Known only from a single coin in the Richard Burn collection, on which he is described as a *kshatrapa* and son of a *mahākshatrapa*, Taraṇaḍāsa appears to belong to the family of Rañjuvula, and may have been a son of Śoḍāsha. He ruled from Mathurā. According to some scholars, the name of the *kshatrapa* on the coin may even be Bharaṇaḍāsa, but Allan prefers the reading *Toraṇaḍāsa.*

Hagāna was a Śaka *kshatrapa* of Mathurā, known only from the joint coins he issued with his brother, Hagāmasha. As the name of Hagāna appears before that of Hagāmasha in the obverse legend of their joint coins, the former seems to be the elder of the two brothers. On numismatic grounds, John Allan placed him before Śoḍāsha, but recent writers on the subject, like Michael Mitchiner and R C Senior, would date him after Śoḍāsha. Hagāmasha seems to have started his career as a subordinate of his elder brother, Hagāna, with whom he issued joint coins. Later, he issued his independent coins, showing that he succeeded Hagāna. The relationship of Śivaghosha and Śivadatta, known from coins, with the other Śaka *kshatrapas* of Mathurā, is not clear.

Among the Śaka *kshatrapas* of northwestern India, Kharaösta, described on his coins as son of Arṭa, is also mentioned in two epigraphs. The Mathura lion capital inscriptions of the time of Rañjuvula and Śoḍāsha mention him as *Yuvarāja* Kharaösta, and he was somehow related to Nada Diäka, the chief queen of Rañjuvula (various scholars regard him as either her son, or her father). In the reliquary inscriptions of the time of Kharaösta and Indravarman, the former is described as a *yaguraṁña* (perhaps equivalent to *yabgu,* 'chief'), and as a son of a *mahākshatrapa.* His date is not certain, but there is a suggestion that he may be placed in the last two decades of the first century BC. He might have ruled over some territories to the north of Takshaśilā, perhaps in Hazara. Hajatriä, known from coins as a son of Kharaösta, might be identical with Hayuära mentioned in the Mathura lion capital inscriptions of the time of

Rañjuvula and Śoḍāsha. He seems to have ruled over some territories to the north of Takshaśilā, perhaps in Hazara.

Liäka Kusulaka is mentioned in the Taxila copperplate inscription of year 78 as the *kshatrapa* of Chukhsa (most probably, modern Chach along the river Indus), perhaps serving under Maues; Marshall would assign to Liäka Kusulaka a much more extensive satrapy, comprising the Peshawar valley to the west of the river Indus, and a large part of Hazara, Attock, and Mianwali regions to its east. According to one view, his main duty was 'the guarding of the northern frontiers and the Indus crossings'. He appears to be the son of *Mahākshatrapa* Patika of the Mathura lion capital inscriptions of the time of Rañjuvula and Śoḍāsha, and the father of *Mahādānapati* Patika. Zeionises, on numismatic grounds, seems to be associated with western Punjab and eastern parts of Hazara-Kashmir, and to be a contemporary of Azes II. His coins describe him as a *kshatrapa* and a son of *Kshatrapa* Maṇigula. A Taxila inscription of [Vikrama *saṁvat*] 191 (= 134 AD) refers to one Jihoṇika as a *kshatrapa* of Chukhsa (modern Chach, northwest of Taxila, although Pushkalāvatī, or some region in Kashmir, have also been proposed as possible identifications). The inscription also refers to him as *maharajabhrata*, but the identity of this *maharaja* is not clear. Jihoṇika seems to be a Prakrit rendering of Zeionises, and Zeionises of the Taxila inscription seems to be a grandson of Zeionises, son of Maṇigula, known from coins. R C Senior regards him as a successor of Azilises in the Hazara-Kashmir region.

The first mention of the *Apracharajas* occurs in the Shinkot Bajaur relic casket inscriptions of the time of Menander, Viyakamitra, and Vijayamitra. Viyakamitra was, very probably, a feudatory of Menander. Vijayamitra is also styled *apracharaja*, and he, too, served as a feudatory under the Śaka-Pahlavas. But his overlord is not mentioned in the Shinkot Bajaur relic casket inscriptions, or in the other inscriptions of the Apracha family mentioning Vijayamitra. He seems to have become virtually independent after the death of Azes I, towards the beginning of the ninth decade of the first century BC. His rule was confined to the Swat valley. Indravasu, the son of Vijayamitra, is known both from coins and an inscription. Perhaps, following the Śaka-Pahlava tradition of co-rule, in which both the senior and the junior co-rulers assumed equivalent titles, Indravasu ruled for some time as the co-ruler of Vijayamitra, as per the evidence of the reliquary inscriptions of the time of Kharaösta and Indravarman. He also seems to have served as a subordinate of the Śaka-Pahlava ruler, Azes II, as per the testimony of their joint coins. Vijayamitra is mentioned as ruling in later inscriptions also, while in the Indravarman reliquary inscription of Azes year 63, we find Vishṇuvarman co-ruling as *apracharaja* with *Apracharaja* Vijayamitra. From this, it appears that Indravasu predeceased his father, some time before Azes year 63 (= 5 AD), the date of the Indravarman reliquary inscription. The rarity of the coins of Indravasu suggests a short career for him. Indravarman, the son of Vishṇuvarman, also ruled as an *apracharaja*. His son, Aśpavarman, is known to have served the Śaka-Pahlava ruler, Azes II, as *strategos*. We also have his joint coins with Gondopharnes. As seen above, it appears that when Gondopharnes invaded the kingdom of Azes II, *Strategos* Aśpavarman sided with the invader, and when Azes II had been defeated, the victorious invader rewarded Aśpavarman by allowing him to continue as *strategos*. He also added the Takshaśilā region to the charge of Aśpavarman, as per the numismatic and epigraphic evidence. Sasan, the nephew of Aśpavarman, started his career as a subordinate of Gondopharnes, but asserted independence on the death of his overlord, and ruled over an extensive area for some time. Two rulers of the lower Indus valley, namely Sapedana and Satavastra, known from some silver coins from Taxila, also seem to belong to the Apracha family.

The Western Kshatrapas : The Kshaharāta and Kārddamaka families

The Western Kshatrapas were rulers of Śaka origin, who held sway over the western parts of India, particularly in Gujarat, Maharashtra, Rajasthan, and Malwa, and most of them assumed the title of *kshatrapa* or *mahākshatrapa*. Three branches of these Western Kshatrapas—Kshaharāta dynasty, Kārddamaka dynasty, and the Kshatrapas of Vidarbha, are known so far. These Western Kshatrapas ruled for over 300 years. The Vidarbha branch of the Western Kshatrapas is represented only by *Mahākshatrapa Kumāra* Rupiämma, known from an inscription. On palaeographical grounds, he appears to have ruled sometime in the first century AD. There is a suggestion that the rule of the Vidarbha branch of the Western Kshatrapas might have been brought to an end by Gautamīputra Sātakarṇi, some time in the first quarter of the second century AD.

The Kshaharāta Kshatrapas. One of the three branches of the Western Kshatrapas, the Kshaharātas seem to have started their career as the provincial governors of the Kushāṇas in the southwestern parts of the empire, as shown by the use of the title of *kshatrapa* by Ābhīraka and Bhūmaka on their coins, and the titles of *kshatrapa* and *mahākshatrapa* by Nahapāna in his inscriptions, although doubts have recently been expressed from certain quarters regarding the subordinate status of the Kshaharāta Kshatrapas. But Nahapāna, on his coins, uses the title of *rājan*, which shows an increase in the power and prestige of the dynasty during his reign. Various interpretations of the family name, Kshaharāta, have been suggested. According to H C Raychaudhuri, it may be identical with Karatai, a branch of the Śakas mentioned by Ptolemy. Michael Mitchiner has tried to associate the Kshaharāta Kshatrapas with Ladhanes, a nephew of Gondopharnes, mainly on the basis of certain coins, on which he reads the name *Chaharata*, together with Ladhanaputra. But what he has read as *Chaharata*, is regarded as *Parama* or *Parata* (= Pārada) by other scholars. The Taxila copper-plate inscription of Patika refers to his father, Liäka Kusulaka, as *Kshahara Chukhsasa cha kshatrapa*, *kshatrapa* of Chhahara and Chukhsa (?), Chhahara being a place name in the vicinity of Taxila. There is a suggestion that the Kshaharāta branch might have derived its name from this place, which might have been its original home. If this Chhahara has anything to do with Kshaharāta, this Western Kshatrapa branch might have been related to the family of Liäka Kusulaka and Patika also.

Ābhīraka seems to be the earliest known Kshaharāta Kshatrapa. His copper coins have been found from the Kachchh and Junagarh regions of Gujarat. The legends on these coins, in both Greek and Brāhmī, seem to give the name of his family as Kshaharāta, and his title as *kshatrapa*. The name on the coins is not very clear, and had earlier been read as Aghudaka or Abhedaka. But R C Senior has now read it as Ābhīraka. The use of Nike as a coin device by him seems to place him before Bhūmaka. This is supported by the find of a coin of Ābhīraka, which was counterstruck by Bhūmaka.

Bhūmaka is one of the earliest known *kshatrapas*, who was appointed by the Kushāṇa ruler to administer the southwestern parts of the empire, although doubts have recently been expressed, from certain quarters, regarding his subordinate status. The find of his coins from the coastal regions of Gujarat, parts of Malwa, and the Ajmer region of Rajasthan, give us an idea of the territories under his rule. The use of both Brāhmī and Kharoshṭhī scripts on his coins shows that he also ruled over the western Rajasthan and Sind regions, where Kharoshṭhī was prevalent, although there is a view that the ancestors of the Kshaharāta rulers might have brought this script to the Deccan from the 'North-west'. Sylvain Lévi's view, that Bhūmaka should be identified with Ysāmotika, the father of Chashṭana, as *ysama* is the Śaka word for the earth (Sanskrit, *bhūmi*), does not seem to be convincing. No inscription of this ruler is known so far.

Nahapāna seems to have succeeded Bhūmaka as the *kshatrapa* of the Kushāṇas, but the relation between these two Kshaharāta rulers is not known for certain. He has been identified with Nambanus of the *Periplus*, and with Naravāhana or Navavāhana of certain Jaina texts, like the *Harivaṁśa*. No inscription issued by Nahapāna himself is known so far, but several inscriptions, issued in his time by his son-in-law, Ushavadāta (a great donor and the governor of the southern province of the Kshaharāta kingdom), daughter Dakshamitrā, and *Amātya* Aryaman, are known from the Nasik, Karle, and Junnar regions of Maharashtra. These inscriptions bear dates, ranging from year 41 to 46. If they are indeed dated in the Śaka era, as has been suggested by a number of scholars, he ruled in the first half of the second century AD. However, scholars like A S Altekar, Karl Khandalavala, Amiteshwar Jha and Dilip Rajgor, A M Shastri, and R C Senior, have pointed out certain difficulties, mainly chronological, in referring the dates, mentioned in these inscriptions, to the Śaka era. They regard these dates to refer to the regnal years of Nahapāna, but have proposed different dates for this ruler—Altekar places him between 55 and 105 AD; Khandalavala opines that he began his rule some time between 55 and 64 AD, and it came to an end between 101 and 111 AD; Jha and Rajgor feel that his reign may be placed between 48 and 94 AD or 52 and 98 AD; Senior regards the second last decade of the first century BC as representing the middle of Nahapāna's reign.

The external and internal evidence of these inscriptions, as also the findspots of his coins, shows that his rule extended from Ajmer in the north to Nasik-Pune in the south, and from Gujarat and northern Konkan in the west to Malwa in the east. The use of the title *rājan* on his coins, instead of the mere *kshatrapa* met with on the coins of Bhūmaka, shows that he enjoyed a position, superior to that of his predecessor. His overlord is not mentioned in any source. One of the Nasik inscriptions of his son-in-law informs us that Ushavadāta defeated the Mālayas (Mālavas settled in Rajasthan) at the command of the *Bhaṭṭāraka*. But Nahapāna ultimately had to suffer defeat at the hands of the Sātavāhana ruler, Gautamīputra Sātakarṇi, as attested by epigraphic, numismatic, and perhaps, also literary, sources. A Sātavāhana epigraph claims that Gautamīputra Sātakarṇi totally uprooted the Kshaharāta dynasty (above, Chapter III).

The Kārddamaka Kshatrapas. One of the three branches of the Western Kshatrapas, the Kārddamakas ruled over western parts of India for a period of nearly 300 years. The dynastic name, Kārddamaka, is mentioned in an inscription of the *amātya* of the daughter of Rudradāman I from Kanheri, and some scholars relate it with the river Kardama in Bactria. Satya Shrava, however, feels that it is associated with Kardama, a territory identified with modern Sidhpur in Gujarat, and proposes that the branch might have originally hailed from that region. However, in the Gadha inscription of Rudrasena, the name of the family is given as Bhadramukha. The royal house of the Kārddamaka Kshatrapas was established by Chashṭana, who was the son of Ysā(Ghsā)motika, and, perhaps, the first known ruler of his family. The probable discovery of his statue from the Kushāṇa *devakula* at Mat, near Mathurā, seems to indicate some relation with the Kushāṇas. He is believed to have started his career as a governor of the southwestern provinces of the Kushāṇa empire, especially entrusted with the task of recovering the territories lost to the Sātavāhanas, as a result of the defeat of Nahapāna at the hands of Gautamīputra Sātakarṇi, which task, as per the numismatic evidence, he succeeded in accomplishing to a certain extent. Scholars like Oldenberg and Jouveau-Dubreuil expressed the possibility of his being initially a governor of the Sātavāhana ruler, Gautamīputra Sātakarṇi. But, recently, doubts have been expressed as to his ever occupying a subordinate position under any political power. On his early coins, he uses the title of *kshatrapa*, but on later coins, he calls himself *mahākshatrapa*. V V Mirashi has read the name of this ruler and the date of year 6 in an inscription from Daulatpur. A recently discovered Andhau inscription of year 11 also seems to mention him, although, according to R C Senior, the name is not clear in the inscription, and has been proposed as Chashṭana only because the ruler is mentioned as *Ghsāmotikaputra*. However, with the discovery of Dāmaghsada I as another son of Ghsāmotika, this identification can no longer be regarded as certain. Another Andhau inscription, this one dated Śaka year 52 (130 AD), refers to him as *rājan*.

From Ptolemy, who apparently refers to Chashṭana as Tiastenes, it is known that Ujjayinī (Ozene) had become the headquarters of the Kārddamaka Kshatrapas, as early as the time of Chashṭana himself. But the use of the Kharoshṭhī script on his coins shows his hold over some Kharoshṭhī areas, like Sind, also. On epigraphical grounds, he is assigned the dates 84-130 AD, but Jaina sources would show that he was ruling even in 78 AD. Chashṭana seems to have appointed his son, Jayadāman, as *kshatrapa* on his own elevation to the position of *mahākshatrapa*. But Jayadāman predeceased Chashṭana, and the former's son, Rudradāman I, was appointed as heir-apparent. This seems to be indicated by the Andhau inscription of year 52, which refers to both Chashṭana and Rudradāman I as *rājan*.

Recently, R C Senior has reported some billon and copper coins, bearing the name of Dāmaghsada. The billon issue has a Brāhmī legend on the reverse, which seems to refer to Dāmaghsada, with the titles of *rājan*, *svāmin*, and *mahākshatrapa*, and as the son of Ysā(Ghsā)motika. This would make Dāmaghsada I a brother of Chashṭana. R C Senior regards Dāmaghsada I as the elder brother of Chashṭana, and, perhaps, 'the first Satrap of the dynasty'. But at another place, in the same work, he states that he would 'opt for the later date for Dāmaghsada', and places him after Chashṭana.

Some time after the date of the Andhau inscription of Śaka year 52 (130 AD), which refers to both Chashṭana and Rudradāman [I] as *rājan,* Rudradāman I succeeded his grandfather as *mahākshatrapa.* The Khavada inscription, which refers to him independently for the first time, is believed to be dated in the year 5[3]. If this reading of the date be correct, he would have succeeded Chashṭana before a year had elapsed since the issue of the Andhau inscription of year 52. But, according to the Junagarh rock inscription of Śaka year 72 (150 AD), a very important source of information about the reign of this ruler, Rudradāman I himself attained the designation of *mahākshatrapa,* and men of all the *varṇas* chose him as protector. From this, it has been inferred that, probably, 'the power of his house had been shaken by some enemy, and he had to restore the supreme satrapal dignity by his own prowess'. The enemy, in this context, might have been the Sātavāhanas. The absence of any reference to the Kushāṇas in his records seems to indicate that he ruled as a sovereign king, for all practical purposes.

The Junagarh inscription gives a list of the regions, over which Rudradāman I exercised authority. These included Pūrvvāparākarāvanti (eastern and western Malwa), Anūpa-nivṛit (the Māhishmatī region), Ānartta (territory around Dvārakā, in northern Kathiawar), Surāshṭra (territory around Girinagara, in southern Kathiawar), Śvabhra on the river Sabarmati, Maru (in the Rajasthan desert of Marwar), Kachchha, Sindhu (western parts of the lower Indus valley), Sauvīra (eastern parts of the lower Indus valley), Kukura (near Ānartta, in western Rajasthan), Aparānta (northern Konkan), and Nishāda (western Vindhya and Aravali). Thus, he seems to have ruled over all the territories, extending from Multan in the north to Nasik and Sopara in the south.

Of these territories, Ākarāvanti, Anūpa, Surāshṭra, Kukura, and Aparānta formed parts of the empire ruled by Gautamīputra Sātakarṇi, as per the testimony of the Nasik cave inscription of year 19 of Vāsishṭhīputra Puḷumāvi. These territories must have been acquired by Rudradāman I from some Sātavāhana ruler. The Junagarh inscription informs us that Rudradāman I twice defeated a Sātavāhana ruler, lord of the *dakshiṇāpatha*, and recovered most of the territories the Kshaharāta Kshatrapas had lost to the Sātavāhanas. But he did not destroy that ruler because of 'not distant' relationship. The defeated Sātavāhana ruler is identified variously as Gautamīputra Sātakarṇi, Vāsishṭhīputra Puḷumāvi, Yajña Sātakarṇi, etc. The clue to the close relationship between Rudradāman I and the Sātavāhanas is supplied by a Kanheri inscription, according to which, Vāsishṭhīputra Sātakarṇi, the son of Gautamīputra Sātakarṇi, was the son-in-law of *Mahākshatrapa* Ru[drāman] of the Kārddamaka family.

In the Junagarh inscription, Rudradāman I also claims to have defeated the Yaudheyas, who were famous among the kshatriyas for their valour. They seem to have inhabited southern Punjab and its adjoining areas. The Suivihar inscription of Kanishka I shows his hold over the lower Indus region. In his Junagarh inscription, Rudradāman I mentions the Sindhu-Sauvīra region as a forming part of his dominions, and he would have wrested these territories from some successor of Kanishka I.

Rudradāman I was a great conqueror, an able administrator, a person well-versed in grammar, polity, music, and logic, and an accomplished composer of Sanskrit verse and prose. He was handsome to behold, and won the hands of a number of princesses in several *svayaṁvaras.* He worked tirelessly for the welfare of his subjects. The Junagarh inscription records that, when the Sudarśana embankment developed a breach, he got it rebuilt, and the lake reconstructed, by 'expending a great amount of money from his own treasury, without oppressing the people of the town and the province by exacting taxes (*kara*), forced labour (*vishṭi*), benevolences (*praṇaya*), and the like'.

Rudradāman I was succeeded on his son, Dāmajadaśrī I. After the end of his reign, there seems to have taken place a struggle for succession between his son, Jīvadāman, and younger brother, Rudrasiṁha I. According to Rapson, Rudrasiṁha I contested the succession of Jīvadāman after the death of Dāmajadaśrī I, but was initially not successful, and had to serve Jīvadāman as a *kshatrapa.* But from Śaka year 103 to 110, and from Śaka year 113 to 118, he ruled as *mahākshatrapa,* on the basis of which, Rapson postulated that, after the initial success, Jīvadāman was removed from the position of *mahākshatrapa* by his uncle. This view is based on Rapson's reading of the date of year 1[00] on a silver coin of Jīvadāman as *mahākshatrapa.* However, Amiteshwar Jha and Dilip Rajgor doubt this reading and suggest that there is no evidence of a struggle between Rudrasiṁha I and Jīvadāman. They are of the view that Rudrasiṁha I initially served as a *kshatrapa* under his brother, and had a 'smooth elevation' to the office of *mahākshatrapa.* They also read the dates of years 100 to 102 on a number of coins mentioning Rudrasiṁha I as *mahākshatrapa.* But the evidence of the Gunda inscription of year 103, which refers to the Rudrasiṁha I as *kshatrapa* only, would seem to go against this theory. However, Jha and Rajgor give preference to the numismatic evidence over epigraphic evidence. Between Śaka year 110 and 112, Rudrasiṁha I issued coins as *kshatrapa* only, either because Jīvadāman had again occupied the position of *mahākshatrapa*, or because of the rise of the power of the Ābhīra (?) chief, Īśvaradatta, or because Yajña Sātakarṇi had eclipsed the power of the Kārddamaka Kshatrapas during this period. By Śaka year 119, Rudrasiṁha I had been succeeded as *mahākshatrapa* by Jīvadāman. If this internal feud did, indeed, take place, it is suggested that the Sātavāhanas seem to have taken advantage of the situation and occupied some of the southern territories of the Kārddamaka Kshatrapas, towards the end of the second century AD. But, ultimately, there seems to have been a *rapprochement* between the two rival claimants to the position of *mahākshatrapa*, for Rudrasena I, the son of Rudrasiṁha I, apparently served as a *kshatrapa* under Jīvadāman, during the second reign of the latter as *mahākshatrapa*.

Rudrasena I was succeeded by Saṅghadāman, Dāmasena, Yaśodāman I, Vijayasena, Dāmajadaśrī III, Rudrasena II, Viśvasiṁha, and Bhartṛidāman. There were also some members of this family, who served only as *kshatrapa*, and could never attain the position of a *mahākshatrapa*, like Jayadāman, Satyadāman, Pṛithvīsena, Damajadaśrī II, Vīradāman, and Viśvasena. The last-mentioned ruler seems to have been supplanted by Rudrasiṁha II, who appears to be closely connected with the family of Chashṭana, but whose father, Jīvadāman, is not given any royal title in the legend of the coins of Rudrasiṁha II. Next came Yaśodāman II. Viśvasena, Rudrasiṁha II, and Yaśodāman II ruled as *kshatrapa* only, indicating a temporary eclipse of the power of the Kārddamaka rulers.

The end of the reign of Yaśodāman II is followed by an interval of 16 years, when we do not hear of any Kārddamaka *kshatrapa* or *mahākshatrapa*. But when, in Śaka year 270, Rudrasena III issued coins as a *mahākshatrapa*, he refers to his father, Rudradāman II, also as a *mahākshatrapa*, although the coins of the latter are not known. The reign of Rudrasena III was not a peaceful one, and saw the invasion of Samudragupta, who claims to have defeated one Rudradeva in his Allahabad pillar inscription. The Sassanian ruler, Shapur II, of Iran, also seems to have invaded the Kārddamaka kingdom. Rudrasena III was succeeded by his sister's son, Siṁhasena, and the latter, by Rudrasena IV and Satyasiṁha, respectively. Apparently, the last-known Kārddamaka ruler was Rudrasiṁha III, who was, perhaps, defeated by Chandragupta II, towards the close of the fourth century AD, or the beginning of the fifth century AD. There is, however, evidence to show that a brother of Rudrasiṁha III, as well as another relative of the latter, also issued coins, although their names have so far baffled all attempts at decipherment.

Chapter VI

The Kushāṇas and their Successors

Origin and early history of the Kushāṇas

According to traditional scholarship, based on the combined testimony of the *Sse-ki*, the *T'ien Han-shu*, and the *Hou Han-shu*, about 165 BC, there was much political upheaval in Central Asia, as a result of which, the Hiung-nu (Hūṇa) tribe was displaced from its original homeland. This tribe, in its turn, forced the Yüeh-chih tribe out of its original habitat in Central Asia. While one branch, Little Yüeh-chih, moved towards Tibet and settled there, the other one, the Greater Yüeh-chih, reached northwestern India by way of Seistan and Bactria. Chinese sources inform that in Bactria, the Yüeh-chih had five small principalities, four of which were subjugated by K'ieou-tsieou-k'io (Kujula Kadphises), the chief of the fifth one, the Kouei-chouang. However, according to some recent writers, the Kushāṇas were a branch of the K'ang-chü race, which was of Skythian descent, and originally belonged to the lower Jaxartes region. This branch allied itself with the Yüeh-chih, and settled in Ferghana. The capital of Ferghana was called Erh-shih around 101 BC, but by 36 BC, it was called Kuei-shan, perhaps after its founder who belonged to Kuei-shang branch of the K'ang-chü. Kushāṇa coins are reported from as remote regions as Ethiopia and Iraq.

Although Kujula Kadphises was the first important Kushāṇa ruler, coins reveal the names of some of his predecessors, who belonged to the period when the Kushāṇa power was on the rise. Of these, Hyrkodes is known from his silver coins, which come from the 'Bactrian side of the Caucasus'. The reverse of some of his coins has the forepart of a bridled horse, a device seemingly borrowed from the Seleukids. The coins of Phseigacharis, all in silver, too, are known from Bactria. Some silver coins bear the name of the issuer, read variously as Sapadbizes or Sapaleizes, on the obverse, and the figure of a lion and the legend, *Nanaia*, on the reverse. The reverse inscription, perhaps referring to the goddess, *Nana*, seems to place Sapadbizes among the Kushāṇa rulers, who mostly mention the name of the deity depicted on the coin, in the reverse label inscription. The popularity of the worship of Nana, among the Kushāṇas, is also testified to by the Rabatak inscription of Kanishka I, which says that the Kushāṇa ruler had obtained kingship from Nana, and from all the gods.

As regards Heraos, the reading of the name of this predecessor of Kujula Kadphises on coins is doubtful, and some scholars suggest it to be Miaos. Cunningham regards him as the father of Kujula Kadphises, and Tarn, as his grandfather. Tarn also suggests that Heraos was not a full king, as he is referred to on his coins as *tyrannountos*. There is a possibility that he married a daughter or sister of the Indo-Greek ruler, Hermaios. The coins of Heraos mostly come from Bactria, north of the Caucasus.

The *Hou Han-shu* informs us that K'ieou-tsieou-k'io, the chief of Kouei-chouang, one of the five Yüeh-chih principalities in Bactria, conquered the other four principalities, and adopted the title of *wang* (king). The Kouei-chouang of this account is identified as Kushāṇa, and K'ieou-tsieou-k'io as Kujula Kadphises. The same source also reveals that Kujula Kadphises later led an expedition against the Arsakids of Parthia, conquered the Kabul valley, and overran Po-ta near Kabul, as also Ki-pin (Kafiristan and the adjoining areas), before he died at the age of over 80 years. The date of Kujula Kadphises is not certain, although attempts have been made to place him between *c* 25 BC and 25 AD; Osmund Bopearachchi dates his reign from *c* 30 AD to 80 AD, which would seem difficult if Kanishka I ascended the throne in 78 AD, and founded the Śaka era. There are some copper coins, which bear the name and/or bust of Hermaios on the obverse, and the name and titles of Kujula Kadphises on the reverse. The suggestions, on the basis of these coins, that Kujula Kadphises was a subordinate ruler or an ally of the Indo-Greek king, are hardly tenable, as there is a long gap between the end of the reign of Hermaios and the accession of Kujula Kadphises (above, Chapter IV). These coins might have been issued by Kujula Kadphises, either as propaganda coins, or as imitation coins.

Earlier, it was believed that among the Kushāṇas, there was only one ruler with V'ima as his forename, namely V'ima Kadphises, and he was regarded as the son and successor of Kujula Kadphises. However, in recent years, epigraphic and numismatic evidence has been forthcoming to the reveal the existence of a Kushāṇa ruler with V'ima as his forename, the last component of the name being read variously as *Takpio*, *Takta*, *Taktoo*, *Takkashama*, *Takshoıno*, or *Takshuma*. Of the epigraphic sources, the first inscription is engraved between the feet of a seated royal statue, discovered in the Kushāṇa *devakula* at Mat, near Mathura. Five inscriptions, two in Graeco-Bactrian, two in Kharoshṭhī, and one in 'an unknown script (and language ?)', were discovered on a peak of Mount Qarabayu, to the west of Dasht-i-Nawur, in Afghanistan. The Graeco-Bactrian inscription refers to *Ooemo Tak[..]o*, while a Kharoshṭhī inscription refers to the reign of Vhama Kuśa. The recently discovered Rabatak (Baghlan) inscription, from northern Afghanistan, refers to the construction of certain divine images for the *devakula*, for the merit of four generations of Kushāṇa kings—Kanishka [I], and his father, grandfather, and great-grandfather, who are all mentioned by name, followed by the title of *shao* in each case. The names of Kanishka [I] (*Kaneshko*), his father V'ima Kadphises (*Ooemo Kadphiso*), and great-grandfather Kujula Kadphises (*Kozoulo Kạdphiso*), are quite clear. But the left side of the rock, on which the inscription is engraved, is badly damaged, and, consequently, the name of Kanishka's grandfather in line 13 is not fully legible. While Sims-Williams restores it as *Taktoo*, Senior proposes *Takkashama* as an alternative reading, which seems 'compatible' with the Kharoshṭhī form, *Takshuma*, met with in the coin legends, and the Brāhmī form, *Tākshuma*, met with in the Mat inscription. The inscription states that the statues of these four Kushāṇa rulers, too, were to be constructed and installed in the *devakula*. According to Sims-Williams, this Kushāṇa *devakula* was different, from the one found at nearby Surkh Kotal.

There are certain coins known from the region, extending from Peshawar and into the Russian Turkestan to Mathurā, and even a[illegible] far east as Varanasi and Ghazipur in eastern [illegible] Pradesh, [illegible]which bear the legend, *Basileos basil*[illegible]*ter megas*, w[illegible]out mentioning the name of the issuer. Earlier scholars had conjectured about the identity of this ruler. But, in view of the evidence available from inscriptions and coins, it has now been suggested that this 'nameless king' should be identified with V'ima Takshuma, the son of Kujula Kadphises. The vast number of the coins of V'ima Takshuma, and the extensive area from which they are reported, 'testify to a long and powerful reign'. But a very long independent reign for V'ima Takshuma is apparently precluded by the fact that his father, Kujula Kadphises, is known from the *Hou Han-shu* to have ruled till (at least) the age of 80. There is a suggestion that V'ima Takshuma served as the governor of his father in the northern provinces of the Kushāṇa empire for a long time, before his accession to the throne, which is hardly surprising in view of the above. V'ima Takshuma, during this period, very probably had his seat at Balkh or Bactria.

According to the *Hou Han-shu,* Kujula Kadphises was succeeded by his son, Yen-kao-chen, who conquered India and appointed military commanders as governors there. This Yen-kao-chen should now be identified with V'ima Takshuma.

V'ima Kadphises, the son and successor of V'ima Takshuma, occupies an important place in Kushāṇa numismatics, as he was, perhaps, the first ruler of his dynasty to issue profusely in gold. The obverse of the silver and copper coins of V'ima Kadphises has the figure of the king sacrificing at an altar, a device which seems to be imitated from the Arsakid coins of Parthia. On this basis, as also on the basis of the information supplied by the *Shahnamah* of Firdausi, B N Mukherjee has concluded that he occupied some Arsakid provinces. The reverse always bears the representation of Śiva, usually with his mount, the bull; however, in some cases, the presence of Śiva is shown symbolically through the *triśūla-paraśu* only. The appearance of Śiva or Śaiva symbol on the reverse of all his coins, together with the use of the title *mahiśvara* (= *māheśvara*, great devotee of Śiva), shows that V'ima Kadphises had adopted Śaivism.

The acme of Kushāṇa power

Kanishka I was, perhaps, the greatest, and certainly the most famous, of the Kushāṇa kings. He is known, from the combined testimony of the literary, epigraphic, and numismatic sources, to have ruled over an extensive dominion extending from Bihar in the east to Khorasan in the west, and from Khotan in the north to, perhaps, Konkan in the south.

There is no unanimity among scholars regarding the date of his accession. The inscriptions issued by him and his successors show that he founded an era which, however, is not named in these epigraphs. Consequently, the name of Kanishka I is associated with the various eras—Vikrama, Traikūṭaka-Kalachuri-Chedi, etc, and his accession is placed in the respective initial years of these various eras. Thus, Fleet, Cunningham, Dowson, Franke, and Kennedy, identify the era founded by Kanishka I as the Vikrama era, and place his accession in 58/57 BC, but the gold coins of Kanishka I are influenced by Roman coins of the first century AD. Scholars, like Marshall, Sten Konow, and Smith, regard 125 AD as the date of his accession, while Roman Ghirshman would place the event in 144 AD, although no Indian era is known to have begun in the first half of the second century AD. R C Majumdar identifies the era founded by Kanishka I as the Traikūṭaka-Kalachuri-Chedi *saṁvat*, beginning 248 AD, while R G Bhandarkar would place the accession of Kanishka I in 278 AD. However, this would make

Vāsudeva I, who is known to have ruled over Mathurā about a hundred years after the accession of Kanishka I, a contemporary of the Imperial Guptas. A vast majority of scholars agrees with Fergusson, who regards him as the founder of the Śaka era, beginning 78 AD with his accession.

On the basis of the dates and findspots of some of the inscriptions of Kanishka I—Kosam inscription dated year 2, Sarnath inscription dated year 3, Mathura inscription dated year 4, Suivihar inscription dated year 11, and Manikiala inscription dated year 18, it was suggested by scholars, like Fleet, that Kanishka I a Kushāṇa chief, who belonged to the Little Yüeh-chih branch settled in Tibet, entered India through Kashmir, carved out a principality for himself somewhere in Uttar Pradesh, some time after the death of V'ima Kadphises, and then extended his sway towards the west and the northwest. However, the recently discovered Rabatak inscription shows that he was, in fact, the son and successor of V'ima Kadphises.

The *Kalpanāmaṇḍitikā* of Kumāralāta reveals that Kanishka I attained several military successes in the east. According to the *Śrīdharmapiṭakasampradāyanidāna*, he invaded Pāṭaliputra. When he returned to his capital, Purushapura, from Magadha, he carried away with him, the begging bowl of the Buddha, a magical cock, and the Buddhist scholar, Aśvaghosha. The discovery of his coins in Bengal and Orissa should, however, not be taken as indicative of his sway over these territories, in the absence of any corroborative evidence.

According to the *Rājataraṅgiṇī* of Kalhaṇa, Kanishka I conquered Kashmir. Hiuen-tsang refers to his authority over Gandhāra, and to his capital at Purushapura (modern Peshawar). The *Śrīdharmapiṭaka* refers to his expedition against the Parthians, in which he is reported to have achieved success.

The most notable achievement of Kanishka I was his subjugation of the Central Asian provinces of Kashghar, Yarqand, and Khotan. These successes of the Kushāṇa ruler towards the north made the Chinese wary of his intentions. Pan-chao, the general of the Chinese emperor, Ho-ti (89-105 AD), started making preparations for an invasion of the Kushāṇa empire. Alerted by this, Kanishka I proclaimed his equality with the Chinese emperor by demanding his daughter in marriage, and assumed the title of *devaputra* (son of god), the Indian equivalent of *t'ien-tzu* (son of heaven), the title of the Chinese emperor. Pan-chao regarded this as a challenge to his emperor. Kanishka I dispatched his viceroy, Hsï, at the head of 70,000 horsemen, across the Taghdumbash Pamir to give battle to Pan-chao. This expedition was, however, unsuccessful due to the hardships of the mountainous terrain, and, according to a legend, Kanishka lamented this failure about the time of his death.

Kanishka I appears to be a devout Buddhist, who, as per the testimony of Hiuen-tsang and Alberuni, got a grand monastery constructed at Purushapura. He is associated with the Fourth Buddhist Council, which he is said to have convoked on the advice of Pārśva. In this Council, Vasumitra acted as the president, and Pārśva, as vice-president. According to most of the traditions, the Council met at Kuṇḍalavanavihāra at Kashmir, but some sources would have us believe that it was held in Gandhāra, or at Jālandhara, and prepared the *Vibhāshāśāstra* commentary on the *Tripiṭaka*. Although Kanishka is generally regarded as a Buddhist, the deities, from varied pantheons, appearing on the reverse of his coins, seem to show 'a sort of religious eclecticism'.

Vāsishka is generally believed to be a co-ruler, associated in administration by Kanishka I, towards the end of his own reign. He seems to have succeeded Kanishka I as an independent ruler, and appointed Huvishka as his junior co-ruler. He appears to be an ephemeral ruler. He is mentioned in two inscriptions from Sanchi, dated years 22 and 28, respectively, and in a *yūpa* pillar inscription from Isapur near Mathura, dated year 24. The Ara inscription, of the year 41, mentions him as the father of Kanishka [II]. He has been identified with Jushka of Kalhaṇa. Earlier, it was believed that he did not issue any coins. But some time back, two types of gold coins, bearing the name of Vāsishka, have been published by R Göbl. A number of scholars, like Craig Alden Burns, Gritli von Mitterwallner, B N Mukherjee, and Sarojini Kulashreshtha, however, place these Vāsishka coins in the period following the death of Vāsudeva I, and regard the Vāsishka of these coins as a successor of that king. It is interesting to note that, initially, R Göbl also ascribed these coins to a Vāsishka II.

Huvishka seems to have started his career as a junior co-ruler of Vāsishka, and later succeeded him as an independent ruler. His inscriptions are dated between 106 and 138 AD. Kanishka II of the Ara inscription of 119 AD seems to have ruled as his junior co-ruler, although there are suggestions that there were two Kushāṇa kings bearing the name of Huvishka, with Huvishka I ruling before Kanishka II, and Huvishka II ruling after him. On the basis of the Mat *devakula* inscription, which seems to indicate that V'ima was the grandfather of Huvishka, A L Basham regards Huvishka I as the son of Kanishka I; there is a possibility that Huvishka II was the son and successor of Kanishka II.

But the present state of our knowledge precludes any definite conclusions in this matter. Huvishka apparently ruled over most of the territories, brought under Kushāṇa sway by Kanishka I. His hold over Afghanistan is testified to by his inscription from Wardak near Kabul. He is identified with Hushka of Kalhaṇa. A Mathura inscription seems to refer to the construction of a *vihāra* by Huvishka, but a seal-matrix apparently represents him as a Vaishṇava.

Vāsudeva I was the last great Kushāṇa ruler, who was reigning about a hundred years after Kanishka I. His dated inscriptions from Mathura attest to a reign of over 20 years. There is evidence of disturbances in northwestern India, Afghanistan, and Russian Central Asia during or after his reign. This was, perhaps, the consequence of the Sassanian onslaught, against which power he seems to have sought Chinese help and formed an alliance with the Armenians.

The decline of the Kushāṇas

The Kushāṇa empire started disintegrating after the reign of Vāsudeva I. The obverse of the gold coins, issued during the declining phase of Kushāṇa power, bears some Brāhmī letters in the right, central, and left fields. The letters in the right field are taken by most of the scholars to be abbreviations of the names of provincial governors, showing that, during this period, the central authority had weakened, and the political influence of the provincial governors had increased, to such an extent that their names had to be mentioned on the obverse of the gold coins in order to satisfy them. The names of some of the Kushāṇa kings, who ruled during this declining phase, are known from coins. Of these, Kanishka III was one of the successors of Vāsudeva I. The legend, distributed on the obverse and reverse of an interesting copper coin, discovered during the excavations at Sonkh, near Mathura, has been read by P L Gupta as *Huvishkasya-putra Kaṇikas[ya].* If this reading be correct, Kanishka III would appear to be a son of Huvishka, as suggested by B N Mukherjee. Huvishka could not have been the father of Kanishka I, who ruled before Huvishka, or of Kanishka II, who is described as the son of Vajeshka (= Vāsishka), in the Ara inscription, of Śaka year 41. The reverse of one type of the coins of Kanishka III has the figure of *Ardochsho*, while that of the other bears the figure of Śiva. Cunningham and Altekar suggest that the reverse device of *Ardochsho* was popular in the eastern provinces of the Kushāṇa empire, while that of Śiva gained popularity in the western provinces. As Kanishka III issued coins bearing both these devices, he appears to have succeeded in retaining hold over the eastern as well as the western provinces.

Vāsudeva II was among the last rulers of the Kushāṇa dynasty. His gold coins have the figure of Śiva, which device was popular in the western provinces of the Kushāṇa empire. As he did not issue coins with *Ardochsho* reverse, it has been suggested that he had lost the eastern provinces, where coins with *Ardochsho* reverse were popular.

The Successors of the Kushāṇas

Taking advantage of the decline in the power of the Kushāṇas, and the disintegration of their empire, some powers, which were initially subordinate to the Kushāṇas, carved out principalities for themselves, and asserted their independence. Some of these powers were of indigenous origin, and have been discussed in Chapter II, while the others were of foreign origin, like the Kidāra-Kushāṇas, Gaḍaharas, Shākas, and Shilādas.

The *Wei-shu*, and Ma-twan-lin, inform us that Ki-to-lo, a king of the Kushāṇa stock, finding himself threatened by some rival tribe (Juan-Juan or Hiung-nu), led his people towards the west, crossed the Hindukush, subjugated Gandhāra, and established his capital at Fu-leu-cha (Peshawar). This Ki-to-lo is identified with *Kidāra Kushāṇa Shāh* of coins, found in large numbers from northwestern India. Around the middle of the fourth century AD, Kidāra Kushāṇa was forced to acknowledge the supremacy of the Sassanian ruler, Shapur II, but later, he asserted his independence, founded his line of kings known as the Kidāra Kushāṇas or Kidarites after his name, and issued his own coins. From the account of the Armenian historian, Faustos of Byzantium, he even appears to have inflicted at least two defeats on the Sassanians in 367-368 AD. There is a suggestion that, in view of the threats he had to face from the Sassanians and the ruling tribes in Bactria, Kidāra Kushāṇa might have maintained cordial relations with the Imperial Guptas, and he might be the *Daivaputrashāhi-shāhānushāhi*, mentioned in the Allahabad pillar inscription, as acknowledging the political supremacy of Samudragupta. Kidāra Kushāṇa was succeeded by his son, Piro, who was forced by Shapur III to acknowledge Sassanian sovereignty. Piro's successor, Varahran, too, served under the Sassanians. There is also a suggestion that the Kidāra Kushāṇas may be identical with the *mlechchhas* defeated by Skandagupta, as per the testimony of the Junagarh rock inscription, although most of the scholars tend to the regard these *mlechchhas* as Hūṇas.

The Gaḍahara tribe, which appears to be of foreign extraction, seems to have asserted its independence, and issued coins of its own, around the fourth century AD. Their coins, in gold, and found in the Punjab and its adjoining regions, bear legends like *Peraya*, *Kirada*, and *Samudra*, along with the tribal name, *Gaḍahara*. While the first is regarded as the name of the tribal chief, Kirada is believed by certain scholars to be a variant of the tribal name Kidāra Kushāṇa, and this variant actually occurs on some of the coins of the Kidāra Kushāṇas. On this basis, it has been suggested that at some stage, the Gaḍaharas might have been subject to the Kidāra Kushāṇas. Samudra on the Gaḍahara coins might be the name of a Gaḍahara chief, but in view of the similarity between this coin type and the coins of the Imperial Gupta ruler, Samudragupta, it has been suggested by a number of scholars that this Samudra should be identified with Samudragupta, who might have imposed his authority over the Gaḍaharas. Interestingly, a coin bearing the tribal name, *Gaḍahara*, and a legend, tentatively read as *Chandra*, has been described by Smith. Could the Gaḍaharas have continued under the authority of the Imperial Guptas during the reign of Chandragupta II, as well ?

Similarly, taking advantage of the weakening authority of the Kushāṇas, the **Shāka** tribe seems to have asserted its independence, and issued coins of its own, around the fourth century AD. They appear to be of some foreign stock, like the Kushāṇas. Their coins, in gold and found from the Punjab and its adjoining regions, bear the names of chiefs, like Sya, Śayatha, Sita, and Sena (or Seṇa), along with the name of the tribe. Some scholars, however, regard Shāka as the name of some chief. The reverse of their coins has the symbol of Vāsudeva I, in a slightly modified form.

The Shilāda tribe, which appears to be of some foreign stock, like the Kushāṇas, seems to have asserted its independence, and issued coins of its own, around the fourth century AD. Their coins, in gold and found from the Punjab and its adjoining regions, bear the names of chiefs, like Bhadra, Bacharṇa, and Pāshaṇa, along with the name of the tribe. Some scholars, however, regard Shilāda as the name of a chief, and also propose to the read it as Kshiṇatha. The reverse of their coins, too, has the symbol of Vāsudeva I, in a slightly modified form.

Chapter VII

The Early History of the Imperial Guptas

The age of the Imperial Guptas is generally taken to begin *c* 319 AD, with the accession of Chandragupta I, his assumption of the sovereign title of *mahārājādhirāja*, and, perhaps, the founding of the Gupta era. However, Imperial Gupta genealogies, as found in their inscriptions and on their seals, mention two predecessors of Chandragupta I, namely *Mahārāja* Gupta and *Mahārāja* Ghaṭotkacha. If the title of *mahārāja* was given to them because they had actually ruled, even if as subordinate rulers, and not just out of respect for the ancestors of Chandragupta I, as has been suggested by some scholars, their reign would fall towards the close of the period under study here, that is in the last quarter of the third century AD, and the first quarter of the fourth century AD.

The original home

The age of the Imperial Guptas occupies an important place in the ancient history of India. A few scholars refer to it as the golden age of ancient Indian history, although the background for it had already been prepared in the Kushāṇa and the post-Kushāṇa periods. The age of the Imperial Guptas saw all round progress in the fields of political life, society, economy, religion, and art.

There is some controversy among scholars regarding the original home of the Imperial Guptas. John Allan suggested that, as Pāṭaliputra was the capital of the Imperial Guptas since the start of their rule, they would have been the original inhabitants of Pāṭaliputra, and the regions in its neighbourhood, in Magadha. But, on the basis of a statement of the Chinese pilgrim, I-tsing, D C Ganguly regards Murshidabad in Bengal as their original home. Hui-lun informs us that 40 *yojanas* to the east of Nālandā is a place, called Mi-li-kia-si-kia-po-no, where Che-li-ki-to got constructed a temple for the convenience of the Chinese pilgrims. Since 40 *yojanas* is equivalent to about 228 miles, this temple would have been located about 228 miles to the east of Nālandā. This, according to Ganguly, would be the Murshidabad region in Bengal. Identifying Che-li-ki-to with [Śrī-]Gupta, the first known Imperial Gupta ruler, Ganguly says that, if Gupta had got constructed a temple in the Murshidabad region in Bengal, and donated 24 villages in that area for its upkeep, that region would have been the original home of the Imperial Guptas. R C Majumdar agrees with this, but while the earlier writers, like Chavannes, rendered Mi-li-kia-si-kia-po-no of the Chinese pilgrim as *Mṛigaśikhāvana*, Majumdar proposes to render it as *Mṛigasthāpanā*, which he identifies as the Mṛigasthāpanā-*stūpa* at Vārendra, illustrated in a Cambridge manuscript, dated 1015 AD.

Jagannath Agrawal and B P Sinha would identify Mi-li-kia-si-kia-po-no with the *mṛigadāva* (deer park) at

Sarnath, where the Buddha delivered his first sermon. Ashvini Agrawal suggests that, if this identification be correct, and if the first Imperial Gupta ruler got a temple constructed at Sarnath, and donated 24 villages in that area for its upkeep, the Imperial Guptas would have been the original inhabitants of Uttar Pradesh, as no other region is known to have been so intimately associated with the Imperial Guptas since the initial phase of their rule. The Imperial Guptas appear to have been the original inhabitants of some region in Bihar, Bengal, or eastern Uttar Pradesh, although it is not possible to identify this original home for certain.

The *varṇa* of the Guptas

The origin of the Imperial Guptas, like their original homeland, is a subject of debate among scholars. K P Jayaswal identifies Chaṇḍasena of the *Kaumudīmahotsava* of Vijjakā, with Chandragupta I of the Imperial Gupta dynasty. In that work, Chaṇḍasena is described as a Kāraskara. In the *Baudhāyanadharmasūtra*, the Kāraskaras are mentioned together with Madras, Āraṭṭas, and some other Jat tribes of Punjab. On this basis, K P Jayaswal proposes to identify the Imperial Guptas as Jats. But most of the scholars do not favour Jayaswal's identification of Chaṇḍasena of the *Kaumudīmahotsava* with Chandragupta I.

A S Altekar, on the basis of the *gupta*-ending names of the rulers of the Imperial Gupta dynasty, suggests that the Imperial Guptas would have been vaiśyas, as, in the dharmaśāstra works, *gupta*-ending names are regarded as appropriate for persons of that *varṇa*. However, there are instances of *gupta*-ending names being assumed by non-vaiśyas, the most notable among them being Vishṇugupta, the brāhmaṇa author of the *Arthaśāstra*, and the brāhmaṇa astronomer, Brahmagupta.

A few scholars regard the Imperial Guptas as brāhmaṇas. In Vākāṭaka inscriptions, dhāraṇa is said to be the *gotra* of Prabhāvatīguptā, the daughter of Chandragupta II and the wife of the Vākāṭaka Rudrasena II. It is known from Vākāṭaka epigraphs that the *gotra* of the Vākāṭakas was vishṇuvṛiddha. Thus, dhāraṇa would have been the paternal *gotra* of Prabhāvatīguptā, that is the *gotra* of the Imperial Guptas. In the Kurud inscription of Narendra, Bhaśrutasvāmin is mentioned as a brāhmaṇa of the dhāraṇa *gotra*. This would show that, in the age of the Imperial Guptas, dhāraṇa was a *gotra* of the brāhmaṇas, and the Imperial Guptas, who were of the dhāraṇa *gotra*, were brāhmaṇas. But Ashvini Agrawal is of the opinion that dhāraṇa in the Vākāṭaka inscriptions is not the *gotra* of Prabhāvatīguptā, but that of her mother, Kuberanāgā, and that it would not be proper to reach any conclusions regarding the *varṇa* of the Imperial Guptas on this ground.

Ashvini Agrawal himself proposes that, as the Imperial Guptas are known to have had matrimonial relations with some brāhmaṇa ruling families—the Vākāṭakas of the vishṇuvṛiddha *gotra*, and the Kadambas of the mānavya *gotra*, they themselves would have been brāhmaṇas. However, political considerations often played a more important role in matrimonial alliances between ruling families, than considerations of *varṇa* or *jāti*. If the evidence of the Allahabad pillar inscription of Samudragupta is to be believed, a number of political powers of foreign extraction, like the later Kushāṇas, Śakas, and Muruṇḍas, and the inhabitants of Sri Lanka and the islands of southeast Asia, offered to marry their daughters in the Imperial Gupta family. Even prior to the

Imperial Guptas, it is known that a daughter of the Kārddamaka ruler, Rudradāman I, was married in the Sātavāhana family. Under such circumstances, it would not be appropriate to regard the Imperial Guptas as belonging to the brāhmaṇa *varṇa*, merely on the basis of their matrimonial relations with some brāhmaṇa ruling families of the time.

Gupta

The genealogy of the Imperial Guptas, available from their inscriptions and seals, begins with Gupta, although in some Vākāṭaka records, Ghaṭotkacha is mentioned as the first ruler. V A Smith earlier regarded Śrīgupta as the name of the first Imperial Gupta ruler. However, in Imperial Gupta genealogy, the names of all the rulers are preceded by the honorific title, *śrī*, and, had the name of the first Imperial Gupta ruler been Śrīgupta, he would have been mentioned in the genealogy as Śrī-Śrīgupta, which is not the case. On this basis, scholars, like J F Fleet, John Allan, and, later on, even Smith, regard the name of the first Imperial Gupta ruler as Gupta, which, according to B Ch Chhabra, is one of the thousand names of Vishṇu.

In Imperial Gupta genealogy, Gupta has been given the title of *mahārāja*, which, in the age of the Imperial Guptas, was a subordinate title. Hence, Gupta would have been a subordinate ruler. Some scholars, however, do not agree with this : a few of them regard him as an independent ruler, while others believe that he was a commoner, who was given the title of *mahārāja* in genealogy, simply because he was the grandfather of *Mahārājādhirāja* Chandragupta I. Among the scholars, who regard Gupta as a subordinate ruler, R D Banerji suggests that he ruled under the Kushāṇas, while K P Jayaswal, Sudhakar Chattopadhyaya, and S K Maity suggest that he served under the Lichchhavis or the Vākāṭakas. Ashvini Agrawal is of the view that, taking advantage of the political instability, following the decline of the Kushāṇa power in northern India, Gupta carved out a small independent kingdom for himself.

The Chinese pilgrim, I-tsing, mentions Che-li-ki-to, who has been identified with Gupta by Allan. According to I-tsing, he ruled 500 years before his visit to India. Fleet is not in favour of identifying Che-li-ki-to with Gupta. His first objection is that the Indian rendering of Che-li-ki-to would be Śrīgupta, while the name of the first Imperial Gupta ruler was Gupta. Moreover, according to I-tsing's account, Che-li-ki-to ruled 500 years before the visit of the Chinese pilgrim to India, which would place Che-li-ki-to around 175 AD, a date too early for the first Imperial Gupta ruler. But Allan argues that Chinese writers often tend to use the honorific title *śrī* with Indian names, and that '500 years', in the account of I-tsing, need not be taken literally. Most of the scholars place Gupta between *c* 275 and 300 AD.

No inscription or coin of Gupta is so far available. The legend on a seal, published by E J Rapson, has been read as *Gutasya*, while that on a seal, published by Jagannath Agrawal, as *Śrīrguptasya.* However, in the absence of any royal title for Gupta in these seal legends, some scholars are not in favour of identifying the owner of these seals with Gupta, the first Imperial Gupta ruler, although royal seals, referring to kings, without using royal titles for them, are known.

Ghaṭotkacha

Gupta was succeeded by his son, Ghaṭotkacha, *c* 300 AD. He, too, is called a *mahārāja*, in Imperial Gupta genealogy, and, on this basis, he is regarded as a subordinate ruler by most of the scholars. The name, Ghaṭotkacha, has been read on a sealing, published by T Bloch; the legend on a gold coin, in the Leningrad Museum, has been read as *Ghaṭo*, and that on another gold coin, published by A Ghosh, as *Kramāditya*. But most of the scholars identify this Ghaṭotkacha Kramāditya with Ghaṭotkachagupta, the younger brother of Kumāragupta I, mentioned in the Tumain and Ramtek inscriptions.

Ghaṭotkacha, the son of Gupta, appears to be an ambitious ruler. It has been suggested that, in order to enhance the power and prestige of his family, he managed to get his son, Chandragupta I, married with the Lichchhavi princess, Kumāradevī. According to Smith, this marriage took place *c* 308 AD, when Chandragupta I was about 25 years of age. If Chandragupta I founded the Gupta era in 319 AD, at the time of his accession, Ghaṭotkacha would have ruled up to that year.

The accession of Chandragupta I

Chandragupta I was the first Imperial Gupta ruler to assume the title of *mahārājādhirāja*, on the basis of which, it is presumed that he was the first sovereign ruler of his family. Probably, his marriage alliance with the Lichchhavis might have been helpful in this endeavour. According to Smith, at that time, Pāṭaliputra was ruled by the Lichchhavis, and the establishment of Imperial Gupta authority over the region might have been the result of the marriage between Chandragupta I and Kumāradevī. Chandragupta I would have assumed the sovereign title of *mahārājādhirāja*, after he gained in political power and prestige, as a consequence of this matrimonial alliance. But Allan does not agree with this. He believes that Imperial Guptas exercised authority over Pāṭaliputra, right from the time of Gupta. He suggests that Chandragupta I defeated the Lichchhavis, following which, a treaty was finalized between the Imperial Guptas and the Lichchhavis. The marriage of Chandragupta I and Kumāradevī was one of the terms of this treaty. The social prestige of the Imperial Guptas increased as a result of this marriage. No wonder, Samudragupta, the son of Chandragupta I and Kumāradevī, is found issuing the Chandragupta I-Kumāradevī type of gold coins, to commemorate this marriage; and, no wonder, Samudragupta is hailed as *Lichchhavidauhitra*, 'daughter's son of the Lichchhavis', in Imperial Gupta genealogy. Altekar, however, argues that, had Chandragupta I defeated the Lichchhavis, his son would not have proudly proclaimed his relationship with those vanquished people, who are called vrātya kshatriya in Indian literature.

Appendix 1

The Far South — Cholas, Pāṇḍyas, Cheras, Toṇḍaiyar and Pallavas

The country, to the south of river Krishna, is known as the Far South, where three powers—Choḷas, Pāṇḍyas, and Cheras, played a major role, and vied for supremacy, since the earliest times; some Pāṇḍya and Chera rulers might have led victorious arms, as far north as the Himalayas. The credit for establishing the first contact, between the vedic people of northern India and the Tamiḷs of the Far South, traditionally goes to Agastya. He was a vedic *ṛishi*, who finds mentions in the *Ṛigveda*, though not specifically in connection with his migration to southern India. According to the *Mahābhārata*, he went to southern India to seek a gift of wealth from Ilvala, the king of Manimaṭi, in order to fulfil the demands of Lopāmudrā, a princess of Vidarbha and his bride-to-be. The story occurs, in a slightly modified form, in the *Rāmāyaṇa*. Nachchinārkkiniyar, a commentator of the fourteenth-fifteenth century AD, would have us believe that, after establishing his *āśrama* on Podiyil, a hillock in the Western Ghats (the Bettigo of Ptolemy), Agastya sent his pupil, Triṇadhūmāgni (that is Tolkāppiyan, the celebrated author of the *Tolkāppiyam*), to fetch Lopāmudrā from northern India. His disciples and followers (including an agricultural population) also arrived from northern India, and, together, they appear to have worked towards the Aryanization/Sanskritization of southern India. Traditional accounts portray Agastya as the *kulaguru* or royal chaplain of the Pāṇḍyas. The *Maṇimekhalai* associates him with two Choḷa kings as well. One of these was Kānta, who requested Agastya to release the waters of the Kāverī from his *kamaṇḍalu*. Another Choḷa king instituted an annual festival in honour of Indra at Puhār, on the advice of Agastya.

Another legendary figure, who seems to have played a role in the Aryanization/Sanskritization of southern India, was Bāvari, a contemporary of the Buddha. He is mentioned in the Buddhist text, *Suttanipāta*, as a learned scholar of the veda, hailing originally from Kosala, and settling in a village, in the Assaka *janapada* of the *dakshiṇāpatha*.

In legendary accounts, a number of Choḷa, Pāṇḍya, and Chera kings are said to have 'fed, maintained and conditioned' the rival armies of the Kauravas and the Pāṇḍavas, during the Bhārata war. The region had trade contacts with northern India, with articles, like pearls from the Pāṇḍya territories, spices, and cotton fabric, forming the chief commodities of trade. Māmūlanār refers to *vamba Moriyar* (Maurya upstart, most probably Chandragupta Maurya) as having sent a large army, with the Vaḍugar forming the vanguard, to assist the Kośar, in their struggle against the chief of Mohūr, indicating that the Mauryas actively intervened in the politics of the Tamiḷ country. Megasthenes, the envoy of Seleukos to the court of Chandragupta Maurya, speaks of Pandaia, a Pāṇḍya queen, as a daughter of Herakles. Aśoka mentions Choḍā (the

Choḷas), Pāḍā (the Pāṇḍyas), and Ketalaputa (the Cheras), speaks of them in the same breath as the Satiyaputa (earlier identified as the Kośar tribe of the Kongu region, but now regarded as identical with the Adigaimān/Adiyamān chiefs of Tagaḍūr), and treats them at par with Taṁbapaṁṇi (Sri Lanka) and the Hellenistic kingdoms, as objects of *dhaṁmavijaya.* According to one view, Khāravela of Kaliṅga destroyed a confederacy of Tamiḷ states, which had existed for a long time. He is also said to have received hundreds of pearls, as well as others precious stones, horses, and elephants, from the Pāṇḍya kingdom.

For the history of the period under study, one has to depend on Śaṅgam literature, which is generally dated to the 'first three or four centuries' of the Christian era. This literature refers to a number of Choḷa, Pāṇḍya, and Chera rulers, as also some minor princelings. But, as has often been observed, these are mostly unrelated names, a continuous genealogy being available therein only in the case of the Chera kings. This renders a reconstruction of a regular history of the period rather difficult.

The Choḷas

The Choḷas occupied the delta of the river Kaveri, and its adjoining territories. The origin of the name, Choḷa, is shrouded in mystery. Parimelaḷagar, in his gloss over *Kural* 955, makes it the name of a 'ruling family or clan of immemorial antiquity', like Chera and Pāṇḍya. There is a story of three eponymous brothers, Cheran, Śolan, and Pāṇḍiyan, which is hardly convincing. Similar is the fate of those theories, which endeavour to connect Choḷa with Sanskrit *kāla* (black), or *chora* (thief), or with Tamiḷ *cholam* (millet). Notwithstanding this state of affairs, in practice, the name Choḷa denotes the people and the country subject to the rulers of the Choḷa dynasty. Other names used for the Choḷas are Kiḷḷi, Vaḷavan, and Śembiyan.

Mention is made above of two Choḷa kings, whom tradition portrays as contemporaries of Agastya. The most famous of the early Choḷa rulers was Karikāla, the son of Iḷañjeṭchenni. According to the Paṭṭinappālai, in the *Pattuppāṭṭu*, one of his earliest achievements was his escape from the fetters of his enemies, and regaining kingship. When the Pāṇḍya and Chera kings, together with 11 minor chieftains, formed a confederacy against him, he defeated his enemies at Veṇṇi, located about 15 miles to the east of Thanjavur. The Chera king, Perum Śeral Ādan, is said to have ended his life, through *vaḍakkiruttal* or slow starvation. He also won an important victory at Vāh(k)aippaṟandalai, and established his authority over nine minor princes. According to the Paṭṭinappālai, the Oḷiyar, perhaps a nomadic tribe of the nāga stock, submitted to him, and were 'converted to a settled life'. Nothing definite can be said about the reliability of the tradition, which ascribes to him the conquest of Kāñchī. Another major political event of the reign of Karikāla was his invasion of Sri Lanka, in the course of which he attained singular success. The *Mahāvaṁsa* does not allude to this event, but later chronicles mention it in some detail. The Choḷa is said to have carried away captive, 12,000 inhabitants of the island, and employed them in the fortification of Puhār, the sea-port at the mouth of the Kaveri.

A number of legends grew around the personality of Karikāla, and Tamiḻ poets go so far as to project him as the conqueror of the whole of India. For instance, the *Śilappadikāram* would have us believe that he led an expedition as far north as the Himālaya, in the course of which, the kings of Vajra, Magadha, and Avanti, either submitted to him, or became his allies. It appears from the *Śilappadikāram* that he made an attempt at reconciliation with the Cheras, by marrying his daughter, named Ādi Mandi, to a Chera prince, Āṭṭan Atti.

His peacetime achievements are no less significant. He is credited with the construction of the Grand Anicut Srirangam; this allowed the waters of the Kaveri to flow into the arid regions of southern Thanjavur, through a new channel, which we now know as Veṇṇār. Thus, he laid the foundations of an ambitious project of the construction of a system of canals, which carried the overflow of the river, to irrigate the water-starved regions of Thanjavur. He is also remembered as a patron of arts and Tamiḷ literature.

Kovūr Kiḷār refers to a civil war among two Choḷa princes, Neḍuṅgīḷḷi and Nalaṅgiḷḷi Śeṭchenni, who are believed to have belonged to the rival Puhār and Uṟaiyūr branches of the Choḷas, respectively. The former prince was besieged at least twice—once, at Āvūr by Māvaḷattān, the younger brother of Nalaṅgiḷḷi, and, perhaps later, at Uṟaiyūr by Nalaṅgiḷḷi himself. The strife finally ended with the death of Neḍuṅgīḷḷi in a battle fought at Kāriyāṟu; according to the *Maṇimekhalai*, this battle also saw the defeat of a Pāṇḍya and a Chera prince.

Perunaṟkiḷḷi seems to have been a powerful Choḷa ruler, as he is the only known king of the Śaṅgam age to have performed the *rājasūya*, which was attended by the Chera king, Māri Veṅko, and the Pāṇḍya king, Ugrapperuvaḷudi. Iḷañjeṭchenni Neydalaṅgānal is famous for wresting the fortress of Pāmaḷūr from the Cheras, while another Choḷa prince, bearing the same name of Iḷañjeṭchenni, has been given the epithet, Śeruppāḷi-yeṟinda, perhaps because of his conquest of the fortress of Śeruppāḷi. Towards the end of the Śaṅgam age, there ruled Śeṅgaṇān, who is famous for having defeated and captured the Chera king, Kaṇaikkāl Irumpoṟai, in the battle of Por, although the poet, Poygaiyār, in the *Kaḷavaḷi*, locates the battlefield at Kaḷumalam, near the Chera capital of Karuvūr. Later on, the captive was released on the intervention of this poet, who happened to be a friend of the Chera king. Śeṅgaṇān was a devout Śaiva, and, according to Thirumangai, he built 70 temples, dedicated to Śiva. The Anbil plates of Sundara Choḷa refer to one Nallaḍikkon as the son of Śeṅgaṇān.

The Pāṇḍyas

The Pāṇḍya country was situated, from coast to coast, to the south of the Choḷa country, with the river Vallaru forming its northern boundary. According to traditional accounts, the Pāṇḍyas were descendants of Śiva and Pārvatī, who were the first king and queen of that royal line. The *Maduraikkāñji* of Māṅguḍi Marudan, also known as Māṅguḍi Kiḷār, refers to an early Pāṇḍya king, Neḍiyon, who is an almost legendary figure. However, in the Veḷvikuḍi plates, the earliest Pāṇḍya ruler is Palśālai Mudukuḍumi Peruvaḷudi, referred to in the inscription as *parameśvara.* He was a warlike prince, and also performed a number of vedic sacrifices. One of his successors was Neḍuñjeḷiyan, who is said to have defeated an army of some power of northern India. According to the *Śilappadikāram*, he died of grief on the death of Kovalan.

This Neḍuñjeḷiyan is to be distinguished from another Pāṇḍya king of the same name—Neḍuñjeḷiyan, the victor of the battle of Talaiyālaṅgānam, who ruled in the first half of the third century AD. He attained kingship at a young age. Shortly after his accession, his kingdom was invaded by the joint forces of the Choḷas, Cheras, and five other minor princes, who reached as far as the Pāṇḍya capital of Madurā. Neḍuñjeḷiyan, however, repulsed the attack, and, pursuing the enemy beyond the borders of his kingdom, he attained a decisive victory over them at Talaiyālaṅgānam, near Thiruvālūr, in the Choḷa country. Thenceforth, he came to be known by the epithet, 'victorious in the battle of Talaiyālaṅgānam'. The Chera ruler, Śey Māndarañjeral Irumpoṟai, was taken prisoner. Other military achievements of Neḍuñjeliyan include his victory over the kings of Kongu and Nīḍūr, which resulted in the annexation of some parts of the dominions of the chieftain of Nīḍūr, and the annexation of the two *kūṟṟam* (provinces) of Miḷalai and Muttūṟu. Māṅguḍi Marudan refers to him as the 'lord of Koṟkai and the warlord of the southern Paradavar'. This Pāṇḍya ruler, too, is credited with the performance of several vedic sacrifices.

The Cheras

The Cheras occupied the land along the western coast of India, up to Konkan in the north. Their capital, Vañji, has been located, variously, at Karūr near Thiruchchhirappalli, or at Thiruvanjikulam near Cochin, on the west coast. The earliest reference to the Cheras is, perhaps, to be found in the *Aitareyāraṇyaka*, which mentions Cherapādāḥ as a people. The following observation, made about the early Cheras, seems to be very apt : 'The Chera ruler joined Pāṇḍya against the Choḷa and the Choḷa against the Pāṇḍya ruler as suited him, but he often fared worst.' For instance, when the Chera ruler, Perum Śeral Ādan, joined forces with the Pāṇḍya king against the Choḷa ruler, Karikāla wounded him, and, perhaps, forced him to starve himself to death. When the Chera ruler, Śey Māndarañjeral Irumpoṟai, who ruled in the early years of the third century AD, joined forces with the Choḷa ruler against the Pāṇḍya king,

Neḍuñjeḷiyan, he was taken prisoner. Another Chera ruler, Kaṇaikkāl Irumpoṟai, suffered the same fate at the hands of the Choḷa king, Śeṅgaṇān.

However, the Chera ruler, Imaiyavaramban Neḍuñjeral Ādan, the son of Udiyañjeral, is credited with achieving victory over the Yavaṇas, whom he carried away captive, and from whom he obtained diamonds and expensive vessels, in profuse quantities, as ransom. These Yavanas have been variously identified as Greek or Arab merchants. Imaiyavaramban Neḍuñjeral Ādan also conquered the coastal region of Kadambu, which has been identified as the region near Vanavāsī, where the Kadambas later rose to power. As is indicated by his epithet, Imaiyavaramban, 'He who had the Himālaya for his boundary', he claims to have ruled over territories, as far north as the Himalayas. He also engaged his contemporary Choḷa king in war, in which both the rivals lost their lives. A son of Imaiyavaramban Neḍuñjeral Ādan was Śeṅguṭṭuvan, who was a contemporary of King Gajabāhu I of Siṁhala (Sri Lanka); his rule is dated to the latter half of the second century AD, on the basis of the date of Gajabāhu (*c* 173-195 AD). Paraṇar ascribes to him a victory over the chieftain of Mohūr, as also some naval successes. He is known to have helped a Choḷa prince ascend the throne, after killing nine of his rival.

Contemporaneous with the rule of these Chera kings, of the line of Udiyañjeral, was that of some kings, celebrated in the *Padiṟṟuppattu*. The earliest of these was the scholarly Anduva; his son, Śelvakkaḍuṅgo Vāḷi Ādan, was the performer of vedic sacrifices, and has been celebrated by Kapilar in a song. Peruñjeral Irumpoṟai, the son of Śelvakkaḍuṅgo Vāḷi Ādan, is known to have ruled towards the close of the second century AD. He is reported to have captured Tagaḍūr (Dharmapuri, near Salem), the centre of power of the Adigaimān chiefs, and the fortress of a chief, named Kaḷuvuḷ. Kuḍakko Iḷañjeral Irumpoṟai, a cousin of Peruñjeral Irumpoṟai, faced the joint forces of the Choḷa and Pāṇḍya kings, and is credited with the capture of five stone fortresses.

The Toṇḍaiyar

Toṇḍai was the name of the country around Kāñchī, as also that of the dynasty which exercised authority over the region. Attempts have to made to associate the Toṇḍaiyar kings with the Pallavas, as both ruled from Kāñchī. Besides, while *toṇḍai* is the 'name of a creeper', *pallava* means 'sprout'. Among the earliest significant rulers of Kāñchī was Toṇḍaiman Iḷandiraiyan. No definite information is available about any ruler, who preceded or succeeded him, although sometimes he is associated with the family of Tiraiyar. There is a view that he might have been a grandson of the Choḷa ruler, Karikāla, or his viceroy at Kāñchī. But most of the scholars believe that he was an independent ruler of Toṇḍai. Claims were made about his descent from Vishṇu. Information about him is vague in nature, making it difficult to form an estimate of him as a ruler. On the one hand, he has been presented as a mighty monarch, commanding the reverence of his contemporary Choḷa, Pāṇḍya, and Chera rulers. On the other hand, he has not even been allotted the status of a sovereign ruler. He might have received Auvaiyār, the envoy of Adigaimān. He is, however, praised for his righteousness. His skill as a poet is attested by four poems attributed to him.

The Pallavas

The origin of the Pallavas of Kāñchī is a matter of intense debate among historians, with various scholars ascribing to them a north Indian, and even a foreign (Pahlava) origin. Reference has been made above to the view that they might be associated with the Toṇḍaiyar of Kāñchī. The combined testimony of two copperplate grants—the Mayidavolu plates and the Hirahadagalli plates, shows that one of the earliest Pallava kings of note was Śiva-Skandavarman. The former inscription refers to him as heir-apparent, clearly indicating that he was not the first ruler of the family. The latter inscription mentions his father, simply as *Bappadeva*, 'revered father', without specifying his name; Nilakanta Sastri would identify him with Siṁhavarman, known from the Guntur charter of Vijaya-Skandavarman, but this identification has not been universally accepted, with S Krishnaswami Aiyangar placing him after Śiva-Skandavarman. Interestingly, the father is said to have granted a hundred thousand ox-plough, which has been taken to indicate that he was largely responsible for the transformation of the forest region into cultivable land. The kingdom of Śiva-Skandavarman is said to have extended up to the river Krishna, in the north, and the Arabian Sea in the west. He appointed the Kadamba ruler, Mayūraśarman, as the ruler of Vanavāsī. The Gaṅga rulers of Mysore, too, seem to have come under Pallava influence. Śiva-Skandavarman performed several vedic sacrifices, like the *agnishṭoma*, *vājapeya*, and, most significantly, the *aśvamedha*. He is generally dated to the last quarter of the third century AD.

In the Guntur charter, the name Skandavarman occurs with the prefix, Vijaya. Scholars, like Nilakanta Sastri and S Krishnaswami Aiyangar, favour the identification of Śiva-Skandavarman of the Mayidavolu and Hirahadagalli plates, with Vijaya-Skandavarman of the Guntur charter. The Guntur charter refers to a grant made by Chārudevī, the wife of Vijaya-Buddhavarman and mother of Buddhyaṅkura. The relationship between Vijaya-Skandavarman and Vijaya-Buddhavarman has not been specified in the charter. However, as Vijaya-Skandavarman is mentioned as the reigning monarch, and Vijaya-Buddhavarman, as the heir-apparent, Nilakanta Sastri and S Krishnaswami Aiyangar might be right in proposing that Vijaya-Buddhavarman might have been a son of Vijaya-Skandavarman. If Vijaya-Buddhavarman attained kingship, he would have ruled in the early years of the fourth century AD. Vishṇugopa, the Pallava ruler of Kāñchī, who was defeated by Samudragupta, as per the testimony of the Allahabad pillar inscription of that Imperial Gupta ruler, appears to have been a scion of this royal family.

The political history of the Śaṅgam age seems to come to an end with Nalliyakkoḍan, celebrated by Nattattanār in the Śiṟupāṇāṟṟuppaḍai, which forms a part of the *Pattupāṭṭu.* Interestingly, he ruled, not from Uṟaiyūr, Madurā, or Vañji, but over the territories comprising the present day district of South Arcot.

Appendix 2

Coinage

Coins form one of the most important sources for the history of the time, especially that of the Indo-Greeks, the Śaka-Pahlavas, and the Western Kshatrapas. The immediate successors of the Mauryas, namely the Śuṅgas and the Kāṇvas, are believed to have struck punch marked coins only. The general features of the coins of other significant successors of the Mauryas have been dealt with, in brief, in this Appendix.

Tribal Coins

The **Audumbaras** are connected with the fig tree (*udumbara*), or a country where fig trees grow in abundance. Audumbara coins have been found from the Pathankot-Gurdaspur region, and a few other sites of Punjab, and at Irippal, district Kangra, and a few other regions of Himachal Pradesh. The tribe seems to have occupied Kangra, Gurdaspur, and Hoshiarpur areas.

The coins of this tribe are divided into two classes. Class I comprises copper coins, which bear, on the obverse, tree-in-railing, forepart of an elephant, and undulating line below, and on the reverse, storeyed temple and trident-battleaxe. The obverse has a Kharoshṭhī legend, mentioning the name of the chief, along with the titles of *raña* (= Sanskrit, *rājña*) and *mahadeva* (= Sanskrit, *mahādeva*); the reverse has a Brāhmī legend, mentioning the name of the tribe, sometimes accompanied by the name of the issuing chief—Śivadāsa, Rudradāsa, Dharaghosha, and Mahādeva. Class II comprises silver coins, which show four varieties, depicting devices like humped bull, lotus flower, *chakra*, and *nandipada*, on the obverse, and elephant, trident, standing figure holding trident-battleaxe, and tree-in-railing on the reverse. One variety has the figure of Viśvāmitra on the obverse. The Kharoshṭhī/Brāhmī legends on these coins mention Mahādeva and Dharaghosha.

On palaeographical grounds, the coins of Class I are placed in the second or first century BC, while those of Class II at the end of the first century BC, or the beginning of the first century AD, on the basis of the Indo-Greek influence on them. The copper coins weigh between 31 and 46 grains, while the silver coins weigh about 40 grains and seem to be based on the weight standard of the Indo-Greek coins of roughly 36 grains.

While the coin legend gives the form Kuṇinda, literature has the forms Kulinda, Kauṇinda, Kaulinda, Kulindrene, etc. Kuṇinda coins have been found at Behat near Saharanpur, Srinagar in Garhwal, and the areas around Jwalamukhi, Karnal, Sunet, Tappa Mewa, and Ropar. They inhabited the strip of land, at the foot of the Siwalik hills, between the Yamuna and the Sutlej, and the territory between the upper courses of the Beas and the Sutlej as their home.

Kuṇinda coins were issued in both silver and copper, and are round in shape. According to Cunningham, they were produced in some mint located at Sugh, while Devendra Handa locates another Kuṇinda mint at Sanghol. The coins have been divided into two series—the Amoghabhūti series, and the *Chatreśvara* series. The weight of the silver coins of the Amoghabhūti series ranges between 21 and 38 grains, and seems to be based on the *hemidrachms* of later Indo-Greek and Śaka-Pahlava kings, adopted with a view to competing in the market with the Indo-Greek silver pieces. The copper coins of this series weigh between 9.5 and 257 grains, while those of the *Chatreśvara* series weigh between 131 and 291 grains; these seem to be based on the Kushāṇa weight standard. Rapson, Powell-Price, and M P Joshi ascribe the Almora coins to a branch of the Kuṇinda tribe.

The **Mālavas** (Malloi) are mentioned by the classical writers as unsuccessfully resisting Alexander, by forming an alliance with the Oxydrakai (= Kshudrakas), in the fourth century BC. In Indian literature, they are often mentioned together with the Kshudrakas. They appear to have migrated to Rajasthan from Punjab under the pressure of the Greek invasion; then they moved further south, and occupied the region in western Madhya Pradesh, now called Malwa after them.

Mālava coins are all in copper, and mostly round in shape, although square and rectangular coins are also known. Their dates range from third-second centuries BC to fourth-fifth centuries AD. The heaviest Mālava coin weighs 43.84 grains, but the smallest coin is only 1.7 grains; most of the other types weigh below 15 grains. The round coins usually have the Brāhmī legend on the obverse, which may be *Mālavānāṁ jaya* or its variant; very few coins of this shape have devices, like tree, lion, or female figure, on the obverse. The reverse bears symbols, like the sun, *nandipada*, vase, tree-in-railing, or undulating line, or devices like, bull, dancing peacock, human head with curly hair, etc.

The square or rectangular coins have been divided into two classes. The coins of Class I have tree-in-railing or solar symbol and the legend, *Mālavānāṁ jaya*, or its variant, on the obverse; the reverse has devices, like vase or bull. The coins of Class II have some enigmatic legends, like *Magaja, Mapojaya, Bhapaṁyana, Yama, Pachha, Jāmaka, Paya, Māśapa, Magachha*, etc. The obverse of these coins is usually occupied by the legend; very rarely, we find symbols, like tree-in-railing, on this side of the coins. The reverse has devices like lion, elephant, or the Mālava symbol.

The *Ashṭādhyāyī* of Pāṇini mentions the Yaudheyas as an *āyudhajīvī saṁgha*. Yaudheya coins have been found in various parts of Punjab, Haryana, Himachal Pradesh, Delhi, Rajasthan, and Uttar Pradesh; or, in other words, from western Uttar Pradesh in the east to eastern Rajasthan in the west, and from Kangra in the north to Sambhar in the south. Sunet near Ludhiana, Khokra Kot near Rohtak, and Naurangabad near Bhiwani, appear to be the great mint sites of the Yaudheyas.

The Yaudheya coins are in silver, copper, potin, and brass. The silver coin weighs about 26 grains; the weight-range of the copper coins is 9.5-200 grains, of potin coins, 14.5-77 grains, and of brass coins, 35.8-42 grains, the heavier weight coins being more common. These coins have been placed between the second century BC and mid-fourth century AD. The Yaudheya coins have been divided into eight classes. Class I has a tree-in-railing, with or without Ujjain symbol, on the obverse, and the reverse is plain.

Class II has either a bull or a horse before *yūpa*, and the legend, *Yaudheyānāṁ bahudhāñake*, on the obverse, and an elephant and *nandipada*, on the reverse.

The silver coin of Class III has the standing figure of six-headed Kārttikeya, holding spear in the right hand, and the legend, *Bhagavata svāmino Brahmaṇya Yaudheya*, on the obverse, and six-headed Shashṭhī, and some symbols, on the reverse. The copper coins of this class have similar devices, but the legend on the reverse reads *Bhagavata svāmino Brahmaṇyadevasya Kumārasya*. Class IV has the figure of Kārttikeya with spear, and traces of a legend, on the obverse, and symbols, like deer, hill, tree-in-railing, *svastika*, *śrīvatsa*, etc, on the reverse. One variety of this class has the figure of Śiva with trident, on the obverse.

Class V has a hill symbol and *svastika*, and a Brāhmī legend, mentioning *Bhānuva*, sometimes with the title, *rājña*, on the obverse; the reverse of various coins of this class have a standard and trident, or some deity, or six-headed Kārttikeya. Class VI has a bull and the Brāhmī legend, *Yaudheyānāṁ*, on the obverse, while the reverse is obliterated. Class VII coins have six-headed Kārttikeya with spear, a peacock, and the legend, *Yaudheyagaṇasya jaya*, on the obverse; the reverse has a female deity, walking. In one variety of this class, the legend, *dvi*, and in another variety, *tri*, has been added. The significance of these additional legends is not certain. Class VIII consists of coins, with the figure of a goddess, or a symbol and the legend, *Rāvaṇa* or *Rāvaṇasya*, on the obverse, and a male figure, or trident, alone or with other symbols, on the reverse. These coins have been attributed to the Yaudheyas, only on stylistic and typological grounds.

Sātavāhana Coins

Sātavāhana coins are known in silver, copper, lead, and potin; some time back, Shobhana Gokhale published some Sātavāhana coins, in electrum, as well. Most of the silver coins are based on the reduced silver standard of 20 *rattīs* (= 36 grains). One coin, bearing the names of Sātakarṇi I and Nāganikā, weighs around 108 grains. The weight standard adopted by the Sātavāhanas, for the coins of other metals, is difficult to determine, as there is a lot of variation in their weights.

The most common modes of fabrication, adopted for Sātavāhana coins, are die-striking and casting; sometimes, blanks were cast in moulds, and then dies were employed to impress devices and legends. The punch-marking technique has been used for manufacturing some coins of the early Sātavāhana rulers, Sāta and Sātakarṇi, found in the region of Vidisha. Sātavāhana coins, from the northern provinces of the empire, are mostly square or rectangular in shape, while those from the southern provinces, round. An oval-shaped coin is known from Kondapur, in Andhra Pradesh.

Except for the coin, bearing the names of Sātakarṇi I and Nāganikā, Sātavāhana silver coins bear the bust of the king, on the obverse, and a group of symbols, on the reverse. The rest of the coins have symbols on both the sides, which have been divided into two categories by I Kartikeya Sarma. The main symbols include bull, lion, elephant, horse, hill, human figure, *chakra*, ship, and portraits, while the auxiliary symbols include Ujjain symbol, triangle-headed symbol, tree-in-railing, crab, *svastika*, the sun and the moon, river with fish, *triratna*, *nandipada*, *śrīvatsa*, lotus, etc. The Ujjain symbol and hill symbol are so common, that Rapson labels them as the dynastic symbols of the Sātavāhanas.

Rapson was, perhaps, the first scholar to point out the local character of Sātavāhana coins. This implies that the coins, issued in a particular region, bear a particular combination of symbols. For instance, the coins of Anantapur and Cuddapah regions bear the figure of a horse, on the obverse, and a *chaitya* and tree, on the reverse; those of the Coromondal coast have the depiction of a ship, on the obverse, and Ujjain symbol, on the reverse; while those of the Malwa region have a combination of elephant, tree, and *chaitya*, on the obverse, and the figure of a man and Ujjain symbol, on the reverse.

The Sātavāhana rulers used Prakrit language, and Brāhmī script, on their coins. The legend gives the name of the ruler, together with the royal title, *raño* (= Sanskrit, *rājña*), and the honorific title, *siri* (= Sanskrit, *śrī*). Quite interesting is the use of metronymics, like Gautamīputra, Vāsishṭhīputra, etc, by kings. The obverse legend, on silver coins, is in Prakrit language, while the reverse legend is the Draviḍa rendering of the obverse Prakrit legend. Although the activities of the Sātavāhana rulers were centred mostly in southern India, Sātavāhana coins are modelled after the coins of northern India.

Indo-Greek Coins

Around the middle of the third century BC, Bactria asserted its independence of the Seleukid emperor, Antiochos II, under its satrap, Diodotos I. Coins reveal the existence of around three dozen Indo-Greek kings and queens, notable among them being Agathokleia, Agathokles, Apollodotos, Demetrios, Eukratides, Hermaios, Kalliope, Menander, Strato, and Zoilos. Indo-Greek rule seems to have come to an end sometime around the middle of the first century BC (above, Chapter IV).

The Indo-Greeks are known to have struck coins in gold, silver, copper, cupro-nickel, lead, and billon. The standard denomination of gold was the *stater* (134.4 grains), that of silver was *drachm* (67.2 grains), and that of copper was *chalkon.* According to Cunningham, the cupro-nickel coin weighing 134.4 grains, was the *obolos.* The gold, silver, and cupro-nickel coins are mostly round in shape; the copper coins in Bactria are round, while those in the Indian territories are square. The coins are all die-struck.

With a few exceptions, the obverse of the Indo-Greek coins bears the realistic head or bust of the king, to the right, and the reverse, the figure or emblem of some deity. The royal bust is absent on the bilingual *drachms* of Apollodotos, Antimachos II, and Telephos. Conjugate busts appear on some coins of Agathokleia with Strato I, of Hermaios with Kalliope, and on the coins struck by Eukratides I in memory of his parents, Heliokles and Laodike. The royal head and bust is invariably shown as wearing a diadem, the symbol of royalty. The deities, appearing on Indo-Greek coins, are mostly from the Greek pantheon—Apollo, Artemis, Athena, Demeter, Dionysos, the Dioskuri, Hekate, Helios, Herakles, Hermes, Nike, Poseidon, Triton, and Zeus. Emblems of deities include the *aegis* of Athena, the *tripod lebes* of Apollo, the palms and *pilei* of the Dioskuri, the *caduceus* of Hermes, and the thunderbolt of Zeus. Some Indian deities, like Balarāma and Vāsudeva-Kṛishṇa, also make their appearance on Indo-Greek coins. Animals, like boar, bull, camel, elephant, horse, and panther, birds, like eagle and owl, and sea creatures, like dolphin, find depiction on Indo-Greek coins.

In case of the Indo-Greek coins in Bactria, the name and title(s) of the issuing monarch appear, on the reverse, in Greek. But in case of the Indo-Greek coins in the Indian territories, they appear, in Greek, on the obverse, and the literal Prakrit translation of this obverse Greek legend, usually written in the Kharoshṭhī script, appears on the reverse; the rare use of the Brahmī script, in place of the Kharoshṭhī, to write the Prakrit legend, may be seen, for instance, on some coins of Agathokles. *Basileus* and *maharaja* are the most common titles. Some Indo-Greek rulers also assumed additional epithets, like *aniketos/apaḍihata*, *autokrator*, *dikaios/dhramika*, *theos*, *megas/mahata*, *nikator/jayadhara*, *soter/tratara*, *philopator/priyapita*, etc. The transfer of the Greek legend, from the reverse to the obverse, affected the size of the royal bust.

The Indo-Greek coins also bear monograms, the exact significance of which has baffled scholars. Indo-Greek coins are generally very artistic, particularly those issued in Bactria.

Śaka-Pahlava Coins

The Śakas were confederations of a number of, apparently, racially and linguistically homogenous tribes or clans, originally from Central Asia, although sometimes they may have also assimilated other ethnic nomadic tribes. Some Śakas from the Ili valley crossed the Pamirs, and entered India, settling in the Hazara-Kashmir region. Maues belonged to this branch of the Śakas. Another branch, moving from Sogdia, first occupied Merv and northern Bactria, and then crossed the Hindukush into India, occupying Kapiśā, the Kabul valley, and western Gandhāra, that is they advanced east into the Indo-Greek territories. Vonones and the related rulers, Spalahora, Spalagadama, Spalirises, Azes I, Azilises, and Azes II, belonged to this branch of the Śakas. The Parthian emperor, Mithridates II, settled the Śakas in Drangiana, which, henceforth, became known as Sakastene (Seistan). Orthagnes, Gondopharnes, Guḍa, Abdagases, and perhaps, also Pakores, might have belonged to this branch of the Śakas from Seistan, although there is a strong possibility that they were related to the family of Vonones. Gondopharnes was the last great Śaka-Pahlava ruler; after him, the empire disintegrated. There are also certain satrapal families, like those of Rañjuvula and Śoḍāsha; of Hagāna and Hagāmasha; of Kharaösta and Hajatriä; of Patika and Liäka Kusulaka; and of Zeionises (above, Chapter V).

The Śaka-Pahlava rulers do not appear to have had any numismatic tradition of their own, and their coins are mostly, but crude imitations of the Indo-Greek coins, with certain features of the Arsakid coins of Parthia. They issued coins in silver, copper, bronze, and billon, their weight standard being based on that of the Indo-Greek coins of these metals. The coins of the Śaka-Pahlavas are both round and square in shape, though later, there is a greater preponderance of round coins than the square ones; the billon coins are always round. All the Śaka-Pahlava coins appear to have been manufactured by the die-striking method.

By the time the Śaka-Pahlavas reached the Kabul valley, they had established their characteristic type of 'Mounted king : Deity'. On some types, the king is being crowned by some deity, usually Nike. Some rulers, like Orthagnes, Gondopharnes, and the Śaka Kshatrapas of Mathurā, issued coins showing the bust of the king, on the obverse. Coins of some rulers, like Azes, bear armed king, seated crosslegged, on a cushion. Enthroned king may also sometimes be seen, as, for instance, on some coins of Gondopharnes. The reverse of Śaka-Pahlava coins is usually occupied by the figure of some deity, but sometimes, a divine figure may be seen on the obverse as well. These deities are from both the Greek and Indian pantheons; city deities are also often depicted. The deities depicted of these coins include Apollo, Artemis, Athena, Demeter, the Dioskuri, Helios, Hephaistos, Herakles, Hermes, Indra, Lakshmī, Nike, Poseidon, Selene, Śiva, Tyche, and Zeus. In certain cases, the deities may be represented by their emblems, like the *aegis* of Athena, the *tripod lebes* of Apollo, the bow-and-arrow of Artemis, the thunderbolt of Zeus. Besides the horse as the mount of the king, animals represented on Śaka-Pahlava coins include maneless lion, humped bull, and elephant. Birds are, however, not seen on Śaka-Pahlava coins.

Śaka-Pahlava coins bear legends, usually on both the sides, but sometimes only on one side. The language of the obverse legend is Greek, while that of the reverse legend is Prakrit, written in the Khroshṭhī script. Sovereign Śaka-Pahlava rulers use the title, *basileos basileon megalos*/*majaraja rajaraja* (or *rajatiraja*) *mahata*, while subordinate rulers use *basileus*/*maharaja*. Besides, on various coins, we come across additional epithets, like *adelphou tou basileos*/*maharajabhrata*, 'brother of the king', or *basileuontos basileon*, *dikaios*/*dhramika*, *soter/tratara*, *autokrator*, *epiphanes*, *theos*, *satrapei*, *devavrata*, *apratihata*, *apratihatachakra*, *stratega*, etc.

Western Kshatrapa Coins

Some rulers, of Śaka extraction, held sway over parts of western India, and are known as Western Śaka Kshatrapas. Two prominent branches of the Western Kshatrapas are the Kshaharāta and the Kārddamaka.

The Kshaharātas seem to have started their career as the provincial governors of the Kushāṇas, in the southwestern parts of the empire, as shown by the use of the title of *kshatrapa*, by Ābhīraka and Bhūmaka, on their coins, and the titles of *kshatrapa* and *mahākshatrapa*, by Nahapāna, in his inscriptions, although doubts have recently been expressed, from certain quarters, regarding the subordinate status of the Kshaharāta Kshatrapas. Nahapāna, on his coins, uses the title of *rājan*, which shows an increase in the power and prestige of the dynasty, during his reign. The rule of the dynasty was brought to an end by the Sātavāhana ruler, Gautamīputra Sātakarṇi (above, Chapter V).

Kshaharāta coins are available in silver, copper, lead, potin, and an alloy of copper and lead. The silver coins seem to be based on Indo-Greek coins. The device of arrow on left, thunderbolt on right, and discus in the centre, occurs on the obverse of the copper coins and the reverse of the silver coins. The legends on the Kshaharāta coins are in Prakrit, written in both Brāhmī and Kharoshṭhī. Ābhīraka used Greek and Brāhmī on his coins. On the silver coins of Nahapāna, the obverse legend is written in mixed Greek and Roman characters, which, according to the Rapson, reads *Raño Kshaharātasa Nahapānasa*.

The Kārddamakas ruled over western parts of India, for a period of nearly 300 years. The royal house of the Kārddamaka Kshatrapas was established by Dāmaghsada I, or by Chashṭana, who is believed to have started his career as a *kshatrapa*, under the Kushāṇas, but attained the position of a *mahākshatrapa*. Jayadāman, the heir-apparent of Chashṭana, died during the lifetime of his father, and was replaced by his son, Rudradāman I, who was perhaps the greatest, and certainly the most famous, of the Kārddamaka rulers. Other rulers of this family include Dāmajadaśrī I, Rudrasiṁha I, Jīvadāman, Rudrasena I, Saṅghadāman, Dāmasena, Yaśodāman I, Vijayasena, Dāmajadaśrī II,

Rudrasena II, Viśvasiṁha, Bhartṛidāman, Satyadāman, Pṛithvīsena, Damajadaśrī III, Vīradāman, Viśvasena, Rudrasiṁha II, Yaśodāman II, Rudrasena III, Siṁhasena, Rudrasena IV, and Satyasiṁha. The last-known Kārddamaka ruler was Rudrasiṁha III, who was, perhaps, defeated by Chandragupta II (above, Chapter V).

The Kārddamaka Kshatrapas issued coins in silver, copper, potin, and lead; some coins reveal an admixture of copper and lead. All these rulers struck coins in silver, with the exception of Jayadāman. Copper coins were issued by Chashṭana, Jayadāman, Rudradāman I, and, perhaps, also by Rudrasiṁha I. Potin coins of Jīvadāman and Rudrasiṁha I, and of the period of Rudrasena I and Dāmasena, are available. Lead coins were issued during the reigns of Chashṭana and Rudrasena III. The silver and potin coins are round in shape, while the copper and lead coins are square. All these coins have been manufactured by the die-striking method.

The obverse of the silver coins is occupied by the bust of the king. Coins of the other metals usually have a humped bull, while the copper coins of Chashṭana have a horse. The reverse of most of the Kārddamaka coins has a combination of the symbols—crescent-on-hill, star, crescent, and curved line. The legend, which occurs on the reverse, is in Prakrit, sometimes influenced by Sanskrit. The script is mostly Brāhmī, Kharoshṭhī being used, in addition to Brāhmī, on the coins of Chashṭana, Dāmaghsada I, and Jayadāman only. The silver coins mention the name and titles of the father of the issuer, along with those of the issuer himself. The coins of the baser metals and alloys, when inscribed, do not usually mention the father of the issuer. From the time of Rudrasiṁha I or Jīvadāman onwards, we start getting the date of the issue of the coin, in the Śaka era.

Kushāṇa Coins

The Kushāṇas are believed to be a branch of the Yüeh-chih tribe, which was displaced from its original habitat, in Central Asia, by the Hiung-nu (Hūṇa) tribe, in the course of the political upheaval in Central Asia, about 165 BC. Chinese sources inform that, in Bactria, the Yüeh-chihs had five small principalities, four of which were subjugated by K'ieou-tsieou-k'io (Kujula Kadphises), the chief of the fifth one, the Kouei-chouang. Kujula Kadphises was followed by his son, V'ima Takshuma, and grandson, V'ima Kadphises. After him came Kanishka I, who ruled over an extensive dominion, extending at least up to Vārāṇasī in the east, and Kashghar, Yarqand, and Khotan in the north, and was succeeded by Vāsishka, Huvishka, Kanishka II, Vāsudeva I, etc. The Kushāṇa empire started disintegrating after Vāsudeva I (above, Chapter VI).

The Kushāṇas were the first power in India to issue profuse gold coinage. Besides, they also struck abundant copper coins, and rare silver ones. The gold coins of the Kushāṇas were based on the weight standard of the Roman *aurei*, and weighed around 123 grains. The copper coins are available in three weights—260 grains, 130 grains, and 65 grains. The silver coins are so few, that nothing definite can be said about their weight standard. The Kushāṇa coins are manufactured by the die-striking method, and are invariably round in shape.

The obverse of the coins of Kujula Kadphises bears the bust of the Indo-Greek ruler, Hermaios, or his own helmeted head; one type even has the figure of a bull on the obverese. But from the time of V'ima Kadphises onwards, the device of king sacrificing at an altar becomes common, Huvishka being the only ruler, not using it on his coins. Other Kushāṇa obverse devices include bust of the king, or king seated on a throne, or on cushions, or on clouds, or reclining on a couch, or riding an elephant. The reverse of the coins of Kujula Kadphises bears, variously, 'Macedonian soldier' or camel; V'ima Kadphises depicted Śiva, anthropomorphically or symbolically. The reverse of the coins of Kanishka I and Huvishka are interesting for the great variety of deities appearing on them. These deities belong to a varied pantheon—Indian, Central Asian, West Asian, Zoroastrian, Graeco-Roman. Among Zoroastrian deities, we have depictions of *Ardochsho, Athsho, Mao, Miiro, Lrooaspo, Oado, Orlagno, Oanindo, Pharro,* etc. The Graeco-Roman deities include *Elios* (Helios), *Selene, Uron* (Ouranos), *Ephaistos* (Hephaistos), *Erakilo* (Herakles), *Riom*, etc, usually in Iranian garb. Indian deities, like Śiva, Umā, Kārttikeya as Skanda-Kumāra, Viśākha, and Mahāsena, and the Buddha, also find depiction. Such representations reflect the spirit of eclecticism, with which the Kushāṇa kings seem to be imbued.

The obverse legend on the coins of the Kadphises group of kings is in Greek, while the reverse legend is in Prakrit language and Kharoshṭhī script. These legends give the name and titles of the issuing king. But the rulers of the Kanishka group used only Greek language, written in Graeco-Kushāṇa script. The obverse legend gives the name and titles of the issuing king, while the reverse legend gives the name of the deity represented, thus helping us in identifying the deity represented, when the depiction is indifferent.

Appendix 3

Select Inscriptions

Inscriptions form a very important source of information about the history of this period. A brief introduction to the significant epigraphs of the period, and a few words about their historical importance, would not be out of place here.

The **Hathigumpha inscription of Khāravela,** engraved on the wall of the cave, locally known as Hathigumpha, on one of the hills of the Udayagiri-Khandagiri range, occupies a unique place in ancient Indian epigraphy, in that it describes the event in the life and reign of a king in a chronological order. The language of the inscription is Prakrit, and the script, Brāhmi of the latter half of the first century BC. The name of the king was correctly read as Khāravela, for the first time, by Bhagvanlal Indraji. The main purpose of the 17 line inscription is, apparently, to record the construction of cave-dwellings and an assembly hall, for the use of Jaina monks, by Khāravela.

The inscription refers to Khāravela as a Chedi, and a scion of the Māhāmeghavāhana family. He spent the first 15 years of his life, engaged in games suitable for a prince. He also gained proficiency in the drawing of royal charters, and in currency, accountancy, protocol, and law. Then, for nine years, he served as *yuvarāja*, and attained practical experience of administration. On completing 24 years of age, he was coronated as the third ruler in the dynasty of Kaliṅga. Then follows the description of thirteen years of his reign.

In the first year of his reign, Khāravela, repaired the fortifications and buildings of Kaliṅganagarī, which had been damaged by a cyclone; caused the construction of ponds, tanks, and dams; revived the parks; and spent 35 lac coins on the entertainment of his subjects. The next year, he sent a large army towards the west, unmindful of Sātakarṇi. This army reached the banks of Kaṇhabeṁṇā, and caused consternation to the residents of Asikanagara. The identity of the river and the city, and even the reading of the name of the city, are subjects of debate among scholars. The language of the inscription leaves little doubt that the expedition was mounted as a challenge to the power of the Sātavāhana ruler, and did not produce any concrete results. However, it was presented in Kaliṅga as a successful expedition, and the king arranged for festivities for his subjects, in the third year of his reign.

In his fourth regnal year, Khāravela sent an expedition, against the Raṭhikas of Khandesh and the Bhojakas of Berar, and forced them to pay homage to his feet. The bone of contention seems to be the Vijādharādhivāsaṁ, which might have been some place sacred to the Vidyādhara sect of the Jainas. In the fifth year, he extended, up to his capital, by way of Tanasuliya, the system of canals, which had been dug by the Nanda king, three hundred years earlier. In the sixth year, Khāravela made a show of kingly pomp, by granting his subjects exemption from taxes. This cost the royal exchequer, several lacs of the current coins. The portion describing the seventh year of his reign is difficult to read. According to K P Jayaswal, it recounts that his wife, who belonged to the Vajiradhara family, attained motherhood.

In his eighth regnal year, Khāravela sent a large army towards northern India, conquered Gorathagiri (Barabar hills, near Gaya in Bihar), and caused consternation to the residents of Rājagṛiha. On hearing of these exploits of the ruler of Kaliṅga, the Yavana king, Ḍimita (Demetrios or Diomedes ?), abandoned his army and mounts, and retreated to Mathurā. Khāravela spent the ninth year of his reign in liberality to the brāhmaṇas. He also built a palace, named Mahāvijaya, at the cost of 38 lac coins.

In his tenth regnal year, Khāravela embarked upon a victorious campaign in Bhāratavarsha, presumably northern India, and, after putting his enemies to flight, wrested jewels and precious stones from them. In the eleventh year of his reign, he attacked Pithuṁḍa (Pithundra of Ptolemy) in the south, razed the city to the ground, and ploughed it, with ploughs yoked to asses. The same year, he also seems to have destroyed a confederacy of Tamiḷ states, which had been in existence for 1,300 or 113 years (?).

In the twelfth year of his reign, Khāravela led another expedition towards *uttarāpatha.* The elephants and horses of his army drank the waters of the Gaṅgā. Bahasatimita, the ruler of Magadha, paid obeisance at his feet. This king has been identified with Bṛihatsvātimitra, a local ruler, known from the Mora and Pabhosa inscriptions. Khāravela returned to Kaliṅga, with the wealth of Aṅga and Magadha. The same year, he also obtained pearls and jewels from the Pāṇḍya ruler.

The inscription ends with the description of the pious works, executed by Khāravela, in the thirteenth year of his reign, and the history of Kaliṅga, once again, plunges into darkness.

The **Nasik inscription of the time of Vāsishṭhīputra Puḷumāvi, year 19**, is an important source of information about the career and personality of the Sātavāhana ruler, Gautamīputra Sātakarṇi. During his reign, Gautamīputra Sātakarṇi had started the construction of a cave, on Triraśmi hill, to be donated to the Bhadrayānīya sect of Buddhism. But the work was completed by Gotamī Balaśrī, the mother of Gautamīputra Sātakarṇi, only during the reign of his son and successor, Vāsishṭhīputra Puḷumāvi. In the nineteenth year of the reign of Vāsishṭhīputra Puḷumāvi, the cave was donated by Gotamī Balaśrī, along with the nearby village of Piśāchīpadraka, which was donated by Vāsishṭhīputra Puḷumāvi. The main object of the inscription is to record the performance of these pious acts. But the 'disconsolate mother' used this opportunity to make a 'funeral oration' about her deceased son. The language of the inscription is Prakrit, and the script, Brāhmī.

The power of the Sātavāhanas was eclipsed for a few decades, following the end of the rule of Sātakarṇi I, mainly due to the rise of the Kshaharāta branch of the Western Kshatrapas. But the dynasty made a complete recovery during the reign of Gautamīputra Sātakarṇi. The present inscription informs us that he completely destroyed the Kshaharāta dynasty, and re-established the power and prestige of the Sātavāhana dynasty. It is also told therein that he put to the sword, the Śakas, Yavanas, and Pahlavas, and defeated a confederacy of enemies in several battles. The Śakas seem to belong to the Kārddamaka branch of the Western Kshatrapas; the Yavanas were occupying western *dakshiṇāpatha*, from where their donative inscriptions have been found; it is difficult to ascertain the identity of the Pahlavas. These rulers of foreign extraction seem to have formed a confederacy against the Sātavāhanas, and in support of the Kshaharāta Kshatrapas. But when Gautamīputra Sātakarṇi embarked upon a campaign to exterminate the Kshaharāta Kshatrapas, he seems to have worsted the Śakas, Yavanas, and Pahlavas, as well.

Right at the outset, the inscription gives a list of the regions, over which Gautamīputra Sātakarṇi held sway, by referring to him as the ruler of Asika, Asaka, and Muḷaka (all in northern Maharashtra), Suraṭha (Saurashtra), Kukura (western Rajasthan), Aparānta (northern Konkan), Anūpa (Narmada valley), Vidarbha (Berar), Ākara (eastern Malwa), and Avanti (western Malwa). This includes, not only the erstwhile Sātavāhana provinces of Ākara, Avanti, Anūpa, Vidarbha, Asika, Asaka, Muḷaka, and Aparānta, which had been conquered from them by the Kshaharāta rulers, but also the Kshaharāta territories of Kukura and Suraṭha. There is a suggestion that, although Ānartta (territory around Dvārakā, in northern Kathiawar), Śvabhra (along the Sabarmati), and Maru (Rajasthan desert) are not mentioned in the inscription, as expressly under the authority of Gautamīputra Sātakarṇi, he would have ruled over them, as they were located between the Sātavāhana regions of Kukura, Suraṭha, and Avanti.

The inscription also mentions some mountains, which were located within the realm of Gautamīputra Sātakarṇi. These include Vijha (eastern parts of the Vindhya range), Achchhavata (Ṛikshavat), Pārichāta (the Aravali and the western Vindhyas), Sahya (northern parts of the Western Ghats), Kaṇhagiri, Macha-Siriṭana-Malaya (southern parts of the Western Ghats), Mahida (Mahendra hill in the Eastern Ghats), and Chakora (southern parts of the Eastern Ghats). References to Mahida and Chakora are interesting, as Gotamī Balaśrī, by stating that Gautamīputra Sātakarṇi was the lord of these mountains, seems to be claiming that her son exercised authority over parts of Kaliṅga and Andhradeśa as well.

Thus, Gautamīputra Sātakarṇi not only recovered those regions, which were earlier under Sātavāhana rule, but had later been snatched away from them, by the Kshaharāta rulers, but also established Sātavāhana authority over some Kshaharāta territories, for the first time.

Gotamī Balaśrī praises Gautamīputra Sātakarṇi in conventional style. She compares her son to Rāma, Keśava, Arjuna, and Bhīmasena in prowess, and Nābhāga, Nahusha, Janamejaya, Sagara, Yayāti, and Ambarīsha in lustre. She also says that Vāyu, *garuḍa*, the *siddhas*, the *yakshas*, the *rākshasas*, the *chāraṇas*, the sun, the moon, and the asterisms and planets, descended to the earth, to witness the valour of Gautamīputra Sātakarṇi in battle. He administered his empire on the principles laid down by the lawgivers, tempered with humanism. There was no excessive taxation. He endeavoured to maintain *varṇāśramadharma* within his empire. Although the inscription refers to him as *eka-baṁhaṇa*, 'unique brāhmaṇa', he reveals his spirit of eclecticism, by making donations to the Buddhist monks of the Bhadrayānīya sect. He possessed a pleasant personality, and his gait has been compared to that of a superior elephant in grace.

The Shinkot-Bajaur relic casket inscriptions of the time of Menander and Vijayamitra are etched on a steatite casket, discovered by some tribals, while digging the foundations for a new fort at Sinkot, in the Bajaur region, at a place some 20 miles to the northwest of the confluence of rivers, Panjkora and Swat. It is said that the steatite casket enclosed a silver casket, which contained gold reliquary, and some ashes : the silver and gold articles are no longer traceable. The language of the inscriptions is the northwestern variety of Prakrit, and the script is Kharoshṭhī. These inscriptions have generally been divided into two groups. The first group, which mentions Menander, may be dated to mid-second century BC, on the basis of the date of that Indo-Greek ruler. Earlier, a gap of around 50 years between the two groups of inscriptions had been surmised by scholars, like N G Majumdar and D C Sircar. It is known, from the Indravarman reliquary inscription, that Azes year 63 (= 5 AD) was the twenty-fifth regnal year of Vijayamitra. Thus, Vijayamitra would have ascended the throne *c* 20 BC. The second group of the Shinkot-Bajaur relic casket inscriptions of the time of Menander and Vijayamitra refers to the fifth regnal year of Vijayamitra. Therefore, it must be dated to *c* 15 BC. Thus, there seems to be a gap of over 125 years between the two groups of inscriptions.

The main object of engraving the first group of inscriptions is to record an event of the time of Menander, namely the consecration of the relics of the Buddha, by *Apracharaja* Viyakamitra. The second group of inscriptions informs us that these relics, being broken, were never venerated, and were 'wasting away'. *Apracharaja* Vijayamitra took the casket, used it to enclose a fresh relic, and consecrated it with the usual ceremony.

Reference to Menander, in the context of a work of piety being performed by Viyakamitra, would seem to suggest that the latter was governing the Swat valley, as a subordinate of the Indo-Greek ruler. The Buddhist inclinations of Menander might, or might not, have had anything to do with the performance of this pious act by his subordinate. In the second group of inscriptions, there is no mention of any overlord of Vijayamitra, indicating that, for all practical purposes, he did not owe allegiance to any other power.

Interestingly, the *Buddhavaṁsa* refers to the consecration of the Buddha's relics, at Vajirā, which might have been the ancient name of Bajaur. This would indicate that the Buddhist scholar was aware of the performance of this pious act by Viyakamitra/Vijayamitra.

The Besnagar *garuḍa* pillar inscription of the time of Bhāgabhadra has been found near Bhilsa, the site of ancient Vidiśā, in Madhya Pradesh. The language of the inscription is Prakrit, and the script, Brāhmī. It has been dated to the latter half of the second century BC, on palaeographical grounds. The main purpose of the inscription is to record the erection of a *garuḍa* pillar, by Heliodoros, the envoy of the Indo-Greek ruler, Antialkidas, to the Śuṅga court, in honour of Vāsudeva-Kṛishṇa.

King Bhāgabhadra of the inscription is regarded as some local ruler of Vidiśā by A K Narain, or the fifth Śuṅga ruler, Bhadraka, by scholars like H C Raychaudhuri and J H Marshall. But it seems more appropriate to identify him as the ninth Śuṅga ruler, Bhāgavata. The find of the inscription, near Bhilsa, indicates that ancient Vidiśā was a part of the dominions of the later Śuṅgas, and might have been an important centre of their power.

Antialkidas is one of the very few Indo-Greek kings, who find mention in inscriptions. He is believed to be a great-grandson of Eukratides, and a son of Heliokles II. His coins are concentrated at Taxila, thereby indicating that it was the centre of his power. This is corroborated by the inscription, which says that his envoy, Heliodoros, came to the court of Bhāgabhadra, from Taxila, and from near Antialkidas. Heliodoros refers to Bhāgabhadra as *trātā*, the Prakrit equivalent of Greek *soter*, 'saviour'. This has led to the suggestion that Bhāgabhadra might have rendered some help to Antialkidas, perhaps against some rival, like Apollodotos.

Śuṅga rule is marked by the revival of Brahmanism. The inscription records the erection of a *garuḍa* pillar, in honour of Vāsudeva-Kṛishṇa, by Heliodoros. This shows the popularity of the Vaishṇava sect, not only among Indians, but also among persons of foreign (Greek) origin, like Heliodoros. The erection of the *garuḍa* pillar, near Vidiśā, indicates the emergence of that region as an important centre of the sect by that time.

The **Mathura lion capital inscriptions of the time of Rañjuvula and Śoḍāsha** are engraved on the surface of the red sandstone capital, found embedded in the steps of an altar, presently dedicated to Goddess Śītalā. The language of the inscriptions is Prakrit, and the script is Kharoshṭhī. The various inscriptions, engraved on the lion capital, have been divided into three groups. The first group records the consecration of the relics of the Buddha, the erection of a *stūpa*, and the construction of a *vihāra*, by the chief-queen of Rañjuvula, and her relations. The main object of the second group of inscriptions is to the record the donation of a cave-dwelling, by Udayana Āryamitra, the disciple of Āchārya Buddhadeva, to Budhila, a Sarvāstivādin monk of Nagarahāra (modern Jalalabad). The main purpose of engraving the inscriptions of the third group is to record the construction of a *stūpa* by some person, again to be donated to Budhila. The performance of these pious acts seems to have followed some military achievement, as the inscription mentions the military camps of Veyaüdirna and Busaparo.

Rañjuvula, Śoḍasha, and most of the persons mentioned in the inscriptions, belong to the Śaka race. Their presence at Mathurā, on the occasion of the performance of the pious acts related to Buddhism, would indicate their Buddhist leanings, despite their foreign (Śaka) origin. There are indications in the inscriptions that these Śakas favoured the Sarvāstivādin sect of Buddhism, and might have been biased against the Mahāsāṅghikas.

According to F W Thomas' interpretation of the first five lines of the inscriptions, the chief-queen of Rañjuvula was the mother of *Yuvarāja* Kharaösta. If this Kharaösta be regarded as the son of Arṭa, known from coins, the inscription would hint at the prevalence of widow remarriage, or of divorce and remarriage of the divorcee, in Śaka society.

The phrase, *sarvasa Sakrastanasa puyaë*, in the inscriptions, shows that the memory of Śakasthāna, the common ancestral home, served as a powerful unifying factor among the various Śaka chiefs, who find mention in the inscriptions.

The **Junagarh inscription of Rudradāman I, [Śaka]** year 72 (150 AD), is the main source of our information about achievements and personality of the Kārddamaka Śaka ruler, Rudradāman I. The inscription is engraved on the same rock, which bears the set of the fourteen Major Rock Edicts of Aśoka, and the famous Junagarh inscription of the Gupta emperor, Skandagupta. The 20 line inscription has been composed in chaste Sanskrit, and engraved in the Brāhmī script of the Kushāṇa period. The main object of the inscription is to record the repair of the Sudarśana dam, by Pahlava Suviśākha, the governor of Saurāshṭra. The dam had been damaged due to severe floods in the rivers, Suvarṇasikatā and Palāśinī, and caused great hardships to the residents. Rudradāman released money from his personal treasury, and instructed his governor to get the dam repaired, for the welfare of his subjects. The inscription relates that the Sudarśana dam, and the lake of the same name, had been constructed during the reign of Chandragupta Maurya, by his governor, Vaiśya Pushyagupta. During the reign of Aśoka, his governor, Yavanarāja Tushāspha, dug a system of canals from the lake, presumably for the supply of water to the residents.

The inscription informs us that Rudradāman was the grandson of Chashṭana, and the son of Jayadāman. Chashṭana had nominated Jayadāman as his heir-apparent, but the latter seems to have predeceased his father, and the Andhau inscription of Chashṭana, year 52 (130 AD), shows that Chashṭana then nominated his grandson, Rudradāman, as his *kshatrapa*. On the death of his grandfather, Rudradāman should have succeeded him, as *mahākshatrapa*, by virtue of being the heir-apparent. However, the Junagarh inscription states that Rudradāman attained for himself the title of *mahākshatrapa*, and that persons of all the *varṇas* chose him as their lord. This has led to the suggestion that Rudradāman had to strive to ascend to the position of *mahākshatrapa*, perhaps due to the rise of the Sātavāhana power.

The Junagarh inscription provides a list of the provinces of the kingdom of Rudradāman. This included Ākarāvanti (eastern and western Malwa), Anūpa-nivṛit (the Māhishmatī region), Ānartta (the territory around Dvārakā, in northern Kathiawar), Surāshṭra (Saurashtra, in southern Kathiawar), Śvabhra along the Sabarmati, Maru (Rajasthan desert), Kachchha (Kutch), Sindhu (western parts of the lower Indus), Sauvīra (eastern parts of the lower Indus), Kukura (adjacent to Ānartta), Aparānta (northern Konkan), and Nishāda (western parts of the Vindhya range and the Aravali).

Of these provinces, Ākara, Avanti, Surāshṭra, Kukura, Aparānta, and Anūpa are expressly mentioned in the Nasik inscription of the time of Vāsishṭhīputra Puḷumāvi, year 19, as forming parts of the dominions of Gautamīputra Sātakarṇi, and Rudradāman would have wrested them from the Sātavāhanas. No wonder, the Junagarh inscription states that he defeated Sātakarṇi, the lord of *dakshiṇāpatha*, twice. However, as he was a near relation, Rudradāman did not destroy him. The defeated Sātavāhana ruler has been identified, variously, as Gautamīputra Sātakarṇi himself, or Vāsishṭhīputra Puḷumāvi, Vāsishṭhīputra Sātakarṇi, Yajña Sātakarṇi, or Śivamaka. Of these, Vāsishṭhīputra Sātakarṇi was the son-in-law of Ru[dradāman I], as per the evidence of an inscription from Kanheri, making the Sātavāhanas, 'not distant' relations of Rudradāman.

The inscription includes Sindhu and Sauvīra, in the lower Indus valley, among the dominions of Rudradāman. The Suivihar inscription of Kanishka I testifies to the hold of that Kushāṇa ruler over the lower Indus valley. If the reign of Kanishka I is placed between 78 AD and 101 AD, then Rudradāman I would have established his authority over the region by defeating some Kushāṇa king.

The Junagarh inscription also informs us that Rudradāman I defeated the Yaudheyas, who were renowned among the *kshatriyas* for their valour. However, the authority of the Kārddamaka Kshatrapas over this republican tribe could not have been lasting, as, shortly afterwards, we find the Yaudheyas issuing independent coins, fashioned after the Kushāṇa module.

The inscription describes Rudradāman as proficient in grammar, polity, music, logic, and other branches of knowledge. He was a just ruler, and deeply interested in the welfare of his subjects. He commissioned the repair of the Sudarśana dam at great personal expenditure, and did not resort to special taxes, forced labour, and other forms of oppression. He possessed an arresting personality, and a number of princesses chose him as their husband in *svayaṁvaras.* He restored a number of deposed rulers on their throne. He had taken a vow of never killing a living being, except in battle. The inscription is secular in nature, and does not reveal the religious leanings of the Kārddamaka ruler.

The Rabataka inscription of Kanishka I was brought to light, in 1993, as a result of the efforts of Sayyid Ja'far, the governor of the Afghan province of Baghlan, and Tim Porter, a British philanthropist. The Greek inscription, consisting of 23 lines, was inscribed on a rectangular stone piece, about 50 cm high and 25 cm thick, and found in a hill, locally known as Kafirs' Castle, at Rabatak in Baghlan. The main purpose of the inscription is to record the construction of a sanctuary for housing the images of a number of deities—Umma, Nana, Ahuramazda, Sroshard, Narasa, Mihr, Mahāsena and Viśākha. The images of these deities, too, were made, at the orders of the king. He also ordered the construction of the statues of himself, and his three ancestors, thus hinting at the existence of a Kushāṇa *devakula,* at the site (above, Chapter I). The work of construction of the sanctuary was executed by Shafar, the *karalrang,* and the service by led by Nukunzuk. The king also performed some other pious acts, and made endowments to the gods. The inscription is undated, but is believed to refer to years one to six of Kanishka, thus leading to the inference that it cannot be earlier than year 6 of that Kushāṇa ruler.

The works of the construction of the sanctuary, and the divine and royal images, were done for Kanishka I himself, and also for his father, V'ima Kadphises, his grandfather, V'ima Taktu/Takshuma, and great-grandfather, Kujula Kadphises. The king desires that the deities, who images were to be installed in the sanctuary constructed at his orders, would grant him everlasting health, security, and victory.

The inscription is quite interesting from several points of view. For the first time, we get the genealogy of the Kushāṇa kings, up to Kanishka I. It reveals the name of a king, V'ima Takshuma, who is expressly described as the grandfather of Kanishka I. So far, the name of this ruler was read only on the coins of Soter Megas, and in the Dasht-i-Nawur inscription, but the reading there was tentative, at best.

The inscription makes the extravagant claim, that Kanishka I had brought the whole of India under his authority. The mention of five cities in line 5 of the inscription, too, is interesting. The name of the first city is not legible; the other four are Sāketa, Kauśāmbī, Pāṭaliputra, and Champā.

The cosmopolitan approach of Kanishka I, towards religion, which was gleaned from the depiction of deities, of diverse pantheons—Zoroastrian, Western Asian, Central Asian, Indian, and Graeco-Roman, on the reverse of his coins, is corroborated by this inscription, which refers the construction of a sanctuary, for housing the images of deities, belonging to a varied pantheon.

Select Bibliography

Agrawal, Ashvini 1989. *Rise and Fall of the Imperial Guptas.* Delhi.

Agrawala, V S 1941. Some Notes on New Pañchāla Coins. *Journal of the Numismatic Society of India* 3, pp. 79-82.

Ahmad, Nisar 1972. The Vemaka Coins. *Journal of the Numismatic Society of India* 34(2), pp. 176-188.

Ahmad, Nisar 1977. The Mitras of Punjab. *Journal of the Numismatic Society of India* 39, pp. 52-68.

Ahmad, Nisar 1993. Coins of the Ārjunāyanas. *Numismatic Digest* 17, pp. 15-24.

Ahmad, Nisar 1996. The Coins of the Śibis. *Numismatic Studies* 4, pp. 31-39.

Allan, John 1914. *Catalogue of the Coins of the Gupta Dynasties, and of Śāśāṅka, King of Gauḍa, in the British Museum, London.* London.

Allan, John 1936. *Catalogue of the Coins of Ancient India, in the British Museum, London.* London.

Altekar, A S 1942. New Kings and Interesting Coin Types from Kauśāmbī. *Journal of the Numismatic Society of India* 4, pp. 1-16.

Altekar, A S 1942. Further New Coins from Kauśāmbī. *Journal of the Numismatic Society of India* 4, pp. 133-145.

Altekar, A S 1942. A Coin of Vaṅgapāla, A King of Kauśāmbī. *Journal of the Numismatic Society of India* 4, pp. 19-20.

Altekar, A S 1946. Some Rare Indo-Bactrian Coins. *Journal of the Numismatic Society of India* 8(1), pp. 51-59.

Altekar, A S 1954. *Catalogue of the Gupta Gold Coins in the Bayana Hoard.* Bombay.

Altekar, A S 1957. *The Coinage of the Gupta Empire.* Corpus of Indian Coins 4. Varanasi.

Audouin, R, and P Bernard 1973. *Trésor de Monnaies Indiennes et Indo-Grecques d'Aï Khanoum* (Afghanistan). *Revue Numismatique*, pp. 238-289.

Bachhofer, L 1941. On Greeks and Śakas in India. *Journal of the American Oriental Society*, pp. 223ff.

Bajpai, K D 1953. New Pañchāla and Kauśāmbī Coins. *Journal of the Numismatic Society of India* 15(1), pp. 42-45.

Bajpai, K D 1960. New Copper Coins from Kauśāmbī and Vidiśā. *Journal of the Numismatic Society of India* 22, pp. 131-133.

Bajpai, K D 1962. New Pañchāla Coins and the Problem of Pañchāla Chronology. *Journal of the Numismatic Society of India* 24(1), pp. 9-19.

Bajpai, K D 1963. The Joint Issues of the Kshatrapas Hagāna and Hagāmasha. *Journal of the Numismatic Society of India* 25(1), pp. 102-103.

Bajpai, K D 1964. Fresh Light on the Post-Aśokan History of Kauśāmbī. *Journal of the Numismatic Society of India* 26(1), pp. 1-6.

Bajpai, K D 1965. A Seal of King Dhanabhūti and a Coin of Śuṅgavarmā from Kauśāmbī. *Journal of the Numismatic Society of India* 27(2), pp. 188-190.

Bajpai, K D 1966. Anamitra—A New Pañchāla Ruler. *Journal of the Numismatic Society of India* 28(1), pp. 43-44.

Bajpai, K D 1973. Yaudheya Coins—A Critical Study. *Journal of the Numismatic Society of India* 35, pp. 90-94.

Bajpai, K D 1976. *Indian Numismatic Studies.* New Delhi.

Baldev Kumar 1973. *The Early Kuṣāṇas.* New Delhi.

Banerji, R D 1933. *The Age of the Imperial Guptas.* Manindra Chandra Nandi Lectures, 1924, revised by the author in 1929-1930. Varanasi.

Basham, A L 1953. A New Study of the Śaka-Kuṣāṇa Period (review of J E van Lohuizen-de Leeuw, *The "Scythian" Period*). *Bulletin of the School of Oriental and African Studies* 15, pp. 80-97.

Basham, A L 1957. The Succession of the Line of Kanishka. *Bulletin of the School of Oriental and African Studies* 20, pp. 77-88.

Bayer, T S 1738. *Historia Regni Graecorum Bactriani.* St Petersbourg.

Bhandarkar, D R 1913-1914. Kshatrapa Coins from Sarvania. *Archaeological Survey of India—Annual Report 1913-1914*, pp. 227-245.

Bhandarkar, D R 1984. *Carmichael Lectures on Ancient Indian Numismatics.* Reprint, Patna.

Bhandarkar, D R 1981. *Corpus Inscriptionum Indicarum* 3. Inscriptions of the Early Gupta Kings. Ed by B Ch Chhabra and G S Gai. New Delhi.

Bhandarkar, R G 1895. *Early History of the Deccan.* 2nd edition. Bombay.

Bivar, A D H 1953. The Indo-Greek Victory Medallions. *Spink's Numismatic Circular* 61, cols 201-202.

Bivar, A D H 1956. The Kushāṇo-Sassanian Coin Series. *Journal of the Numismatic Society of India* 18, pp. 13-46.

Bivar, A D H 1965. Indo-Bacrtrian Problems. *Numismatic Chronicle* 1965, pp. 73-108.

Bopearachchi, Osmund 1993. *Indo-Greek, Indo-Scythian and Indo-Parthian Coins in the Smithsonian Institution.* Smithsonian Institution, Washington D C.

Bopearachchi, Osmund 1994. Recent Discoveries : Hoards and Finds of Ancient Coins from Afghanistan and Pakistan. *Yavanika* (Journal of the Indian Society for Greek and Roman Studies) 4, pp. 3-30.

Bopearachchi, Osmund 1997. Nasten, A Hitherto Unknown Iranian Ruler in India. *Studies in Silk Road Coins and Culture* : Papers in the Honour of Professor Ikou Hirayama. The Institute of Silk Road Studies, Kamakura, pp. 67-74.

Bopearachchi, Osmund 2004. Two Rare Pre-Kushan Coins. *Newsletter of the Oriental Numismatic Society* 178, pp. 18-20.

Bopearachchi, Osmund, and Wilfried Pieper 1998. *Ancient Indian Coins.* Brepols, Turnhout.

Bopearachchi, Osmund, and A U Rahman 1995. *Pre-Kushāṇa Coins in Pakistan.* Islamabad.

Burns, Craig Alden 1984. Later Kushan Conflict. *Numismatic Digest* 8, pp. 54-66.

Burns, Craig Alden 1985. Last Kushan Decades. *Numismatic Digest* 9, pp. 55-71.

Chakrabortty, S K 1931. *A Study of Ancient Indian Numismatics* (Indigenous System) from the Earliest Times to the Rise of the Imperial Guptas. Mymensingh.

Chattopadhyay, Bhaskar 1967. *The Age of the Kushāṇas—A Numismatic Study.* Calcutta.

Chattopadhyaya, Sudhakar 1955. *The Śakas in India.* Santiniketan.

Chattopadhyaya, Sudhakar 1958. *Early History of North India.* Calcutta.

Cribb, Joe, and Nicholas Sims-Williams 1995-1996. A New Bactrian Inscription of Kanishka the Great. *Silk Road Art and Archaeology* 4, The Institute of Silk Road Studies, Kamakura, pp. 75-142.

Cunningham, Alexander 1962. *Later Indo-Scythians.* Reprinted from *Numismatic Chronicle* 1893-1895. Indian reprint, Varanasi.

Cunningham, Alexander 1967. *Coins of Mediaeval India.* Reprint, Delhi.

Cunningham, Alexander 1970. *Coins of Alexander's Successors in the East.* Reprint, Varanasi.

Cunningham, Alexander 1971. *Coins of the Indo-Scythians, Sakas, Kushans.* Reprinted from *Numismatic Chronicle* 1888-1892. Indian reprint, Varanasi.

Cunningham, Alexander 1971. *Coins of Ancient India.* Reprint, Varanasi.

Dani, A H 1992. Greek Monograms. D W Macdowall, Savita Sharma, and Sanjay Garg (ed), *Indian Numismatics, History, Art, and Culture* (Essays in the Honour of Dr P L Gupta), (Delhi, 1992), pp. 99-114.

Dar, M B L 1940. Some Rare Pañchāla Coins from the Site of Ancient Ahichchhatra, Bareily District. *Journal of the Numismatic Society of India* 2, pp. 115-117.

Dasgupta, K K 1974. *A Tribal History of Ancient India—A Numismatic Approach.* Calcutta.

Deb, H K 1934. Indo-Greek Coin-Types. *Indian Historical Quarterly*, pp. 509-522.

Deyell, J S 1984. Indo-Greek and Kshaharāta Coins from the Gujerat Seacoast. *Numismatic Chronicle*, pp. 115-127.

Dobbins, K W 1970. The Question of the Imitation Hermaios Coinage. *East and West* 20, pp. 307-326.

Dobbins, K W 1973. *Śaka-Pahlava Coinage*. Memoirs of the Numismatic Society of India 5. Varanasi.

Dobbins, K W 1980. *A Schema of Indo-Baktrian Coinage*. Numismatic Notes and Monographs (Numismatic Society of India) 13. Varanasi.

Fleet, J F 1888. *Corpus Inscriptionum Indicarum* 3. Inscriptions of the Early Gupta Kings and their Successors. Calcutta.

Furdoonjee, D J Paruck 1976. *Sassanian Coins*. New Delhi.

Fussman, G 1974. *Documents Épigraphiques Kouchans, "I. –Inscriptions et Antiquités du Dašt-e Nāwur". Bulletin de l'Ecole Française d'Extreme-Orient* 61, pp. 2-50.

Gardner, Percy 1887. New Greek Coins of Bactria and India. *Numismatic Chronicle*, pp. 177-181.

Gardner, Percy 1918. *A History of Ancient Coinage (700 BC – 300 BC)*. Oxford.

Gardner, Percy 1971. *Catalogue of the Coins of the Greek and Scythic Kings of Bactria and India, in the British Museum, London*. Indian Reprint, New Delhi.

Ghirshman, Roman 1948. *Begram. Mémoires de la Délégation Archéologique Française en Afghanistan* 13. Cairo.

Gopalachari, K 1941. *Early History of the Andhra Country*. Madras.

Goyal. S R 1994. *Indigenous Coins of Early India*. Jodhpur.

Goyal, S R 1995. *The Dynastic Coins of Ancient India*. Jodhpur.

Goyal, S R 1995. *The Coinage of Ancient India*. Jodhpur.

Goyal, S R 2005. *The Imperial Guptas.* Jodhpur.

Gupta, P L 1977. Coins of the Ārjunāyanas. *Numismatic Digest* 1(1), pp. 14-18.

Gupta, P L 1980. Western Kshatrapa Coins from Karnataka. *Numismatic Digest* 4(2), pp. 10-12.

Gupta, P L 1998. *The Imperial Guptas* 1. Varanasi.

Gupta, P L 2004. *Coins.* Reprint, NBT, New Delhi.

Gupta, P L, and Sarojini Kulashreshtha 2004. *Kuṣāṇa Coins and History.* New Delhi.

Handa, Devendra 2003-2004. Coins of King Magha. *Numismatic Digest* 27-28, pp. 39-42.

Handa, Devendra 2007. *Tribal Coins of Ancient India.* New Delhi.

Haughton, H L 1943. A Note on the Distribution of Indo-Greek Coins. *Numismatic Chronicle,* pp. 50-59.

Haughton, H L 1946. Notes on Greek and Kushan Coins from the North-West Frontier of India : (a) The Bajaur Hoard of 1942; (b) Some Rare Copper Coins from the North-West Frontier of India. *Numismatic Chronicle,* pp. 141-145.

Haughton, H L 1948. The Silver Coinage of Strato and of Agathocleia. *Numismatic Chronicle,* pp. 134ff.

Head, Barclay V 1906. The Earliest Graeco-Bactrian and Graeco-Indian Coins. *Numismatic Chronicle,* pp. 1-16.

Head, Barclay V 1911. *Historia Numorum.* London.

Herzfeld, Ernst 1932. *Sakastan.* Berlin.

Herzfeld, Ernst 1998. *Kushano-Sasanian Coins.* Memoirs of the Archaeological Survey of India 34. Reprint, New Delhi.

Holt, Fr 1980. The Euthydemid Coinage of Bactria : Further Hoard Evidence from Ai Khanum. *Revue Numismatique,* pp. 7-44.

Huxley, George 1983. Geography in the *Acts of Thomas. Greek, Roman and Byzantine Studies* 24, pp. 71-80.

Jayaswal, K P 1920. The Statue of Wema Kadphises and Kushan Chronology. *Journal of the Bihar and Orissa Research Society* 6, pp. 12-22.

Jayaswal, K P 1933. *History of India, 150 AD – 350 AD.* Lahore.

Jenkins, G K 1955. Indo-Scythic Mints. *Journal of the Numismatic Society of India* 17(2), pp. 1ff.

Jenkins, G K 1977. Kushan Coins from Iraq. *Numismatic Digest* 1(2), pp. 26-29.

Jenkins, G K, and A K Narain 1957. *The Coin-types of the Śaka-Pahlava Kings of India.* Numismatic Notes and Monographs (Numismatic Society of India) 4. Varanasi.

Jha, Amiteshwar, and Dilip Rajgor 1994. *Studies in the Coinage of the Western Kshatrapas.* Nashik.

Joshi, M C 1962. Kuṇinda Coinage : A Review (with Special Reference to Later Series). *Bhāratīya Vidyā* 22 (1-4), pp. 45-50.

Joshi, M P 1989. *Morphogenesis of Kuṇindas—A Numsimatic Overview.* Almora.

Jouveau-Dubreuil, G 1920. *Ancient History of the Deccan.* Translated from French by V S Swaminadha Dikshitar. Pondicherry.

Kangle, R P 2000. *The Kauṭilīya Arthaśāstra,* 3 parts. Reprint, Delhi.

Keith, A B 1920. *A History of Sanskrit Literature.* London.

Konow, Sten 1929. *Corpus Inscriptionum Indicarum,* 2(1). Kharoshṭhī Inscriptions with the Exceptions of those of Aśoka. Calcutta.

Konow, Sten 1933. Notes on Indo-Scythian Chronology. *Journal of Indian History* 12, pp. 1-46.

Kosambi, D D 1965. *The Culture and Civilization of Ancient India.* London.

Kothari, Narendra 1991. New Kauśāmbī Coins. *Numismatic Digest* 15, pp. 10-17.

Kovalenko S 1995-1996. The Coinage of Diodotus I and Diodotus II, Greek Kings of Bactria. *Silk Road Art and Archaeology* 4, The Institute of Silk Road Studies, Kamakura, pp. 17-74.

Kraay, Colin M 1985. Demetrius in Bactria and India. *Numismatic Digest* 9, pp. 12-30.

Krishnaswami Aiyangar, S 1980. Southern India and Ceylon. Chapter XV, in R C Majumdar, A D Pusalker, and A K Majumdar (ed), *The Age of Imperial Unity.* The History and Culture of the Indian People 2, (Bombay, 1980), pp. 228-242.

Krishnaswami Aiyangar, S 1923. *Some Contributions of South India to Indian Culture.* Calcutta : University of Calcutta.

Kulashreshtha, Sarojini 1986. Coins of Vāsishka—Historical Implications. *Numismatic Digest* 10, pp. 70-80.

Kulashreshtha, Sarojini, and P L Gupta 2004. See under Gupta, P L, and Sarojini Kulashreshtha 2004.

Lahiri, A N 1954. Coins of Queen Agathocleia and the Attribution of the Legendless Indo-Greek *Staters. Journal of the Numismatic Society of India* 16(2), pp. 189-196.

Lahiri, A N 1965. *Corpus of Indo-Greek Coins.* Calcutta.

Lahiri, A N 1971. Early Indigenous Coins of Northern India. D C Sircar (ed), *Early Indian Indigenous Coins,* (Calcutta, 1971), pp. 48-77.

Lahiri, Bela 1974. *Indigenous States of Northern India* (circa *200 BC to 320 AD).* Calcutta.

van Lohuizen-de Leeuw, J E 1949. *The "Scythian" Period : An Approach to the History, Art, Epigraphy and Palaeography of North India from the 1st century BC to the 3rd century AD.* Leiden.

Lüders, Heinrich 1961. *Mathura Inscriptions*, edited by K L Janert. Gottingen.

MacDonald, D, and R C Senior 1998. *The Decline of the Indo-Greeks—A Re-appraisal of the Chronology from the Time of Menander to that of Azes.* Hellenic Numismatic Society, Monograph Series 2.

Macdonald, George 1987. The Hellenic Kingdoms of Syria, Bactria, and Parthia. Chapter XVII, in E J Rapson (ed), *The Cambridge History of India* 1, (reprint, New Delhi, 1987), pp. 384-419.

MacDowall, D W 1968. *Soter Megas*, the King of Kings, the Kushāṇa. *Journal of the Numismatic Society of India* 30, pp. 28-48.

MacDowall, D W 2002. The Rabatak Inscription and the Nameless Kushan King, in *Cairo to Kabul : Afghan and Islamic Studies Presented to Ralph Pinder-Wilson* (London), pp. 163-169.

Maity, S K 1970. *Early Indian Coins and Currency System.* New Delhi.

Majumdar, R C 1960. *The Classical Accounts of India.* Calcutta.

Majumdar, R C, A D Pusalker, and A K Majumdar (ed) 1980. *The Age of Imperial Unity.* The History and Culture of the Indian People 2. Bombay.

Majumdar, R C, A D Pusalker, and A K Majumdar (ed) 1988. *The Classical Age.* The History and Culture of the Indian People 3. Bombay.

Majumdar, R C, and A S Altekar (ed) 1986. *The Vākāṭaka-Gupta Age (c 200 – 550 AD).* A New History of the Indian People 6. Delhi.

Majumdar, R C, and K K Dasgupta (ed) 1981. *A Comprehensive History of India (AD 300 – 985)* 3(1). New Delhi.

Mani, B R 1978. Determining the Type and Substantival Attribution of *Kāḍasa* Coins. *Journal of the Numismatic Society of India* 40, pp. 9-12.

Mann, Richard D 2007. Yaudheya Chronology and Coinage : An Analysis. *Numismatic Digest* 31, pp. 47-113.

Marshall, J H 1936. *A Guide to Taxila.* 3rd ed, Delhi.

Marshall, J H 1947. Greeks and Śakas in India. *Journal of the Royal Asiatic Society of Great Britain and Ireland*, pp. 3ff.

Marshall, J H 1975. *Taxila*, 3 vols. Indian Reprint, Delhi.

McCrindle, J W 1901. *Ancient India as described in Classical Literature.* Westminster.

Mirashi, V V 1982. *Sātavāhanoṁ aura Paśchimī Kshatrapoṁ kā Itihāsa aura Abhilekha* (Hindi). Lucknow.

Mitchiner, Michael 1975-1976. *Indo-Greek and Indo-Scythian Coinage*, 9 vols. London.

Mitchiner, Michael 2001-2002. The Kushan King, Vima Takshuma, Son of Kujula Kadphises : A Discussion of his Name. *Numismatic Digest* 25-26, pp. 43-50.

von Mitterwallner, Gritli 1986. *Kuṣāṇa Coins and Kuṣāṇa Sculptures from Mathurā.* Mathura.

Mukherjee, B N 1960. The Prototype of an Obverse Device of Kushāṇa Coinage. *Journal of the Numismatic Society of India* 22, pp. 109-112.

Mukherjee, B N 1967. *The Kushāṇa Genealogy.* Studies in Kushāṇa Genealogy and Chronology 1. Calcutta.

Mukherjee, B N 1969. *An Agrippan Source—A Study in Indo-Parthian History.* Calcutta.

Mukherjee, B N 1972. *The Pāradas.* Calcutta.

Mukherjee, B N 1981. *Mathura and its Society—The Śaka-Pahlava Phase.* Calcutta.

Mukherjee, B N 1995. The Great Kushāṇa Testament. *Indian Museum Bulletin* 30. Calcutta.

Mukherjee, B N 1997-1998. Vima Taktu, An Alleged Kushana King. *Numismatic Digest* 21-22, pp. 5-10.

Narain, A K 1953. Remarkable Discovery of Some Indo-Greek Victory Medallions. *Journal of the Numismatic Society of India* 15(2), p. 213.

Narain, A K 1955. *The Coin-types of the Indo-Greek Kings.* Numismatic Notes and Monographs (Numismatic Society of India) 1. Bombay.

Narain, A K 1957. *The Indo-Greeks.* Oxford.

Narain, Sudha 1956. The Twenty-*Stater* Gold Piece of Eukratides I. *Journal of the Numismatic Society of India* 18(2), pp. 217-218.

Nilakanta Sastri, K A 1935. *The Coḷas* 1. Madras University Historical Series 9. University of Madras.

Nilakanta Sastri, K A 1958. *A History of South India, from Prehistoric Times to the Fall of Vijayanagara.* (2nd ed). OUP.

Nilakanta Sastri, K A (ed) 1957. *A Comprehensive History of India* 2. Indian History Congress. Place of publication, not mentioned.

Oikonomides, A L N 1973. Soter the Great—The Last of the Indo-Greek Kings. *Journal of the Numismatic Society of India* 35, pp. 82-89.

Petitot-Biehler, C Y 1975. *Le Trésor d'Aï Khanoum. Revue Numismatique*, pp. 23-57.

Pieper, Wilfried 2005. Achyu Coins of Ahichhatra and Their Late 4th Century Derivatives. *Newsletter of the Oriental Numismatic Society* 184, pp. 13-14.

Powell-Price, J C 1945. Kuṇindas and Katyuras. *Journal of the UP Historical Society* 18, pp. 214-218.

Prinsep, James 1858. *Essays on Indian Antiquities, Historic, Numismatic, and Palaeographic.* Edited by E Thomas, 2 vols. London.

Puri, B N 1965. *Indian under the Kushāṇas.* Bombay.

Rajgor, Dilip 1991. Recent Researches in Kṣatrapa Numismatics. *Numismatic Studies* 1, pp. 33-44.

Rajgor, Dilip 1992. An Inventory of Dates known on the Coins and Inscriptions of the Western Kshatrapas. *Numismatic Studies* 2, pp. 87-105.

Rama Rao, M 1961. *Sātavāhana Coins in the Andhra Pradesh Government Museum.* Andhra Pradesh Government Series 2. Hyderabad.

Rapson, E J 1897. *Indian Coins.* Strassburg.

Rapson, E J 1906. Coins of the Graeco-Indian Sovereigns Agathocleia, Strato I Soter, and Strato II Philopator. *Corolla Numismatica* (Numismatic Essays in Honour of Barclay V Head), (Oxford, 1906), pp. 245-258.

Rapson, E J 1914. *Ancient India, from the Earliest Times to the First Century AD.* London.

Rapson, E J 1975. *Catalogue of the Coins of the Andhra Dynasty, the Western Kṣatrapas, the Traikūṭaka Dynasty, and the "Bodhi" Dynasty, in the British Museum, London.* Indian reprint, New Delhi.

Rapson, E J (ed) 1987. *The Cambridge History of India* 1. Indian reprint, Delhi.

Rawlinson, H G 1912. *Bactria, the History of a Forgotten Empire.* London.

Rawlinson, H G 1916. *Intercourse between India and the Western World.* Cambridge.

Raychaudhuri, H C 1972. *Political History of Ancient India,* from the Accession of Parīkshita to the Extinction of the Gupta Dynasty. 7th ed, Calcutta.

Reddy, D R, and P S Reddy 1983. *Coins of the Satraps of the Sātavāhana Era.* Hyderabad.

le Rider, G 1967. *Monnaise de Taxila et d'Arachosie, Une Nouvelle Reine de Taxila. Revue des Études Grecques* 80, pp. 331-342.

Rosenfield, J M 1967. *The Dynastic Arts of the Kushans.* University of California Press.

von Sallet, A 1883. *Die Nachfolger Alexanders des Grossen in Bactrien und Indien.* Berlin.

Salomon, Richard 1998. *Indian Epigraphy.* New Delhi.

Sarma, I K 1980. *Coinage of the Sātavāhana Empire.* Delhi.

Satya Shrava 1981. *The Śakas in India.* New Delhi.

Satya Shrava 1985. *The Kushāṇa Numismatics.* New Delhi.

Schoff, W H 2001. *The Periplus of the Erythraean Sea.* Reprint, New Delhi.

Scott, H R 1908. The Nasik (Jogelthembi) Hoard of Nahapāna's Coins. *Journal of the Bombay Branch of the Royal Asiatic Society* 22, pp. 223-244.

Senior, R C 1996. The Apracharajas and their Coinage. *Numismatic Digest* 20, pp. 33-40.

Senior, R C 2001. *Indo-Scythian Coins and History,* 3 vols. Lancaster, Pennsylvania, London.

Shastri, A M 1964. Some Observations on Audumbara Coinage. *Journal of the Numismatic Society of India* 26(2), pp. 157-161.

Shastri, A M 1979. *Kaushambi Hoard of Magha Coins.* Nagpur.

Shastri, A M 1995. Jogalthambi Hoard of Nahapāna Coins : Some Aspects. *Numismatic Digest* 19, pp. 73-95.

Shastri, A M (ed) 1972. *Coinage of the Sātavāhanas and Coins from Excavations.* Nagpur.

Simonetta, Alberto M 1957. An Essay on the So-called 'Indo-Greek' Coinage. *East and West* 8, pp. 44-66.

Simonetta, Alberto M 1958. A New Essay on the Indo-Greeks, the Śakas and the Pahlavas. *East and West* 9, pp. 154-183.

Sims-Williams, Nicholas 2008. The Bactrian Inscription of Rabatak : A New Reading. *Bulletin of the Asia Institute* (NS) 18, (2004, released in 2008), pp. 53-68.

Sims-Williams, Nicholas 2012. Bactrian Historical Inscriptions of the Kushan Period. *The Silk Road* 10, pp. 76-80.

Sims-Williams, Nicholas, and Joe Cribb 1995-1996. See under Cribb, Joe, and Nicholas Sims-Wolliams 1995-1996.

Sircar, D C 1939. *The Successors of the Sātavāhanas in Lower Deccan.* Calcutta : University of Calcutta.

Sircar, D C 1965. *Indian Epigraphy.* Delhi.

Sircar, D C 1966. *Indian Epigraphical Glossary.* Delhi.

Sircar, D C 1968. *Studies in Indian Coins.* Delhi.

Sircar, D C 1969. *Ancient Malwa and the Vikramāditya Tradition.* New Delhi.

Sircar, D C 1980. The Yavanas. Chapter VII, in R C Majumdar, A D Pusalker, and A K Majumdar (ed), *The Age of Imperial Unity.* The History and Culture of the Indian People 2, (Bombay, 1980), pp. 101-119.

Sircar, D C 1980. The Śakas and the Pahlavas. Chapter VIII, in R C Majumdar, A D Pusalker, and A K Majumdar (ed), *The Age of Imperial Unity.* The History and Culture of the Indian People 2, (Bombay, 1980), pp. 120-135.

Sircar, D C 1980. The Kushāṇas. Chapter IX, in R C Majumdar, A D Pusalker, and A K Majumdar (ed), *The Age of Imperial Unity.* The History and Culture of the Indian People 2, (Bombay, 1980), pp. 136-153.

Sircar, D C 1980. Northern India after the Kushāṇas. Chapter XI, in R C Majumdar, A D Pusalker, and A K Majumdar (ed), *The Age of Imperial Unity.* The History and Culture of the Indian People 2, (Bombay, 1980), pp. 159-177.

Sircar, D C 1980. The Śaka Satraps of Western India. Chapter XII, in R C Majumdar, A D Pusalker, and A K Majumdar (ed), *The Age of Imperial Unity.* The History and Culture of the Indian People 2, (Bombay, 1980), pp. 178-190.

Sircar, D C 1986. *Select Inscriptions bearing on Indian History and Civilization, from 6 century BC to 6 century AD.* 3rd ed, Delhi.

Smith, V A 1972. *Coins of Ancient India—Catalogue of the Coins in the Indian Museum, Calcutta, including the Cabinet of the Asiatic Society of Bengal* 1. Reprint, Varanasi.

Smith, V A 1999. *The Early History of India.* Third revised and enlarged edition. Reprint, New Delhi.

Srinivasa Iyengar, P T 1929. *History of the Tamils.* Madras.

Srivastava, Prashant 1989. Observations on the Joint Issues of Vaṅgapāla and Damagupta of Pañchāla. *Journal of the Numismatic Society of India* 51, pp. 56-57.

Srivastava, Prashant 1990. *Joint Coin-types of Ancient India.* Numismatic Notes and Monographs (The Numismatic Society of India) 22. Varanasi.

Srivastava, Prashant 1990. Some Observations on the Hermaios-Kalliope Type. *Journal of the Numismatic Society of India* 52, pp. 45-47.

Srivastava, Prashant 1990. The Lysias-Antialkidas Coin. *Bulletin of Museums and Archaeology in UP* 45-46, pp. 81-85.

Srivastava, Prashant 1992. The Joint Rule of Orthagnes and Gondopharnes : A Numismatic Overview. *K D Bajpai Commemoration Volume*, pp. 215-217.

Srivastava, Prashant 1992. On an Ayodhya Coin Bearing the Names of Devamitra and Āyumitra. *Kosala Through the Ages* (Lucknow, 1992), pp. 159-161.

Srivastava, Prashant 1996. *Aspects of Ancient Indian Numismatics.* Delhi.

Srivastava, Prashant 2005. Two Śaka-Pahlava Kings Named Azes ? A K Sinha (ed), *Dimensions of Indian History*, (New Delhi, 2005), pp. 74-79.

Srivastava, Prashant 2005. The Date of Gondopharnes. *Proceedings of the Indian History Congress* (65th Session, Bareilly, 2004), pp. 159-164.

Srivastava, Prashant 2007. *The Apracharajas* (A History based on Coins and Inscriptions). Delhi.

Srivastava, Prashant 2007. Indravasu : A New Apracha King. *Proceedings of the Indian History Congress* (67th Session, Calicut, 2006-07), pp. 128-130.

Srivastava, Prashant 2008. Machene, the Śaka-Pahlava Queen : Some Observations. Pratima Asthana and S Z H Zafri (ed), *Transformations in Indian History*, (New Delhi, 2009, released in 2008), pp. 168-173.

Srivastava, Prashant 2012. *Encyclopaedia of Indian Coins (Ancient Coins of Northern India, up to* circa *650 AD).* 2 vols. Delhi.

Srivastava, Prashant 2014. *Gleanings in Ancient Indian Numismatics.* Delhi.

Srivastava, Prashant, and K K Thaplyal, 1998. *Coins of Ancient India.* Lucknow.

Srivastava, Prashant, and Prachi Srivastava 1993. On the Relationship Between Nikias and Hippostratos. *Milinda,* pp. 97-98.

Tarn, W W 1980. *The Greeks in Bactria and India.* Reprint, New Delhi.

Thaplyal, K K 2012. *The Imperial Guptas : A Political History.* New Delhi.

Thaplyal, K K, and Prashant Srivastava 1998. See under Srivastava, Prashant, and K K Thaplyal, 1998.

Trivedi, H V 1957. *Catalogue of the Coins of the Nāga Kings of Padmāvatī.* Gwalior.

Trivedi, H V 1964. *Western Kshatrapa Coins in the Andhra Pradesh Government Museum.* Hyderabad.

Valentine, W H 1993. *Sassanian Coins.* Reprint, Delhi.

Vanaja, R 1983. *Indian Coinage.* New Delhi.

Warmington, E H 1928. *The Commerce between the Roman Empire and India.* Cambridge.

Watters, T 1961. *On Yuan Chwang's Travels in India.* Edited by T W Rhys Davids and S W Bushell. Reprint, Delhi.

Wheeler, R E M 1954. *Rome Beyond the Imperial Frontiers.* London.

Whitehead, R B 1914. *Catalogue of the Coins in the Punjab Museum, Lahore* 1. The Indo-Greek Coins. Oxford.

Whitehead, R B 1922. *Pre-Mohammadan Coinage of North-West India.* Numismatic Notes and Monographs 13. New York.

Whitehead, R B 1923. Notes on Indo-Greek Numismatics. *Numismatic Chronicle,* pp. 294-343.

Whitehead, R B 1940. Notes on the Indo-Greeks, Part 1. *Numismatic Chronicle*, pp. 89-122.

Whitehead, R B 1947. Notes on the Indo-Greeks, Part 2. *Numismatic Chronicle*, pp. 28-51.

Whitehead, R B 1950. Notes on the Indo-Greeks, Part 3. *Numismatic Chronicle*, pp. 205-232.

Whitehead, R B 1975. Commentary on Rare and Unique Coins. J H Marshall, *Taxila* 2, pp. 830-842.

Wilson, H H 1971. *Ariana Antiqua—A Descriptive Account of the Antiquities and Coins of Afghanistan.* Indian Reprint, Delhi.

Wood, A H 1959. *The Gold Coin-types of the Great Kushāṇas.* Numismatic Notes and Monographs (Numismatic Society of India) 9. Varanasi.

Wroth, W 1903. *A Catalogue of the Greek Coins in the British Museum, London.* Coins of Parthia. London.

Yazdani, Ghulam 1960. *Early History of the Deccan.* London.

PLATES

Plate I

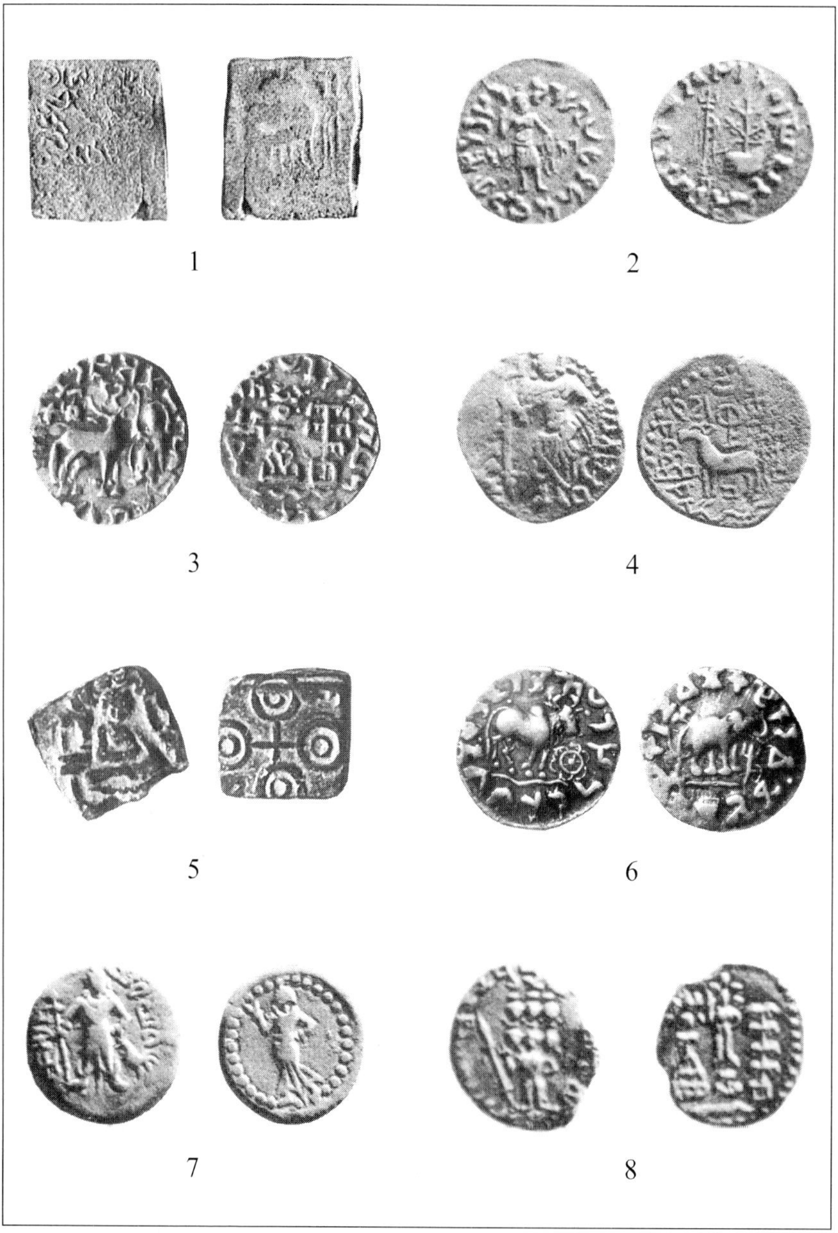

1-2 : Audumbara : Dharaghosha, 3 : Kuṇinda : Amoghabhūti, 4 : Kuṇinda : Chatreśvara, 5 : Ujjayinī, 6 : Vemaki, 7-8 : Yaudheya

Plate II

9

10

11

12

13

14

15

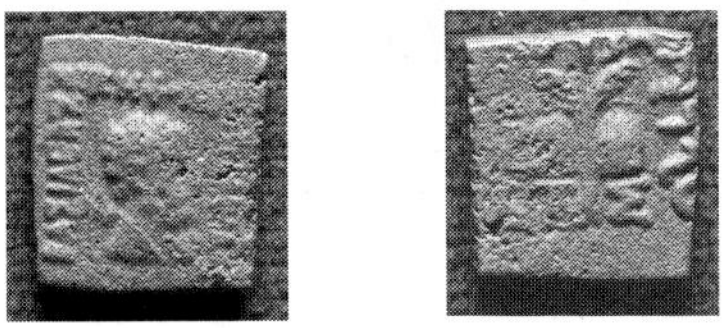

16

9 : Kauśāmbī, 10 : Mathurā, 11 : Pañchāla : Bhānumitra, 12 : Pañchāla : Phalgunīmitra, 13 : Agathokleia with Strato I, 14 : Agathokles, 15 : Amyntas, 16 : Antialkidas

Plate III

17

18

19

20

21

22

23

24

17-18 : Antialkidas, 19-20 : Antimachos, 21-22 : Apollodotos, 23-24 : Archebios

Plate IV

25

26

27

28

29

30

31

32

25 : Demetrios, 26 : Diodotos, 27 : Diomedes, 28 : Epander, 29-30 : Eukratides I, 31-32 : Euthydemcs I

Plate V

33

34

35

36

37

38

39

40

33-34 : Heliokles I, 35 : Heliokles II, 36-37 : Hermaios, 38 : Hermaios with Kalliope, 39-40 : Hippostratos

Plate VI

41

42

43

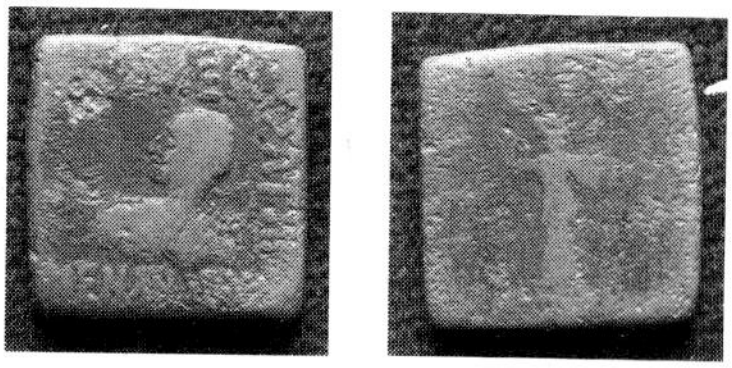

44

45

46

47

48

41 : Lysias, 42-44 : Menander I, 45 : Nikias, 46 : Pantaleon, 47 : Philoxenos, 48 : Strato I

Plate VII

49

50

51

52

53

54

55

56

49 : Telephos, 50 : Zoilos I, 51 : Zoilos II, 52 : Vonones with Spalahora, 53 : Vonones with Spalagadama, 54-55 : Spalirises, 56 : Maues

Plate VIII

57

58

59

60

61

62

63

64

57 : Maues, 58 : Maues, 59-60 : Azes I, 61-64 : Azilises

Plate IX

65

66

67

68

69

70

71

72

65-68 : Azcs II, 69 : Azes II with Aśpavarman, 70 : Gondopharnes with Aśpavarman, 71 : Abdagases, 72 : Sasan

Plate X

73

74

75

76

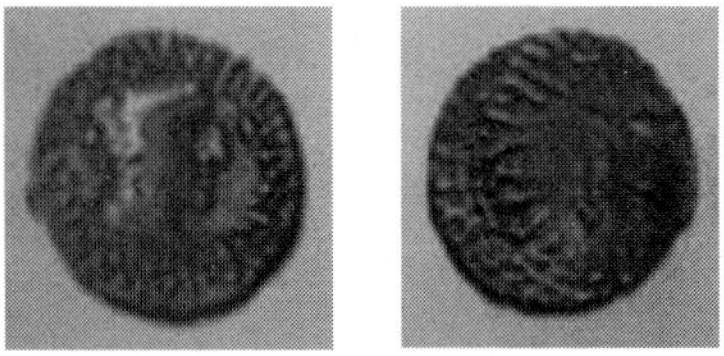

77

78

79

80

73 : Rañjuvula, 74 : Śoḍāsha, 75 : Hagāmasha, 76 : Sanabares, 77 : Kshaharāta : Nahapāna, 78 : Kārddamaka : Jīvadāman, 79 : Heraos, 80 : Kujula Kadphises

Plate XI

81

82

83

84

85

86

87

88

81 : Kujula Kadphises, 82-83 : V'ima Takshuma, 84-85 : V'ima Kadphises, 86-88 : Kanishka I

Plate XII

89

90

91

92

93

94

95

96

89 : Kanishka I, 90-96 : Huvishka

Plate XIII

97

98

99

100

101

102

103

Huvishka, 98 : Vāsudeva I, 99-100 : Kanishka III, 101 : Vāsudeva II, Shāka : Saya, 103 : Chandragupta I-Kumāradevī